The Bear
in the
Back Yard

———

The Bear
in the
Back Yard

Moscow's Caribbean Strategy

Timothy Ashby

Lexington Books

D.C. Heath and Company/Lexington, Massachusetts/Toronto

Library of Congress Cataloging in Publication Data

Ashby, Timothy.
The bear in the back yard.

Includes index.
1. Caribbean Area—Foreign relations—Soviet Union
2. Soviet Union—Foreign relations—Caribbean Area.
3. Caribbean Area—Foreign relations—1945–
    4. Geopolitics—Caribbean Area. I. Title.
F2178.S65A84 1987   327.470729   86-45944
        ISBN 0-669-14768-0 (alk. paper)

Published simultaneously in Canada
Printed in the United States of America
International Standard Book Number: 0-669-14768-0
Library of Congress Catalog Card Number: 86-45944

The paper used in this publication meets the minimum requirements of
American National Standard for Information Sciences—Permanance of
Paper for Printed Library Materials, ANSI Z39.48-1984.

ISBN 0-669-14768-0

87 88 89 90 91 8 7 6 5 4 3 2 1

Contents

Foreword

Edwin J. Feulner, Jr., Ph.D.
President
The Heritage Foundation

What Zbigniew Brzezinski has described as a "fourth central strategic front . . . in the worldwide U.S.–Soviet contest" has opened in the Caribbean and Central America. Never before in history has the U.S. been faced with a national security threat of such proportions so close to its borders. What would have been unthinkable to Americans a generation ago has become reality: the Soviet Union, a rival superpower unprecedented in aggressiveness and strategic capability, has established a major military, espionage, political, and cultural presence in the United States' "back yard." Having tested—and found wanting—the U.S. resolve in protecting its vital Caribbean interests, the Kremlin has declared the Monroe Doctrine dead.

The Kremlin is wrong. The Monroe Doctrine remains the cornerstone of U.S. security policy in the Western Hemisphere. Although the U.S. was passive for many years in its response to Soviet aggression along its vulnerable southern flank, this neglect ended with the Reagan administration. The Grenada Rescue Mission, military aid to the Nicaraguan democratic resistance, and the replacement of rhetoric with action in support for freedom in the Caribbean and Latin America have reinvigorated the Monroe Doctrine.

Fortunately, this book is a timely warning of Moscow's intent in the Caribbean region instead of a history of an irrevocably failed U.S. response. Leaders of the Americas will ignore the message of **The Bear in the Back Yard** at their own, and their peoples', peril. Supporters of political and economic freedom in this hemisphere will prevail only if they are aware of the forces that threaten democracy, and are prepared to defend it.

Introduction

For more than one-and-a-half centuries, the states of the Western Hemisphere—the Americas—have shared a common interest in preventing incursions by extrahemispheric powers. The fragility of political and economic structures in the newly independent American nations of the early nineteenth century invited intervention by the great European empires: Britain, France, Spain, and Russia. As the progenitor of the Western Hemisphere's democratic revolutionary movement, the United States was compelled by both national security and its unique political philosophy to take the lead in countering European expansionism. The U.S. stance on extrahemispheric incursions was articulated in the Monroe Doctrine—a concept designed to serve as the cornerstone of U.S. policy toward Latin America and the Caribbean.

Although the Monroe Doctrine was intended as a geopolitical warning to all the world's empires, it was partially inspired by concern over Russian penetration of the hemisphere.[1] Over the succeeding years, the power of all but one of the great nineteenth-century European empires has declined through decolonization and the ravages of war. The one exception is Russia (now Soviet Russia), which continues its expansionism under the guise of global Marxist-Leninist revolution.

In recent times, this new imperialism has penetrated the Western Hemisphere through its most vital geostrategic area—the Caribbean. Since 1960, the Soviet Union has established a degree of influence approaching hegemony over several heretofore independent nations in the Western Hemisphere: Cuba, Grenada, and Nicaragua. From these bases, the Union of Soviet Socialist Republics

(USSR), together with its proxies, has sought the destabilization of other American nations as a means of weakening the highly strategic southern flank of the United States.

In the sixteenth century, King Philip II of Spain said, "He who owns Cuba has the key to the New World," a maxim that remains valid.[2] The absorption of Cuba into the Soviet system has provided the USSR with one of its most strategically important bastions: an "unsinkable aircraft carrier" ninety miles from the United States that allows the Kremlin a military base in the Western Hemisphere as well as opportunities for power projection on an international scale via its Cuban surrogate.

Cuba serves as a weapons depot and conduit for the export of Soviet-sponsored revolution and subversion. Long-range Soviet aircraft such as the Tu-95 Bear D and Tu-142 Bear F now regularly patrol the U.S. East Coast using Cuban bases. A Soviet electronic intelligence facility on the island monitors sensitive U.S. maritime, space, and telephone communications. Through Cuba, Moscow has provided financial and logistical support for thousands of guerrillas in the Western Hemisphere. Such support has, in turn, been a decisive factor in creating similar Soviet bases in Nicaragua and Grenada (until October 1983).

The Soviet presence in the Caribbean region is an established fact, acknowledged by policymakers and analysts of every ideological persuasion. However, the circumstances of this presence—the intent, the degree, and the threat of Soviet involvement in the Caribbean—are a major point of contention, as is what the appropriate U.S. response should be. Latin American and Caribbean affairs specialists on the left argue that the USSR does not have geostrategic designs on the Western Hemisphere and therefore has no strategy toward the Caribbean. Communist revolutions, they insist, are the result of decade upon decade of economic deprivation and oppression by oligarchs who have often been supported by the United States. Soviet aid to revolutionary governments such as Cuba, Grenada, and Nicaragua represents no threat to the United States; Moscow's influence in these regimes is negligible. Caribbean and Central American revolutionaries have been forced to turn to the Soviet Union for assistance after being rebuffed by the narrow anticommunist policies of the United States.

Other analysts, in the political center and on the right, acknowledge the geostrategic threat posed by Soviet penetration of the Caribbean, but differ among themselves as to the strategic motivations and degree of control of regional client states, as well as the policies or means of dealing with the threat. Some of these specialists side with their colleagues on the left in viewing the root cause of communist revolutions in the Caribbean to be poverty and social inequality.

This book examines the Soviets' Caribbean policies, explores the USSR's strategy toward the area, and analyzes the threat. It concludes that the Soviet Union is following a deliberate and increasingly sophisticated strategy in its penetration of the Caribbean region. In its present form, this strategy incorporates nine identifiable elements designed to achieve the following objectives (see "Elements of the Strategy" in chapter 8 for a detailed discussion of the nine elements):

1. Erosion of the United States' historical predominance in the region.
2. Expansion of Soviet influence and power.
3. Establishment and maintenance of Soviet proxies.
4. Proliferation of Soviet military and C^3I facilities.
5. Forced withdrawal of U.S. influence from other parts of the world due to an enhanced security threat along the U.S. southern flank.

The idea for this book developed during the author's seven-month residence on the island of Grenada, from the fall of 1979 to the spring of 1980. Research for this work is therefore drawn from a variety of sources, beginning with the author's personal observations and experiences in a communist Caribbean nation with strong ties to the Soviet Union and its Cuban proxy. When possible, original documentary sources have been used to support this work, including theoretical writings by Soviet policymakers, official communiqués, and memoirs. Other primary sources used include documents from Cuba, Nicaragua, Grenada, and various other Caribbean regional organizations and governments. Of these, the collection of documents and other archival material found in Grenada after the October 1983 U.S.–OECS intervention provides an invaluable glimpse of this small Caribbean nation's relations with the USSR and its proxies. When compared with the available evidence of Soviet relations with Cuba and Nicaragua, the Grenada documents exhibit a significant number of parallels, offering strong evidence of a coherent Soviet strategic plan for the Caribbean region.

The security interests of the United States and, indeed, of all the Americas, are being threatened in Central America and the Caribbean. This vital issue must be raised from the political and ideological debate currently surrounding it. Only by understanding the implications of Soviet strategic policy toward the Caribbean can all citizens of the Western Hemisphere join forces in a counterstrategy to resurrect and implement the premise of the Monroe Doctrine.

The Bear
in the
Back Yard

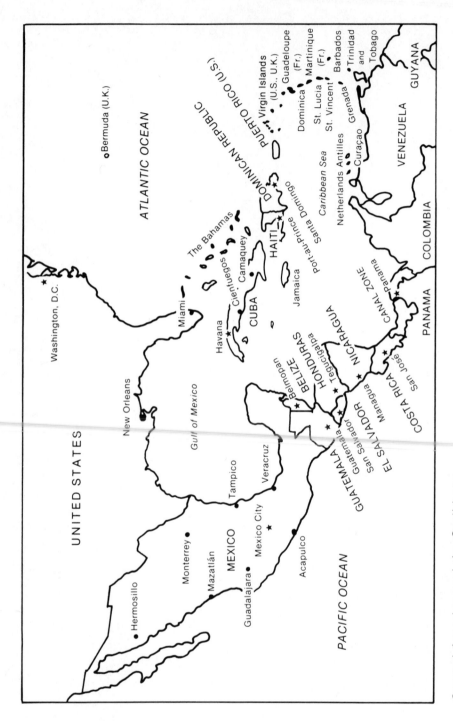

Central America and the Caribbean

1
Historical Soviet Interest in Latin America and the Caribbean

Genesis of a Strategy

It would be a fallacy to assume that Soviet strategic interest in Latin America in general, and the Caribbean basin in particular, is a relatively recent phenomenon. Although a coherent and sophisticated Soviet strategic policy toward the Caribbean region began to crystallize in the early 1960s, its origins can be traced to the ideological forces that have shaped the Union of Soviet Socialist Republics (USSR) since the Bolsheviks seized power in Russia in November 1917. The realization that the expected world communist revolution did not automatically follow on the heels of their coup d'état made the Bolshevik leaders acutely aware of their regime's vulnerability. Thus evolved the salient feature of Soviet geopolitical doctrine: The success of global Marxist-Leninist revolution would guarantee the ultimate national security of the USSR, while, conversely, the Soviet Union's national security was essential for the triumph of world revolution.[1] The roots of this tenet can be traced to the eighteenth-century maxim of an early Russian imperialist: "That which stops growing begins to rot."[2]

The USSR's emphasis on fomenting communist revolution on an international scale is therefore derived from an amalgam of Marxist-Leninist ideology and a quest for national security. Subversion and revolution, having demonstrated their effectiveness over the years, have become both the most durable and the most cost-effective weapons in the Soviet arsenal.

Cases of Soviet-sponsored subversion or covert political activity in Latin America and the Caribbean during the decades preceding 1960 exhibit a general ignorance of local conditions, a concomitant lack of coherent strategy, and tactics based more on theory than reality. Bolshevik leaders who influenced both Soviet and Communist International (Comintern) policy during the early postrevolutionary period were almost completely ignorant about Latin America. Chilean communist leader Elias Lafertte noted in his memoirs his acute dismay at discovering how poorly informed Comintern officials in Moscow were about his country.[3] Víctor Raúl Haya de la Torre, founder of Peru's socialist APRA party, echoed Lafertte's sentiments after a visit to Moscow in 1924 during which he met with Georgi Chicherin, Solomon Lozovski, and other Soviet leaders.[4] Lenin clung to the view that the South American republics were no more than neocolonies—a viewpoint that influenced Soviet/Comintern strategic policy toward the region for decades.[5]

Documented cases of Marxist-Leninist subversion during the period 1920–60 usually involve indigenous Latin American communist parties that were formed after the Russian Revolution and the ensuing schism within the world socialist movement. Actual Soviet influence on these parties dates from the Second Congress of the Comintern, held in Moscow in 1920, during which the leaders of the Comintern issued twenty-one conditions to which all parties had to adhere in order to belong to the organization. The purpose of this was to bring all other communist parties under Moscow's control.[6]

The Comintern and Latin America

Although Lenin had little knowledge of Latin America, his interest in Mexico was aroused by a fortuitous meeting with two Mexican delegates at the Second Congress of the Comintern. One of these Mexican communists reported that Lenin evinced no interest in the Mexican socialist movement (which he considered rudimentary) but rather in Mexico's strategic relationship with the United States:

the "masses of the people" in Mexico, their relation to the United States, whether there was a strong opposition movement to the United States, and if there was a strong peasant base for a communist movement.[7]

Because of its strategic location as well as the chronological parallel of the Mexican and Bolshevik Revolutions, Mexico was seen as logical place to base the Latin American headquarters of the Comintern. The Bolsheviks initiated this by sending their "emissary," Mikhail Borodin, to Mexico City. Borodin, a Russian with a unique American background, was a founder of the Comintern and one of its most important early missionaries. Following his work in Mexico to establish a pro-Soviet communist party and lay the groundwork for the Mexican government's recognition of the USSR, Borodin moved to China where he reorganized the Kuomintang party apparatus along Bolshevik lines.[8]

Borodin was followed in Mexico City by Sen Katayama, one of the founders of the Japanese Communist Party, and Manabendra Nath Roy, a founder of the Communist Party of India, thus establishing early use of "internationalists" as Soviet proxies in Latin America.[9] Roy, an Indian nationalist who had been serving as a German agent in Mexico, was converted to Marxism by Borodin and assigned the task of carrying on his mentor's mission of organizing "what we now call Communist movements in Latin America, with Mexico as the centre. . . ."[10] The Comintern pioneers succeeded in their mission of persuading Mexico to become, in 1924, the first country in the Western Hemisphere to recognize the Soviet Union. However, the Mexican government never consented to the establishment of a formal Comintern office in Mexico City. As its differences grew with the Mexican revolutionary leaders, the Comintern turned against them, declaring that it was "the task of the Mexican Communist Party to destroy the illusions of the masses about the government. . . ."[11] The Mexican Communist Party was successful in organizing the Cuban Communist Party and the Guatemalan Communist Party, which in turn helped to establish the Communist Party of El Salvador.[12]

When the Fifth Congress of the Comintern issued its call for Bolshevization in 1924, the Latin American communists responded by pledging their support for the Soviet Union while simultaneously asking for an increase in assistance from the Comintern. This resulted in the establishment of a South American bureau of the Comintern in Moscow. The Argentine Communist Party, the first in Latin America to formally affiliate itself with the Comintern, apparently made a favorable impression during the Sixth Congress of the Comintern in 1928, leading CPSU theoretician Nikolai Bukharin to declare that "South America is now for the first time widely entering the orbit of influence of the Communist International."[13] Later that year, the bureau was moved from Moscow to Buenos Aires. However, friction developed between the Comintern and the Argentine communists due to the insistence of the Comintern that the interests of Argentine workers be subordinated to the dictates of Moscow.[14] As a result, the Comintern's South American bureau was moved to the Uruguayan capital of Montevido, where the first all-Latin American communist periodical, *El Trabajador Latino Americano (The Latin American Worker)* began publication. The first issue actively took up the Comintern's campaign to "struggle against English and American imperialists and against reaction from within . . . [and to] aid the workers of the distinct countries, whether capitalist or capitalist dictatorships."[15]

El Trabajador's call for "struggle" was the direct result of the Latin American communists' adherence to the Comintern's hard-line tactics laid down at the Sixth Congress. Prior to 1928, the tactics of the Comintern's followers in Latin America had been cautious and relatively low-key, concentrating mainly on infiltrating labor movements and intellectual circles. These early tactics were also dictated by Moscow, as a communiqué issued in the Russian capital in 1927 makes clear. In a message for the Congress of the Latin American Confederation of Labor Unions, Solomon Lozovski, leader of the International of Red Labor Unions, urged caution in the revolutionary struggle, saying, "There is not yet in the interior of your movement sufficient motivational strength to be able to transform all of Latin America overnight."[16]

Such caution was cast aside by the Comintern's Sixth Congress, which had adopted the belief that a "third period" was beginning in the capitalist world during which the masses of the colonial and semicolonial countries were taking to the field in the international revolutionary struggle. As a result, the conference of Latin American communist parties held in Buenos Aires in 1929 adopted markedly aggressive policies, seeking to actively promote and support revolution in Latin America and the Caribbean.[17]

Nicaragua, a highly strategic transit point between the Atlantic and the Pacific Oceans since the 1850s, was singled out for special attention by the Comintern during its Sixth Congress due to the anti-U.S. guerrilla warfare campaign being conducted in that nation by General Augusto César Sandino. The congress approved a resolution, introduced by the communist parties of the United States and Mexico, which stated:

> The Sixth World Congress of the Comintern sends fraternal greetings to the workers and peasants of Nicaragua, and the heroic army of national emancipation of General Sandino, which is carrying on a brave, determined struggle with the imperialism of the United States. We call for all working class organizations and the entire proletariat of all countries to support Sandino.[18]

Nicaragua was an unusual choice for Comintern's attention, as it was one of the few Latin American countries without an indigenous communist movement, and Sandino had no record of strong Marxist leanings. Although Sandino—patron saint of the avowedly Marxist–Leninist Sandinista regime of modern Nicaragua—maintained contact with Hernan Laborde, secretary general of the Mexican Communist Party, he viewed the Comintern with suspicion. An attempt was made by the South American Bureau of the Comintern to raise money for Sandino's cause, but the results were negligible. From April 1930, the devoutly nationalistic Sandino had no further relations either with Laborde or with Farabundo Martí, a Salvadoran communist who served as the Comintern's envoy to Sandino's forces.[19] Following the Nicaraguan guerrilla leader's truce with the Sacasa government in 1933, the Comintern condemned him for "capitulation" and going over to the side of "the counter-revolutionary government."[20]

Nicaragua's neighbor, El Salvador, became the first Latin American nation to experience an attempted communist insurrection. In January 1932, Salvadoran Marxists challenged the results of municipal and congressional elections, claiming that their candidates had won. When the Martínez government refused to recount the ballots, communist leaders organized an uprising among sympathetic units of the armed forces. Alerted to the impending rebellion, the Salvadoran government arrested the ringleaders. The execution or banishment of many communist party leaders and the outlawing of their press served to put an end to Marxist-Leninist activities in El Salvador for a number of years.[21] The U.S., British, and Canadian governments viewed the attempted communist coup d'état as a "serious situation," and sent warships to El Salvador. However, they did not, apparently, consider the incident to be Soviet-inspired.[22]

Partly as a result of the abortive Salvadoran coup, the Seventh Congress of the Comintern, convened in Moscow in 1935, passed a resolution favoring popular insurrections in Latin America. In November of that year, an uprising was launched in Brazil by Luiz Carlos Prestes, a noted soldier and communist leader who had lived in the Soviet Union for the previous four years. With heavy backing from the organized labor movement, Prestes had sponsored a popular front movement called the National Liberation Alliance (ANL). When the organization was legally dissolved by President Vargas, the alliance declared Prestes president of Brazil and fomented uprisings in Rio de Janiero and other cities.[23] The revolt was rapidly suppressed by the Brazilian Army and most communist party leaders were arrested, including Prestes, who was sentenced to life imprisonment. Prestes subsequently found asylum in the Soviet Union after being granted amnesty by a more liberal Brazilian government.

The Soviet Union's rudimentary relations with Latin America soured during the early 1930s due to its support for Comintern's meddling in local politics. In 1929, the increasingly tense Soviet–Mexican relationship came to a head. Misinterpreting a military revolt against the government of president Portes Gil as a sign that the time was ripe for social revolution, the Comintern ordered the Mexican Communist Party to foment armed rebellion among the peasants. Some communist peasant leaders refused to take up arms against the government and were expelled from the party; others, such as Guadeloupe Rodriguez (who had been in Moscow for the tenth anniversary celebration of the October Revolution), obeyed the Comintern's instructions. Rodriguez issued a revolutionary May Day proclamation calling upon the peasants to seize land and the workers to take over factories. However, Rodriguez was executed by the Mexican authorities, leading the Comintern to issue a manifesto urging the Mexican people to rise up against the "Fascist government of Mexico."[24] The Comintern's attacks were promptly echoed by the Soviet press.

In July, the Mexican government formally protested the incitement of the Comintern as well as the hostility of the USSR's official press. In response, Soviet Foreign Minister Litvinov declared that his government could not "hold itself responsible for the contents of articles in the press," and asserted that "the Communist International is a completely autonomous international organization," the activities of which had "nothing to do with the Soviet Government."[25] The USSR continued to dismiss further Mexican protests over the remainder of the year, leading the Mexican government to sever diplomatic relations with Moscow in January 1930. In his memoirs, President Portes Gil said that "the Soviet legation in Mexico was a center for propaganda and political unrest. Meetings of a political nature, which many of our nationals were invited to attend, were frequently held there. These persons were trained in agitation activities and then sent out from it for purely political ends to the different states of our country."[26]

Similar activities caused a rupture of relations with Argentina and Uruguay. Although the Soviet Union did not establish formal diplomatic relations with Argentina until 1946, it was allowed to open an office of *Yuzhamtorg*—a special trading agency—in Buenos Aires in December 1927. Yuzhamtorg served as a cover for the transmission of funds to the Comintern's South American Bureau until it was raided by Argentine police and closed down in July 1931.[27] Following its closure in Buenos Aires, Yuzhamtorg moved to Montevideo, where its subversive activities continued despite the USSR's establishment of formal diplomatic relations with Uruguay. In 1935, after an official diplomatic relationship lasting less than one year, the Uruguayan government expelled Yuzhamtorg and the Soviet embassy staff, citing the Soviet missions' roles in promoting revolutions in Brazil and other countries. The Uruguayans bluntly concluded that "no distinction can be drawn between the Third International of the Moscow Congress and the Soviet Government."[28]

The Kremlin considered the break with Uruguay a serious set-back, for it cost the Soviet Union its last official foothold in Latin America for the remainder of the prewar years.[29] However, the Comintern continued its activities, considerably moderating its tactics in Latin America as a result of the abortive communist coup in Brazil as well as the Popular Front policy adopted during the Seventh Congress of the Comintern.[30] The U.S. government's Good Neighbor policy had also decreased Latin American hostility toward the United States, thereby rendering this popular communist bête noire a less appealing target. Usurping the Pan-American movement as part of their moderate facade, in July 1939 the communist parties of Mexico, Cuba, and Venezuela joined those of Canada and the United States in a joint declaration called "Strengthen Panamerican Democracy."[31] During World War II, Latin American communists gained further legitimacy by supporting the Allied war effort and generally backing the governments of their respective countries. Such moderate tactics served the dual purpose of erasing hostility toward the Soviet Union, thus paving the way for renewed diplomatic relations.

The Role of the Cominform

The Comintern was dissolved in 1943, to be replaced by the Communist Information Bureau (Cominform) in September 1947. The primary function of this resurrected communist international organization was to ensure Soviet control over the various Eastern European communist parties and thus facilitate the integration of the occupied nations of Eastern Europe into the Soviet empire.

At the strategic level, the founding of the Cominform marked the end of the Soviet Union's pretense of cooperation with the West due to the strategic necessity of World War II. Concern about the growing independence of established communist parties, a trend caused by the USSR's wartime beleaguerment and the ostensible dissolution of the Comintern, motivated the Soviet leadership to revive international communist unity and cooperation by the tactical device of emphasizing unequivocal opposition to Western policies.

Most importantly, the Cominform's inauguration indicated that

Moscow's global ambitions were not, as most Western leaders had naively hoped, a discarded imperialist anachronism. Stalin's supposed dissolution of the Comintern in May 1943 had been nothing more than a dramatic ruse to assuage Western fears that the Soviet Union "intends to intervene in the life of other nations and to 'Bolshevize' them,"—one more in a long series of tactics designed to win the support and sympathy of the industrial democracies whose assistance was so vital. In reality, the Comintern apparatus was kept intact until its rebirth as Cominform.[32]

The seminal speech by Andrei Zhdanov at the Cominform's founding conference betrayed both the USSR's strategic interest in the Third World and its recognition of the "correlation of forces" in the immediate postwar era. Zhdanov divided "the international arena" into "two camps": one, "the imperialist and anti-democratic camp," represented by the United States and its allies; the other, "the anti-imperialist and democratic camp," based on the Soviet Union and its Eastern European satellites. Zhdanov tacitly acknowledged the Soviet perception of the United States and other Western spheres of influence by stating that the first camp was also supported by countries that were "politically and economically dependent" on the United States, "such as the Near-Eastern and South-American countries and China." However, Zhdanov also clearly identified nations that were subsequently to become major targets of Soviet influence by informing his audience that "Indonesia and Viet Nam are associated with [the second or anti-imperialist camp]; it has the sympathy of India, Egypt and Syria."[33] In retrospect, this latter remark indicates that all five countries named must have appeared vulnerable to Soviet influence, suggesting some degree of strategic planning years before the Kremlin's involvement with these nations became overt.

As Zhdanov's speech forewarned, the Soviet Union had only a secondary interest in Latin America during the fifteen years following the end of World War II. China and other Asian countries offered far more promising targets of opportunity for strategic gain than did an area which, when viewed from Moscow, appeared literally to reside in the United States' back yard. Soviet policymakers were fully cognizant of the premise of the Monroe Doctrine; however, they perceived it in the context of historical Russian imperialism and current Soviet strategic motivations in Eastern Europe and parts of Asia:

> Pan-Americanism is based on the ideology of American imperialism which alleges an existent community of interests of the countries of the Western Hemisphere, one based on their geographical closeness and an affinity of political ideals and systems. In essence, however, Pan-Americanism is a new edition of the renowned Monroe Doctrine, certifying the domination of the U.S.A. in the Western Hemisphere.[34]

The promulgation of the inter-American system during the postwar years was seen by Soviet policymakers as calculated strategic maneuvering on behalf of the United States. The U.S. sphere of influence was therefore to be acknowledged and overtly respected until an exploitable weakness appeared in the system, as happened in Cuba in 1960.[35]

Although the Soviet Union's strategic attention was focused elsewhere during the remainder of the 1940s and throughout the decade of the 1950s, Latin America and the Caribbean were not forgotten. Diplomatic ties with Mexico and Uruguay had been restored during World War II; Cuba, Venezuela, Colombia, Chile, Argentina, and Brazil established formal diplomatic relations with the USSR between 1941 and 1947. The prospect for strong ties between Chile and the Soviet Union seemed especially promising. President Gabriel González Videla, elected in 1946 with strong communist support, appointed several Chilean communists to his cabinet. Direct shipping connections between Valparaiso and Vladivostok were planned, as was the trading of Chilean nitrates and other commodities for Soviet equipment and raw materials.[36]

In the last months of the war, the Dominican Republic, Costa Rica, Guatemala, Ecuador, and Bolivia extended formal diplomatic recognition to the Soviets without exchanging representatives. This diplomatic thaw was due to a more favorable opinion towards the USSR generated by the wartime alliance as well as by U.S. championing of a Soviet role in the much-vaunted United Nations organization. For example, Argentina only agreed to exchange representatives with the USSR in May 1947 after U.S. Secretary of State Edward Stettinius acted as intermediary.[37]

The reincarnation of the Comintern as Cominform led to a resurgence of Soviet-sponsored subversion in Latin America. Although resident Soviet officials could rarely be directly implicated in destabilization plots,[38] the governments of Colombia, Brazil, and Chile were sufficiently alarmed by the activities of their indigenous pro-Moscow communist parties to sever relations with the USSR.

In 1947, the year of Cominform's founding, Brazil and Chile broke diplomatic ties with the Soviet Union within one day of each other. Colombia followed their example in 1948 after the notorious *Bogotazo* riots. The Colombian government charged that communists had instigated the April 9, 1948, riots in the capital city of Bogotá for the dual purpose of disrupting the Ninth Conference of the American States and overthrowing the administration of President Mariano Ospina Pérez. Fidel Castro and three other young Cubans, including Alfredo Guevara, a communist youth leader at the University of Havana, and Enrique Ovares Herrera, a founder of the Anti-Imperialist Student Union created in Prague in 1946, were in Bogotá at the time to attend a leftist student congress called to coincide with the Conference of the American States. Although Castro participated in the rioting, his exact role remains unclear.[39]

At the instigation of U.S. Secretary of State George Marshall, the Conference of the American States unanimously adopted a resolution urging member states to take measures to control the expansion of communism.[40] These included curtailment or greater control over local communist parties, restrictions on Soviet diplomatic activities, and the exchange of intelligence information on subversion and espionage. The Bogotazo therefore served to gain increased support for the Rio Treaty, signed the previous year, which the United States hoped to use as the basis for an inter-American front against the possibilities of international communist aggression.[41]

Latin American governments needed little urging to curtail communist activities in their countries, for indigenous Marxist-Leninist parties had, following Moscow's example, renewed their propaganda against U.S. imperialism and the doctrine of Pan-Americanism. Less than six months after the end of World War II, the Cuban Communist Party admitted that it had "misinterpreted" the results of the 1943 Teheran Conference and nourished "false illusions" as to the possibility of changes in the international behavior of capitalism.[42] The following year, Rodney Arismendi, a leading Latin American communist theoretician, ratified the anti-U.S. stance that has persisted to this day. Holding up the Soviet Union as an example of a power that "is able to follow and does follow a policy of peace without contradictions," Arismendi said that, in contrast, "Anglo–Yankee financial oligarchies" were "starting to dynamite the foundations of the newly laid peace." Pan-Americanism, a concept postulated by "the obliging lawyers of imperialism," was fundamentally incompatible with the "national sovereignty and liberty of the Latin American countries."[43]

Covert Soviet meddling in other nations' internal affairs followed a pattern dating back to the Treaty of Rapallo.[44] Cominform's alleged involvement in the Bogotazo and other cases of subversion in Latin America are examples of the contradictory nature of Soviet foreign policy throughout the history of the USSR. Because of its basic revolutionary nature, the Soviet government faces the permanent dilemma of reconciling support for indigenous communist groups with the cultivation of good relations with those governments that the Marxist-Leninist revolutionaries are pledged to overthrow. In addition to this inherent contradiction of Soviet foreign policy, the Kremlin's geostrategists during the period from 1920 to 1950 were generally ignorant about Latin America, applying tactics that were largely unsuitable for the region. With remarkable candor, a marxist theoretician writing in the late 1960s admitted the failure of this poorly coordinated strategy, blaming it on "the immaturity of the communist parties" in Latin America as well as on the fact that Soviet communists "mechanically transferred to the specific conditions of Latin America many of the lessons and experiences of the struggle of the European proletariat standing at an entirely different stage of development."[45]

A New Sophistication

As the leadership changed in Moscow in the early 1950s, a new sophistication became apparent in the USSR's relations with Latin America and other parts of the developing world. A return to basic Leninist strategy became evident as Soviet policymakers concentrated on the three-pronged tactic of quietly building trade, diplomatic, and subversive ties while probing for revolutionary opportunities.[46]

The Soviet Union had failed to exploit a revolutionary opportunity that developed in Guatemala during the final months of Stalin's life. The Guatemalan government of Lieutenant Colonel Jacobo Arbenz Guzmán, elected in November 1950, had drifted steadily to the left. Probably due to the influence of his wife, a member of the Guatemalan Communist Party, and her circle of politically active friends, President Arbenz had allowed communists to insinuate themselves into key positions in his government, including the police, the Department of Agrarian Reform, and the trade union movement.[47] In February 1953, Arbenz began expropriating land owned by U.S. companies, a measure that the new Eisenhower administration interpreted as "part of the world-wide Soviet Communist conspiracy."[48]

In reality, no conclusive evidence has appeared that would indicate direct Soviet involvement in Guatemala during this period. The only overt gesture of Soviet support for the Arbenz government was a veto cast in the United Nations (UN) Security Council by the USSR's delegate to forestall a Brazilian and Colombian proposal to allow the Organization of American States (OAS) to mediate the Guatemalan situation.[49] Beyond a doubt, members of the Arbenz regime collaborated with Cominform agents, facilitating a shipment of Czech arms from the Polish port of Szczecin, which Arbenz intended to use to arm "the workers and peasants" as a counterweight to the conservative Guatemalan army. The arms were seized by the army at dockside in May 1954, providing the catalyst that led to the overthrow of Arbenz with CIA backing.[50]

In the unlikely event that the Arbenz regime had been allowed to survive and flourish by the Guatemalan army and the U.S. government, it is conceivable that the Soviets would have initiated an overt relationship with Guatemala. However, the historical timing of the Guatemalan episode probably would have precluded this. Both the leadership struggle in the Kremlin and fear of provoking the militarily superior United States during the early days of the cold war era manifested themselves in a Soviet attitude of "geographic fatalism" toward an obscure, indefensible nation in the U.S. sphere of influence. Regardless of its apparent lack of involvement in the Guatemalan crisis, the USSR observed and analyzed its evolution, applying its lessons to its dealings with Cuba a scant six years later.

The new flexibility in the Soviet Union's foreign policy became evident in its dealings with Latin America as early as 1952, when Soviet officials tried unsuccessfully to mend relations with Brazil by offering the unofficial Brazilian delegation attending the Moscow Economic Conference a million tons of badly needed wheat in return for traditional Brazilian exports.[51] A more sophisticated approach to the possibilities offered by Latin America appeared in the aftermath of the Twentieth Party Congress of the CPSU, convened in February 1956, during which Nikita Khrushchev's significant impact on Soviet foreign policy first became apparent. Khrushchev's speech to the congress on "The Disintegration of the Imperialist Colonial System" carried a message of enticement to all developing nations:

> These countries, although they do not belong to the socialist world system, can draw on its achievements to build up an independent national economy and raise the living standard of their peoples. Today they need not go begging for up-to-date equipment. . . . [T]hey can get it in the socialist countries, without assuming any political or military commitment.
>
> The very fact that the Soviet Union and the other countries of the socialist camp exist, their readiness to help the underdeveloped countries in advancing their industries on terms of equality and mutual benefit, are a major stumbling block to colonial policy. . . .[52]

Although Khrushchev's speech contained no direct references to Latin America or the Caribbean, this omission was remedied by an almost coincidental article that appeared in *Visión*, a Mexican illustrated magazine with a circulation throughout Latin America. In the article, Nikolai Bulganin, chairman of the Soviet Council of Ministers, issued a grandiloquent invitation to all Latin American governments to develop their economies with the aid of the Soviet Union.[53] Even though parliamentary delegations from Uruguay and Brazil visited the USSR for the first time in the summer of 1956, the controversial invitation had little immediate impact on Latin American relations with Moscow, largely because of adverse international reaction to the bloody Soviet suppression of the Hungarian Revolution in October and November of that year.[54]

In an attempt to assure Third World nationalist movements that the Soviet Union was now sincere in encouraging communists to seek power through peaceful, parliamentary means, the Kremlin dissolved Cominform shortly after the close of the Twentieth Party Congress. Though this action was primarily designed to support the Soviet "peaceful coexistence" propaganda campaign, it also served the important purpose of streamlining the USSR's international relations apparatus by shifting greater control over both policy-making and foreign communist parties to the CPSU Central Committee. As a result of the major administrative changes made in the central government from December 1956 to May 1957, responsibility for the Central Committee's Foreign Department was given to two members of the Presidium; its chief answered directly to the first secretary.[55]

As was the case elsewhere in the world, most Latin American governments soon lost interest in the Soviet Union's "police action" in Hungary. In December 1957, Rio de Janiero's communist daily newspaper, *Voz da Unidade,* reported that Khrushchev was very interested in renewing trade relations with Brazil. In response, the head of the Brazilian delegation to the UN told Agence France-Presse that he believed his country should renew diplomatic and commercial relations with *all* communist nations (the Brazilian government had maintained diplomatic ties with Poland, Czechoslovakia, and Yugoslavia after its break with Moscow). The campaign for rapprochement with the Soviets was joined by other prominent Brazilian government officials including the politically ambitious finance minister, who was also leader of the youth wing of the ruling Social Democratic Party (PDS). These individuals pointed out the commercial benefits enjoyed by Argentina's recent trade agreement with the Soviets, who also were assisting the development of Argentina's oil industry.[56]

The Soviets' campaign of commercial goodwill towards Brazil coincided with that nation's deteriorating relations with the International Monetary Fund (IMF). The Brazilians were highly susceptible to nationalistic appeals on behalf of the Soviets, as they considered the IMF's strict loan conditions as both an obstacle to economic progress and symbolic of subservience to foreign capital. At the Inter-American Conference held in Washington, D.C., in November 1958, the Brazilian delegation defiantly announced that their country would henceforth seek trade openings in both the Soviet bloc and communist China. Seven months later, in June 1959, Brazilian President Kutitschek broke off negotiations with the IMF, angrily announcing that the people of Brazil "were no longer poor relations forced to stay in the kitchen."[57]

Despite strong U.S. warnings, a Brazilian trade delegation was sent to Moscow in the fall of 1959, returning with a new Soviet–Brazilian trade document that mentioned the strategically significant "possibility of refining in Brazilian plants [imported] Soviet crude oil."[58] In the interim, the Soviet Union was to supply the Brazilians with industrial machinery and high-quality petroleum products at lower prices than were available anywhere else. In May 1960, Gosbank, the Soviet state bank, signed a clearing agreement with the Banco de Brasil and made arrangements for further commercial exchanges. Pro-Soviet feelings were running so high that Jânio Quadros, one of the Brazilian presidential candidates (who subsequently won the election) visited Moscow during the campaign to emphasize his stance on Brazil's new "independent foreign policy."[59]

The USSR's successful public relations campaign of extending trade and development assistance to Latin America was not confined to Brazil. In 1958, a delegation of the Supreme Soviet visited Uruguay to initiate increased commercial and diplomatic ties. In January 1960 the rightist coalition government of Chile responded to Soviet overtures by dispatching a trade and industry delegation to Moscow to explore economic opportunities. After Chile was struck by a major earthquake later that year, the Soviet Union sent food and medicines, taking full advantage of the favorable publicity this action generated throughout Latin America.

Following the 1959 meeting of Eisenhower and Khrushchev at Camp David, Mexico became the primary target of the new Soviet diplomatic, commercial, and cultural offensive, probably as much as for its proximity to the United States as for its "revolutionary" tradition, which it supposedly shared with the USSR. After the successful Sputnik flight, the Soviets opened a major exhibition in

Mexico City designed to extol the USSR's achievements in science, technology, and culture. The exhibition was designed both for propaganda purposes and to serve as a "legal," yet highly visible, means of testing the United States' reaction to a seemingly benign Soviet incursion into its traditional sphere of influence.

The now half-forgotten exhibition in Mexico City marked the beginning of the Soviet Union's true strategic offensive in the Caribbean region, for it served as a "Trojan horse" for the penetration of Cuba. The fair was opened in November 1959 by Anastas Mikoyan, then deputy premier of foreign and domestic commerce of the Soviet Union. The exhibition moved on to Havana, Cuba, in February 1960, and Mikoyan followed it, opening a completely new chapter in the geostrategic history of the Western Hemisphere.

2
Cuba's Role in Soviet Strategy

The Revolution

Until Fidel Castro's diplomatic overtures in the summer of 1959, the Soviet Union seems to have overlooked the enormous strategic potential of his minor Caribbean republic. The prevalent assumption among Marxist-Leninist theorists was that "the road to socialism" in Latin America lay "basically through a people's democratic revolution," the objective and subjective conditions for which existed in five countries: Argentina, Brazil, Chile, Mexico, and Uruguay. Moscow's limited interest in Latin America was therefore directed toward these nations until the unexpected orientation of the Cuban Revolution brought about an epochal transformation in the Soviet Union's perceptions of the strategic possibilities available to it in the Western Hemisphere.[1]

The Soviet Union's unofficial presence in Cuba, via Comintern and Cominform, preceded the Castro regime by a full generation. The pro-Moscow Cuban Communist Party (which existed under a variety of names after its founding in 1925) had been one of the most politically influential Marxist-Leninist parties in Latin America during the 1930s and 1940s.

Paradoxically, early Cuban communists reached their zenith of political power and legitimacy under Fulgencio Batista. Wishing to legitimize his dictatorship by winning the presidential election scheduled for 1940, Batista began laying the groundwork for an alliance with the still outlawed Cuban communist party (known at

---

Facing page: MiG-23s at an airfield in Cuba. The Soviet-built MiG-23s are the backbone of Cuba's modern air force, which has received 45 of these Mach 2 fighters. *Department of Defense photo*

that time as the *Partido Unión Revolucionario* [PUR]) as early as 1938. The communists were allowed to begin publishing a daily newspaper and open a radio station that had the most powerful shortwave transmitter in Havana. In July 1938, the Cuban Communist Party's Tenth Plenum decided that the party should take "a more positive attitude toward Colonel Batista," concluding that the dictator was "no longer the focal point of reaction, but the defender of liberty."[2]

Two months later, on September 24, 1938, Batista legalized the Cuban Communist Party (which thereupon changed its name to the *Unión Revolucionario Comunista* [URC]), reaping the full benefit of its support in what transpired to be his successful bid for the presidency. This led to one of the most ironic statements in Cuban history from a prominent island communist: "The situation has changed so that the slogan of the Party must be 'With Batista, Against Reaction,' meaning that we must work openly for the support of the masses to Batista's policies."[3]

The URC also scored significant victories in the national elections, electing ten members to the Chamber of Deputies and more than a hundred members to municipal councils throughout Cuba. A communist was also elected mayor of Santiago, the island's second largest city. As an additional reward for their support, Batista turned over the Cuban trade unions to the communists. In January 1943, the party made yet another change in its name, to the *Partido Socialista Popular* (PSP); three months later, with the Soviet Union now an ally of the United States, Batista formally established diplomatic relations with the USSR. The Cuban leader also appointed two PSP members to his cabinet—the first time that an acknowledged communist party member sat in the cabinet of a Western Hemisphere government. One of these ministers, Carlos Rafael Rodríguez, served as an important liaison between the young Castro regime and Moscow, and is currently a vice president of the Cuban Councils of State and Ministers.[4]

The communist hold on Cuban labor unions was broken by Carlos Prío Socarrás after he succeeded Ramón Grau San Martín in the presidency in 1948. Under the Prío administration, the PSP lost most of the political ground it had gained under Batista. In the 1950 elections, the PSP's popular vote dropped from 150,000 to only 55,000 and the party lost its three Senate seats. The communists were therefore pleased when their old ally, General Batista, overthrew President Prío on March 10, 1952.

To win favor with the Eisenhower administration, Batista outlawed the PSP in October 1953. However, his treatment of his former allies was remarkably benign. Prominent communists were occasionally detained and then promptly released, adding to the cynical Batista's reputation in Washington as a bulwark against communism. In reality, the illegal PSP consistently denounced attempts to overthrow Batista by violent means, the most famous case being Fidel Castro's attack on the Moncada Barracks on July 26, 1953, which the communists described as "putschist" and "bourgeois."[5]

Released from prison under a general amnesty in 1955, the Castro brothers, Ernesto "Che" Guevara, and a handful of others launched an "invasion" of Cuba the following year that was partially subsidized by former President Prío, an enemy of the Cuban Communist Party.[6] During the first two years of its limited guerrilla operations in the Sierra Maestra, Castro's Twenty-sixth of July Movement was shunned by the communists. There were several reasons for this. Until well into the year 1957, the older PSP leadership had worked to maintain their entente with Batista. These old guard communists distrusted Castro, viewing him as a radical opportunist whose tactics conflicted with the party's "nonputschist" policy; Castro, in turn, had castigated these Cuban communists as "Nazi gauleiters."[7]

The PSP's assessment of Fidel's opportunism was well-founded. Castro had flirted with utopian socialism since his student days, but had also been a keen admirer of Napoléon and Simón Bolívar.[8] Although Castro's brother Raúl and chief lieutenant Che Guevara had well-established international communist connections,[9] Castro himself had continually reaffirmed the Twenty-sixth of July Movement's allegiance to the Orthodox Party and the ideals of its anticommunist founder, Eduardo Chibás. The PSP, having no formal contact with Castro until 1958, may also have believed *New York Times* correspondent Herbert Mathew's famous interview with Castro, which told the world that "there is no communism to speak of in Fidel Castro's 26th of July Movement," and that the Castroite guerrilla forces were, in fact, "anti-Communist."[10]

Eager to back a winner, younger members of the PSP began to

press for an alliance with Castro in early 1958, largely as a result of the groundswell of anti-Batista sentiment throughout Cuba. This feeling was immeasurably strengthened by the U.S. government's announcement on March 14, 1958, of an arms embargo against the Batista regime—an action with striking parallels to the Carter administration's policy toward the Somoza government in Nicaragua twenty-one years later. When Batista sought arms elsewhere he was turned down, other nations having been told by the U.S. State Department that it looked with disfavor on the sale of arms to the Cuban government. According to the U.S. ambassador to Cuba at the time, President Batista regarded the arms embargo as blatant U.S. intervention on behalf of Castro.[11]

Several weeks after the arms embargo, Castro called for a general strike. This was an action criticized by the communists, who were in turn attacked by the Castro forces for their lack of support when the strike failed. The PSP's position at this time appears to have been approved by Moscow, as evidenced by a contemporary letter written to the Soviet periodical *Partiinaia zhizn'* by a "Comrade P. Lopez." The letter's harsh criticism of Castro's tactics and obvious resentment that the PSP had been left out of his tactical planning lends further credence to the theory that the old guard Cuban communists were not part of the Twenty-sixth of July Movement and only backed Castro when the tide appeared to have turned in his favor.[12] Blas Roca, the PSP party chief, admitted that the Cuban Revolution was "the first socialist revolution that was not made by the Communist Party."[13]

Nevertheless, several youthful communists had joined the Castroite forces in the Sierra Maestra in February 1958, apparently at the instigation of Carlos Rafael Rodríguez. By July, the communist party's hierarchy had made the decision to join forces with the Twenty-sixth of July Movement, and Rodríguez subsequently met with Castro in the mountains to formalize the alliance.

After Castro's accession to power on January 8, 1959, neither the Cuban Communist Party nor the Soviet Union appear to have expected his new regime to be anything more than another "petty radical bourgeoisie" government that would probably make its peace with the United States and maintain the basic social structure.[14] The alliance with Castro's forces was therefore a tactical device, akin to the party's earlier relationship with Batista. Given the presumed omnipotence of the United States in the Caribbean region, this action was probably taken for the primary purpose of assuring legalization of the PSP and some role in the new regime. The application of Lenin's "two-stage" revolutionary strategy (a bourgeois–nationalist coup d'état followed by communist usurpation of the revolution) does not seem to have received serious consideration by the PSP's old guard.

Fidel Castro surprised the PSP as much as he did the U.S. State Department. Castro usurped the communist party, using it to fulfill his own totalitarian political ambitions. He eventually placed the PSP under his discipline by purging much of its old leadership, then cynically used the party as a vehicle for attaining rapid control of Cuba. It was therefore the necessity of holding and extending power that drove Castro to the left, and not doctrinal conviction. For the same motives, Fidel Castro turned to the wary Kremlin for the material assistance to consolidate his revolution and give him the power to achieve his personal dream of becoming the Bolívar of the Caribbean. In doing so, he handed the Soviet Union one of its greatest strategic assets.

The Coming of Soviet Influence

The beginning of the Soviet Union's relationship with the Castro regime remains shrouded by mystery. In accordance with its general policy of fostering commercial, cultural, and diplomatic relations with Latin America, the USSR extended pro forma recognition to the revolutionary government on January 11, 1959. Soon thereafter, Anastas Mikoyan, on a visit to Washington, D.C., attended a dinner party given by Secretary of State John Foster Dulles. Mikoyan reportedly told Dulles and his guests that he was planning a goodwill mission to Cuba in the hope of establishing trade relations with the Castro regime.[15]

In July 1959, Major Ramiro Valdés, chief of Cuban Intelligence, visited Mexico City for a pair of meetings with Soviet ambassador to Mexico, Vladimir Bazikin. Ambassador Bazikin was a crucial contact, responsible for Soviet interests in all of Central America and the Caribbean in addition to Mexico. Following these meetings, the Cuban envoy to Mexico, Salvador Massip, began holding regular conferences with Bazikin, coordinating the clandestine transmission of Soviet agents and funds to Cuba. Direct responsibility for the earliest Soviet penetration of Cuba appears to have been given to USSR Consul General P. Yatskov, who traveled secretly to Havana on at least one occasion.[16]

A team of Soviet labor officials had been in Havana since May to help arrest the growing anticommunist sentiment of the Cuban Confederation of Workers (CTC). These men had most likely come to Cuba at the invitation of old guard communist labor leader Lázaro Peña (who had returned from exile in early January) and PSP Secretary General Blas Roca. This action was known to Fidel Castro and probably would not have been carried out without his approval.[17] The interpreter accompanying the Soviet labor delegation turned out to be a KGB officer named Vadim Kotchergin, who used his official cover to meet with Ramiro Valdés and his deputy, Major Manuel Piñeiro Losado, who is now chief of the Cuban Communist Party's intelligence arm, the *Departamento América* (DA).[18]

Following Mikoyan's arrival in Mexico City on November 18 to open the Soviet industrial exposition, he was approached by Ambassador Massip with a request for a meeting with Che Guevara. Initially, Mikoyan turned down the request, either because of fear that an open meeting with a prominent communist from the Cuban government would endanger the Castro regime and jeopardize what was then a relatively good relationship between the Soviet Union and the United States, or because he lacked instructions from Moscow. The Soviet deputy premier finally agreed to meet with an obscure Castro aide named Héctor Rodriguez Llompart, who was given the rank of ambassador extraordinary and plenipotentiary for the occasion. Accompanied by Ambassador Massip, Llompart held a thirty-five minute meeting with Mikoyan at the Soviet Embassy on the morning of November 27, 1959, and returned to Cuba that afternoon. It is reasonable to assume that Llompart conveyed to Mikoyan the desire of his superiors to conclude a pact with the USSR, receiving in return suggestions for proceeding with negotiations from the man who was Nikita Khrushchev's closest adviser.[19]

On the day before this first high-level Soviet–Cuban meeting, Fidel Castro had appointed Che Guevara to head the National Bank of Cuba. Guevara, a dedicated Marxist-Leninist, promptly set about a radical restructuring of the Cuban economy, bringing in leftist economists from all over Latin America to begin the transformation of Cuba into a "socialist" society. Guevara influenced Castro to accelerate the development of ties with Moscow, asserting that the USSR could provide Cuba with the technicians needed to revive the island's already deteriorating economy. Property expropriations, begun by the Agrarian Reform Law of May 1959, were stepped up, as was Castro's vituperation against the United States.

The growing volume of anti-Yankee propaganda, augmented by diatribes aimed at the OAS, was designed to spread paranoia through the Cuban population, making the people more susceptible to Castro's pro-Soviet turn by creating the impression that their traditional Western Hemisphere allies had grown hostile to Cuba. Fearing imminent U.S. sanctions, Castro agreed with Guevara that he must act quickly to win active Soviet support for his increasingly radical regime. Guevara particularly feared "another Guatemala," a concern fostered by former Guatemalan leader Jacobo Arbenz who, along with leftist members of his cabinet, was invited to take up residence in Cuba.[20]

Shortly after Mikoyan's return to Moscow, and presumably after Castro's offer was discussed in the Presidium, the Soviet Union made a formal offer to the Castro government to stage its cultural and industrial fair in Havana after it closed in Mexico City. Following an unusual amount of favorable publicity in the Cuban Communist Party's organ *Hoy* and the Twenty-sixth of July Movement's *Revolución*, the government announced that it had "acceded to the will of the people" and would accept the USSR's offer. The official government press release added that the exhibition would open to the public in February and that it was "thought" that Anastas Mikoyan would attend the opening.[21]

Over the next six weeks, nearly a hundred Soviet technicians arrived in Havana, ostensibly to supervise the staging of the exhibition and to serve as propagandists. Many of these young men and women were actually Spaniards taken by their communist parents to the USSR after the Spanish Civil War and subsequently trained as Soviet military and intelligence operatives. The majority of these *niños* were to remain in Cuba, some serving as instructors in the guerrilla training schools established by former Spanish Republican General Alberto Bayo. Another Spanish Republican veteran, Enrique Lister Farjan, laid the groundwork for the Committees for the Defense of the Revolution (CDR)—the ubiquitous Cuban neighborhood spy system.[22] KGB officers of Spanish origin also entered Cuba under the cover of technicians and quickly began reorganizing the Cuban intelligence service.[23]

The ruse of infiltrating ethnic Latins into Cuba was both an early manifestation of the Soviet use of proxy forces and a dynamic application of Leninist theory to a tactical problem, that is, the control of risks. In V. I. Lenin's classic work on the problems of communist strategy, *Left-Wing Communism—An Infantile Disorder,* he warned:

> It is folly . . . to deprive ourselves in advance of any freedom of action, openly to inform an enemy who is at present better armed than we are, whether we shall fight him and when. To accept battle at a time when it is obviously advantageous to the enemy, but not to us, is criminal.[24]

For the Kremlin's still-tentative strategic venture in Cuba to succeed, it was essential not to risk early provocation of "the enemy"—the United States—who hovered over Cuba like a slumbering giant befuddled by half-truths and conflicting reports about Castro's ideological orientation. The introduction of the niños was designed to deceive the U.S. government as well as the nationalistic, anti-Soviet members of Castro's own Twenty-sixth of July Movement. The same tactic, only slightly modified, was to be successfully employed later in Grenada, Nicaragua, and other Caribbean countries.

Anastas Mikoyan arrived in Havana on February 4, 1960, to open the Soviet exhibition and hold discussions on economic relations with Cuba. Evidently, Moscow's decision to purchase Cuban sugar and extend other types of aid to the Castro regime had been made prior to Mikoyan's visit, for the Soviet government cabled an order to Havana for 345,000 tons of sugar on February 5, the day the exhibition formally opened. During the course of Mikoyan's nine-day visit to Cuba, he signed other commercial agreements with Castro, including one for a $100 million line of credit to be used for equipment, machinery, materials, and technical assistance from the USSR over a five-year period.[25]

The fanfare attending Mikoyan's visit aroused the expected rumblings in Washington. Only a month earlier, President Eisenhower had told a meeting of Latin American heads of state that the traditional concept of "aggression" had to be updated to include "subversion," and that the United States "would consider it to be intervention into the internal affairs of an American state if any power whether by invasion, coercion or subversion, succeeded in denying the freedom of choice of any of our sister republics."[26] To mollify the lame-duck Eisenhower administration and assure it of the USSR's "peaceful intentions" in the Caribbean, Mikoyan stated at a press conference held on his return to Moscow that Castro had not asked for military aid and that no Soviet armaments would be sent to Cuba.[27] Regardless of this denial, Soviet military instructors, whether proxies or ethnic Slavs, had already begun restructuring the Cuban armed forces, as admitted by Raúl Castro in 1970: "[F]rom 1959 to 1970, our armed forces have worked in closest contact with Soviet troops. . . . [T]hey were the first to help us organize our armed forces, to develop and nurture them."[28]

What Soviet military assistance to the Castro regime there was during the first four months of 1960 was both strictly covert and limited in materiel. Nikita Khrushchev, still basking in the positive international warmth generated by his Camp David meeting the previous September, probably planned an incremental expansion of Soviet influence over a number of years. Khrushchev knew that a sudden infusion of Soviet military equipment into Cuba would almost certainly damage U.S.–Soviet relations and harm the USSR's carefully reconstructed post-Hungary image in the world. The Soviet premier was eager to strut the world stage once again at the Paris summit scheduled for mid-May, and did not wish to jeopardize the possibility of additional Soviet foreign policy successes.

The U-2 incident during the first week of May 1960 provided the catalyst for a considerably more aggressive Soviet involvement with Cuba. Citing the need to salve the USSR's wounded pride and prestige, Khrushchev felt compelled to "stand up to the Americans." Because of his refusal to hold further negotiations with the West while Eisenhower remained in office, Khrushchev no longer felt any restraints in openly strengthening the USSR's relationship with the Castro regime.[29]

A Military Foothold

A prime indication of the Soviet Union's shift in strategy toward Cuba was the decision to give full diplomatic recognition to the Castro regime on May 8, 1960, nearly eighteen months after Batista's overthrow. The Soviet ambassador, Sergei M. Kudriastsev, arrived in Havana in August, nearly a year after his expulsion from Canada for espionage activities.[30]

In what can be seen as an attempt to challenge the Eisenhower administration, Khrushchev issued what appeared to be a direct challenge to the United States on July 9. Stating that the USSR was "raising its voice and extending a helping hand . . . to the Cuban people," the Soviet premier said:

> We shall do everything to support Cuba in her struggle. . . . Now the United States is not so unreachable as she once was. . . . Figuratively speaking, in case of need, Soviet artillerymen can support the Cuban people with their rocket fire should aggressive forces in the Pentagon dare to start an intervention against Cuba. And let them not forget that, as the latest tests have shown, we have rockets capable of landing precisely on a given square at a distance of 13,000 kilometers.[31]

Although Khrushchev's threats were largely bluster, they had the desired effect on the U.S. presidential campaign of 1960, which featured Cuba as a major issue. John F. Kennedy, elected president four months after Khrushchev's belligerent remarks, apparently took them seriously enough to allow them to influence crucial tactical decisions affecting the Bay of Pigs invasion the next spring. Following the debacle, Kennedy told Richard Nixon that he had "opposed armed intervention by U.S. forces" in Cuba because his Russian experts had told him that Nikita Khrushchev was feeling "very cocky."[32]

Khrushchev's bellicose words also had a powerful psychological effect on the Castro regime, bolstering the shaky "Revolution" and encouraging the Cubans to sever their few remaining ties with the

United States. The day after Khrushchev's speech, Che Guevara boasted that Cuba was now defended by the "greatest military power in history." Raúl Castro, on a visit to the Soviet bloc later that month to negotiate military aid, told reporters in Moscow that he was delighted to hear "that the Soviet Union would use every means to prevent any United States intervention against the Cuban Republic."[33]

Emboldened by what it apparently accepted as a genuine Soviet commitment to serve as its unequivocal defender, the Castro government began to reveal its strategic ambitions in Latin America. Speaking on July 26, Fidel Castro told his audience that he would convert the Andes into the Sierra Maestra of the South American continent. Lázaro Peña referred to the communist takeover of Cuba as "only the first step in the liberation of Latin America," while PSP Secretary General Blas Roca said that when communist guerrilla forces in Venezuela achieved victory, "America will be aflame" and Cuba would "no longer be the solitary island in the Caribbean. . . ."[34]

There is evidence that such statements by Cuban officials, in turn, directly influenced the process of changing Moscow's strategic perception of the Western Hemisphere. Regardless of its strong statements of support for the fledgling Castro regime, the Soviet Union had no intention of risking a military confrontation with the far more powerful United States. The Kremlin's public statements and steadily increasing involvement with Cuba were means of testing the Americans, whom they expected to decisively crush Castro once the provocation threshold had been crossed. Unfortunately for the subsequent course of history, the U.S. response, apart from clandestine training of the Cuban exile brigade, was rhetorical, as demonstrated by the empty "Declaration of San José," which indicated that Castro was not viewed as a serious potential threat.[35] This demonstration of the U.S. government's indecisiveness and lack of will was an open invitation for the application of Lenin's classic maxim: "If you strike steel, pull back; if you strike mush, keep going."[36]

As the U.S. blow failed to materialize, the Soviet leadership realized the unprecedented strategic advantage to be gained by establishing a military foothold on Cuba. Whereas Castro and his followers, at that period, confined their revolutionary goals to Latin America, the Soviet Union now viewed Cuba as an asset of great potential in the global struggle to shift the "correlation of forces" in its favor. Soviet writers in the early 1960s were already cognizant of the possibilities Cuba offered as a means of undermining U.S. influence in the Western Hemisphere. The CPSU party school's official history of the USSR's foreign policy from 1917 to 1960, published in 1961, declared that

> [T]he triumph of the revolution in Cuba dispelled the myth of the omnipotent power of American imperialism in Latin America. It showed that the U.S.A. in the present international situation cannot undertake armed intervention in the countries of Latin America with her former ease. . . . The Cuban revolution . . . became the model of national-liberation movements in the Western Hemisphere.[37]

The authors of this work noted that Castro's revolution had "dealt a strong blow to American imperialism in the Western Hemisphere, and constituted a serious defeat for the American policy of 'positions of strength'." Most importantly, the history accurately predicted that the consolidation of the Castro regime was "the beginning of a new stage in the national-liberation struggle of the people of Latin America."[38]

Another factor in the Soviet Union's ardent embrace of Cuba was its rivalry with the People's Republic of China. Guevara and other Twenty-sixth of July veterans made no secret of their admiration for Mao Tse-tung's guerrilla warfare teachings and, to a lesser extent, his interpretation of Marxism-Leninism. Cuban and Chinese leaders enjoyed pointing out the similarities in their respective revolutions, and one of the first publications offered by Imprenta Nacional, the Cuban state printing house, was a Spanish translation of Mao's famous "thoughts" pamphlet.[39]

In July 1960, only one month after Khrushchev's dramatic confrontation with P'eng Chen at the Romanian Party Congress, Fidel Castro received a fourteen-member Chinese delegation led by Deputy Minister of Foreign Commerce Lu Hsu-chang. The People's Republic had already concluded a deal for 130,000 tons of Cuban sugar and was actively pursuing other political and trade negotiations. These contacts were of great concern to the Kremlin inasmuch as they presented fresh challenges to the USSR's self-assumed role as leader of the socialist world.

In retrospect, it seems likely that Fidel Castro used this international rivalry for his own ends, playing on the Soviet fear that Cuban adoption of the Chinese Great Leap Forward model would have severe repercussions on the USSR's influence throughout the Third World. In early September, Castro announced that his government would recognize the People's Republic of China, causing consternation to Nikita Khrushchev, who made a public display of heartily embracing the Cuban leader during Castro's visit to New York only three weeks later to address the United Nations.

Although Castro exchanged ambassadors with the People's Republic of China and maintained good relations with Peking until 1966, his regime never seriously considered following the Maoist model. Regardless of his admiration for Mao's guerrilla tactics, Guevara, the Castro government's chief ideologue, confessed as early as 1957 that he believed "the solution of the world's problems" lay within the Soviet bloc.[40] This orientation was confirmed in December 1960 when Guevara, addressing a major conference of eighty-one communist parties in Moscow, declared that "Cuba wants to tread the path of the Soviet Union."[41]

The Missile Crisis

Soviet deliveries of arms and military personnel were significantly increased over the summer and fall of 1960. In August, seven hundred Soviet bloc "technicians" arrived in Santiago accompanied by huge crates and boxes. Cuban stevedores were forbidden to handle other suspicious cargoes that were unloaded at the northern Cuban ports of Matanzas, Bahía Honda, and Mariel by Russian crews. By official U.S. government estimates, the Castro regime received twenty-two thousand tons of Soviet bloc armaments between August 1 and October 27, 1960, alone, with the final total for the year coming to twenty-eight thousand tons. Some of this Soviet largesse was displayed during an eight-hour military parade commemorating the second anniversary of the Cuban Revolution, including Stalin II and T-34 tanks, Su-100 assault guns, and 76-mm, 85-mm and 122-mm artillery pieces.[42]

In early 1960 the Eisenhower administration had established a supposedly secret program to train and equip a force of Cuban exiles under CIA auspices. No plan to put this force into action had been made by the time John F. Kennedy took office, although the secrecy of the training program had been compromised by numerous publications from October 1960 onward. By the time President Kennedy decided to use the Cuban exile brigade in an direct amphibious invasion without U.S. military support, the expedition was doomed—Fidel Castro was fully aware that an invasion was planned more than a week before the puny attempt was mounted, and lacked only the exact time and place.[43]

The Bay of Pigs debacle proved to be a major propaganda fiasco for the Kennedy administration and a timely boon for the Kremlin. Much of the world, including U.S. allies, joined the Soviet Union in condemning the United States for its ill-disguised role in the invasion. Although the USSR's verbal assaults on the United States were shrill, Khrushchev's earlier threat to use nuclear weapons to defend Cuba did not reappear, the possibility of retaliation now cloaked in the ambiguous warning that "the Soviet government reserves the right, if armed interference in the affairs of the Cuban people is not stopped, to undertake, together with other countries, all measures for rendering the necessary aid to the Republic of Cuba."[44] The phrase "together with other countries" is a significant indication of the USSR's tactical decision to mute its rhetoric and join the chorus of "respectable"international outrage, thus scoring a double propaganda coup against the United States. To further test the new U.S. president, Khrushchev sent Kennedy a gratuitously insulting message after the initial international outcry decreased.

John F. Kennedy's lack of will during the Bay of Pigs invasion was a major factor in the chain of events leading to the Cuban missile crisis. During the remainder of 1961 and most of 1962, Khrushchev formed the opinion that the inexperienced and indecisive Kennedy administration was so much Leninist "mush" that could be manipulated and exploited. The Soviet premier found it hardly credible that the U.S. superpower could refrain from liquidating Castro after his announcements that Cuba was a "socialist" nation and that he was a Marxist-Leninist. In Khrushchev's eyes, Kennedy's weakness was confirmed during the June 1961 Vienna summit when the U.S. president allowed himself to be criticized over the Bay of Pigs to the point where he broke down and confessed his personal responsibility for the debacle to the secretly astonished Soviet leader. Kennedy's easy acquiescence to the bogus "neutralization" of Laos and feeble response to the construction of the Berlin Wall served to embolden Khrushchev for further strategic "thrusts".[45] As the Soviet premier told the poet Robert Frost, it appeared to him that the Western democracies were "too liberal to fight."[46]

A U.S. counterthrust came on October 21, 1961, in the midst of the CPSU's Twenty-second Congress. On that date, U.S. Deputy Secretary of Defense Roswell Gilpatric officially disclosed that the United States had a major advantage over the Soviet Union in tactical and strategic nuclear weapons. Gilpatric's challenging statement that "their Iron Curtain is not so impenetrable as to force us to accept at face value the Kremlin's boasts," again caused a crisis in the Presidium and threatened Khrushchev's political primacy. The Soviet premier therefore found it necessary to find a means of reasserting the USSR's military capability as well as his own leadership.[47]

Khrushchev chose to resolve his dilemma by the highly risky device of emplacing nuclear missiles in Cuba—one of the most blatantly provocative acts possible. According to his memoirs, the Soviet premier believed it was possible to install the weapons secretly and thus present the Americans with a fait accompli which they would come to accept as a modification to the status quo. "In addition to protecting Cuba," Khrushchev reasoned, "our missiles would have equalized what the West likes to call the 'balance of power.' . . . [W]e'd be doing nothing more than giving them a little of their own medicine."[48]

Fearing opposition from his own government, Khrushchev resorted to subterfuge to achieve his strategic objectives. Early in 1962, Aleksei Adzubei, director of *Izvestia* and Khrushchev's son-in-law, arrived in Havana after a tour of the United States during which he had interviewed President Kennedy. Adzubei told Castro that Kennedy had hinted that another Cuban invasion was planned that would employ U.S. forces. Castro was reportedly advised that the only means of forestalling the invasion was to ask the Soviet

Union for "strategic defensive weapons." Khrushchev's memoirs acknowledge that there were "heated arguments" before Castro agreed to accept the missiles. Upon receiving Castro's formal request, Khrushchev used his influence to win his government's acceptance of it, going so far as to replace the commander of the strategic rocket forces, who opposed the deployment, with a more amenable Ukrainian.[49]

The official decision to send Soviet missiles to Cuba was apparently made in April 1962, immediately after another event that Khrushchev probably used as a factor in gaining approval for his plan. At the end of March, Castro had purged Aníbal Escalante, a leader of the Cuban Communist Party's old guard and one of the most important liaisons between the CPSU and the Integrated Revolutionary Organization (ORI)—the party apparatus created the previous year by merging the PSP with the Twenty-sixth of July Movement. Escalante's exile generated concern among the five-member Presidium team responsible for interparty relations, as it was feared that the delicate task of transforming Castro's ORI into a strictly pro-Moscow communist party might be in jeopardy. Khrushchev, the leading member of the team, played on the worries of fellow Presidium members Kuusinen and Suslov, and two secretaries from the Central Committee Secretariat, Andropov and Ponomarev, persuading them that acceding to Castro's spurious defense request would allow the Kremlin more leverage in the molding of his regime. It is interesting to note that the two junior team members, Yuri Andropov and Boris Ponomarev, later played major roles in shaping Soviet policy toward the Caribbean, with Ponomarev in particular emerging as the USSR's leading Latin American strategist.[50]

In late July, Soviet shipping traffic to Cuba increased dramatically. During the month of August, thirty-seven Soviet dry-cargo ships arrived at Cuban ports, at least twenty of them carrying arms shipments. By the end of the month, Soviet military materiel included surface-to-air missiles (SAMs), cruise missiles, Komar-class guided missile boats, some five thousand Soviet personnel, and tons of electronic and construction equipment. The first medium-range ballistic missiles (MRBMs) arrived on September 8 hidden in the hold of a Soviet lumber ship fitted with unusually large hatches.

Throughout September, more MRBMs and support equipment for both MRBMs and intermediate-range ballistic missiles (IRBMs) arrived in Cuba together with prefabricated materials for building nuclear warhead storage bunkers. All of this materiel was rapidly transported to nine missile sites. The September arms deliveries also brought Il-28 bombers, MiG-21 fighters and additional SAMs, cruise missiles, and patrol boats.[51] On September 22, the Soviet Union announced that it had agreed to help Cuba defend itself from "aggressive imperialist quarters" by delivering "armaments and sending technical specialists for training Cuban servicemen."[52]

The Soviet "technical specialists" numbered some twenty-two thousand military and civilian personnel by mid-October. These forces were primarily deployed at four major installations to assemble, operate, and defend the Soviet missiles. These bases were under complete Soviet control and off-limits to all Cubans, including senior members of the Castro government. Each base was guarded by a regimental-sized armored group that included approximately forty T-54 tanks, Frog tactical nuclear weapons, Snapper antitank rockets, and SA-2 SAMs.[53]

The story of the U.S. discovery of the Soviet missiles and the crisis that followed has been told and thoroughly analyzed elsewhere.[54] In retrospect, the USSR's acquiescence to the U.S. demand for removal of the missiles is easily understandable given the USSR's policy of avoiding a serious armed confrontation with the United States. Soviet prestige suffered, as did the subsequent political career of Nikita Khrushchev, yet history has demonstrated that the Soviet Union lost a launching pad for its missiles while gaining an invaluable base for subversion and an equally important proxy.

Contrary to popular belief, the famous Kennedy–Khrushchev "understanding" that led to the resolution of the Cuban missile crisis never really existed in the sense of a formal agreement, either orally or in writing. In the autumn of 1970, Henry Kissinger reported to President Richard Nixon that there was "an implicit understanding" in 1962 that the United States "would agree to give assurances against an invasion of Cuba" if the Soviet Union removed its "offensive missiles from Cuba under UN observation and would undertake, with suitable safeguards, to halt the re-introduction of such weapons' systems into Cuba." However, as Dr. Kissinger told the president, the "agreement" was never completed because the Kremlin would not agree to an acceptable verification system, and the United States, as a result, never made a formal non-invasion pledge. The negotiations to work out a mutually satisfactory means of formalizing the Kennedy–Khrushchev "understanding" eventually "just fizzled out."[55]

It would be scarcely credible to assume that Soviet strategists in the early 1960s saw Cuba as only a launching pad for medium- or intermediate-range missiles or a "bargaining chip" to secure nuclear-free zones in Germany and the Far East.[56] The great Soviet naval strategist Admiral Sergei Gorshkov was already in a position to exert a major influence on the USSR's Caribbean strategy due to the positions he held as commander-in-chief of the Soviet Navy and deputy minister of defense. From Gorshkov's study of the works of the nineteenth-century U.S. strategist Admiral Alfred Thayer Mahan, he was aware of Cuba's commanding position astride the Caribbean's major sea lines of communication (SLOCs).[57] Regardless of Nikita Khrushchev's grasp of the long-term strategic advantages of Cuba as a Soviet base, other Soviet strategists and Latin Americanists—including Mikoyan and Ponomarev—were aware of Cuba's potential as a politico-military asset.[58]

The blow to the Kremlin's international prestige caused by the missile crisis only served to harden its goal of achieving military superiority over the United States. It also bolstered the USSR's determination to maintain Cuba and exploit the island for strategic advantage. In November 1962, Vasiliy V. Kuznetsov, until recently first deputy of the Presidium, told the U.S. special representative to the United Nations, John McCloy, that the Soviet Union would never again back down to U.S. power in a crisis as it had been forced to do in Cuba the previous month.[59]

Soviet Preeminence

Due to the USSR's decision to dismantle its Cuban missile bases without consulting with or informing the Castro government, Soviet–Cuban relations were strained for several weeks after the end of the missile crisis, but not to the serious extent reported by writers such as Theodore Sorenson and Elie Abel.[60] Although Fidel Castro accused Khrushchev of cowardice and angrily refused to allow a UN inspection team into Cuba, his public statements were largely histrionic. The Cuban leader was engaged in a dangerous balancing act. Without Soviet aid his regime was hopelessly vulnerable, yet he knew that his internal support would be threatened if he did not openly identify with the Cuban people's outrage over what they viewed as Soviet disregard for their nation's sovereignty. For the remainder of October and the first week in November 1962, Castro authorized *Revolución* to publish a series of articles extolling his role as the symbol of Cuba's differences with the USSR and exalting Cuban nationalism. After eleven anti-Russian articles had appeared in *Revolución,* Castro personally ordered the editor to "lay off the Soviets."[61]

The hypocrisy of the Cuban media's brief anti-Soviet campaign is illustrated by the muted coverage given to Anastas Mikoyan's arrival in Havana on November 2 to confer with Castro. *Bohemia* magazine covered the official reception at José Martí airport, reporting how Fidel and Mikoyan embraced "more as friends than as officials," while Raúl Castro, Guevara, and "other figures of our national life" looked on.[62] The next day, *Hoy* quoted Mikoyan's pledge to the Cuban people that his countrymen "are by your side, full of scorn for your enemies, and by your side we will fight."[63] The myth that Mikoyan was snubbed by Castro for much of his stay is completely disproved by the November 9, 1962, issue of *Bohemia:*

> The talks between the Vice Prime Minister of the USSR and the Cuban leadership should have begun on Saturday, November 3. But (due to the death of Mikoyan's wife) the meeting was postponed for 24 hours. On Sunday, the 4th, the conference began in the Cabinet Room of the Presidential Palace. Representing the USSR were Mikoyan and Ambassador Alejandro Alexeyev. The Cuban representation consists of Fidel, Dorticos, Raul, Guevara, Carlos Rafael Rodriguez, and Aragones.[64]

During the course of Mikoyan's visit, Castro made a television address to stress his goodwill toward the USSR and defend its decision to withdraw the missiles. "There will be no breaches between Cuba and the Soviet Union," he told his audience, "because we are friends of the Soviet Union." Castro stated that he approved of the missile removal because "the strategic arms are not the property of Cuba. When the Soviet Union decided to withdraw these arms we abided by their decision." Attributing the Cuban people's injured national pride to misunderstanding, he said that "confusion on this point will disappear, little by little." Castro also announced that the USSR had canceled all indebtedness for Soviet bloc armaments sent to the island and lauded the large number of Soviet military and civilian personnel remaining in Cuba as "symbols of all the generosity, all the nobility, and all the friendship which the Soviets have shown us."[65]

While the number of Soviet personnel in Cuba gradually declined, the Kennedy administration remained silent on their presence as well as the three squadrons of MiG-21 aircraft serviced and flown by Russian crews. When pressed by his advisers in August 1963 to issue a public demand for the withdrawal of all Soviet forces in Cuba, President Kennedy refused because he did not wish to place Khrushchev "in a position where he has no alternative except humiliation."[66] Although probably unanticipated by the Kremlin, the Soviet Union had been handed a major victory by the U.S. government in the form of a de facto recognition of its right to maintain military forces in Cuba.

In early 1963, Castro accepted an invitation from Khrushchev to visit the Soviet Union, arriving with his entourage on April 27. The USSR gave him a hero's welcome, deftly playing on his vanity and overriding ambition to be accepted as a world figure. The Cuban leader returned to Havana with glowing reports to his people of the greatness of the Soviet Union and the magnificent qualities of Nikita Khrushchev. Castro announced the contents of a joint Soviet–Cuban declaration that recognized Cuba as a full member of the "great socialist community" and of recognition of the ruling party (renamed the United Party of the Socialist Revolution [PURS] as a genuine Marxist-Leninist "vanguard." The declaration also contained a commitment by the USSR to "defend the liberty and independence of the Republic of Cuba." For their part, the Cubans declared their acceptance of the unity of the socialist camp as defined by the Soviet Union as well as the official Soviet doctrine of peaceful coexistence between socialist and capitalist states.[67]

The declaration was also a minor personal triumph for Nikita

Khrushchev, whose political star had been in decline since the missile crisis. Khrushchev had been forced to scrap his efforts at economic liberalization and reorganization within the USSR while simultaneously trying to cope with the fragmenting of the international communist movement brought about by the break with China. Castro's public acknowledgment of Moscow's socialist preeminence temporarily stymied Khrushchev's opponents on the CPSU Central Committee and eased relations with troublesome members of the socialist bloc. Even the People's Republic of China (PRC), which had lambasted Khrushchev's handling of the missile crisis as "adventurism" and "capitulationism," entered into a brief period of détente with Moscow after Castro's visit.

The Utility of Revolution

The advent of Fidel Castro had inspired a quantum increase in the study of Latin America and the Caribbean within the Soviet Union's academic and intelligence communities. In January 1959, the Soviet government sponsored the Association for Friendship and Cultural Collaboration with the Latin American Countries which, within two years, established contacts with more than four hundred cultural and academic centers in fourteen Latin American and Caribbean countries. In 1961, on the personal recommendation of Anastas Mikoyan, a generously subsidized Latin American Institute was created in Moscow to train experts in Latin American country studies, sociopolitical problems, and economics.[68] As an indication of the institute's role as an adjunct to the foreign policy apparatus, its first director was a senior Soviet diplomat named Sergey S. Mikhailov who left after four years to become ambassador to Brazil. Scholars at the institute were responsible for much of the analysis and theoretical work influencing the steadily evolving Soviet strategy toward the Caribbean. Today, the USSR's Latin American Institute has the largest centrally planned research program on the area in the world. Data collection and collation are given high priority and are coordinated with KGB, GRU (Soviet Military Intelligence), and other operatives at Soviet embassies throughout Latin America. The institute also had a regular exchange program for Latin American students and scholars for the purpose of identifying and training pro-Soviet individuals who may have an influence on future politics of their respective Latin American and Caribbean countries.[69]

The Latin American Institute's first and most seriously studied subject was Castro's revolution and its feasibility as a model for the introduction of communist governments into other Latin American countries. Third World Marxist-Leninists looked to Moscow for help in resolving the dispute then raging over the orthodoxy of the Castroite route to power.[70]

Fidel Castro's dispute over the armed insurrectionary method of achieving power versus peaceful (albeit subversive) means was *not* with the Kremlin but rather with the orthodox, pro-Moscow communist parties of Latin America. Soviet strategists remained largely aloof from the debate on revolutionary strategy during the early 1960s. Although they seriously doubted whether Castroite tactics could succeed unless local political conditions were ripe for revolution, they did not oppose Castro and his followers both for reasons of opportunism and fear of driving Latin American guerrilla movements into the Maoist camp. On the other hand, the Kremlin remained publicly committed to a doctrine of "peaceful coexistence" (to which even Castro paid lip service) and thus could not repudiate the carefully nurtured network of orthodox communists who opposed Castro's approach to winning power.[71]

In 1963, Anatolii F. Shul'govskii (now the USSR's leading specialist on Marxist-Leninist theory in relation to Latin America and head of the Department for Research on Sociopolitical Questions at the Latin American Institute) published a scholarly article on the Cuban Revolution that laid the theoretical foundation for subsequent Soviet strategy toward Latin America and the Caribbean. Shul'govskii recognized Castro's coup d'état as "one of the most important events in modern times" because it signified "an important step in the development of the world-wide national liberation and communist movement." In a straightforward approach unusual in officially sanctioned Soviet theoretical writings, Shul'govskii stated the four aspects of the Cuban Revolution that were "attracting the greatest attention" from Soviet strategists:

1. Castro's triumph was "the first socialist revolution accomplished in the . . . backyard of U.S. imperialism," and, as a

result, Cuba has "become the active vanguard of all the 200 million Latin Americans." Latin America, overlooked by the Kremlin as an area of extreme U.S. vulnerability, had "long been ripe for a revolution of deep social character." This revolution "on a continental scale" was now possible because "Cuba destroyed the myth of geopolitical fatalism with respect to the United States and Latin America."

2. Because the Cuban Revolution had been allowed to thrive "a mere ninety miles from the United States" it demonstrated that "the world had entered a new era characterized by the dominant strength of communism and the socialist camp," an international arena in which "imperialism" could "no longer do whatever it wishes to." Thus, the Cuban Revolution served as "a graphic expression of the new alignment of powers in the world."[72]

3. The Cuban Revolution wrought major revisions ("clarifications") in Marxist-Leninist revolutionary doctrine. It demonstrated "that the genuine revolution will succeed only as a result of a combination of all forms of struggle, with one or another of the forms prevailing depending upon the conjuncture of forces, place, time, and conditions of the moment." Although it was somewhat grudgingly acknowledged that "armed conflict, headed by the rebel army and its leader, Fidel Castro, became the decisive form of the struggle" in Cuba, "it should not be forgotten that preparations for the insurrection were aided greatly" by other actions such as strikes, election boycotts, and so on. In the final analysis, the "Cuban experience conclusively demonstrated that no national-reformist, conciliatory leadership could lead the Latin American countries to socialism."

4. Special attention was given to the carefully worded statement that the Cuban Revolution "in its current second stage" was "the first socialist revolution on the American continent." Of great strategic significance was the Soviet perception that "the transition to the socialist revolution took place in Cuba under conditions of peaceful coexistence, without war"—a

confirmation of the Soviet doctrine that great strategic gains could be made via subversion and other means during periods of détente or "peaceful coexistence" with the West.[73]

The impact of Shul'govskii's theoretical work on actual Soviet foreign and strategic policy became evident in the summer of 1964 by publication of an article in *Kommunist* by M. Kudachkin and N. Mostovets. Mikhail Kudachkin, the politically powerful chief of the Latin American section of the CPSU Central Committee, noted that "events in recent years have proved that the Latin American countries, which the imperialists regarded as their reliable rear guard, are being turned into a scene of anti-imperialist struggle . . . over a vast territory stretching from the Rio Grande on the north to Tierra del Fuego in the South."[74]

The article, "The Liberation Movement in Latin America," was the first official indication of the Kremlin's approval of Castroite insurrectionary movements. Kudachkin and Mostovets said that although the Latin American revolutionaries had "a great deal in common with the anti-imperialist movements of Asia and Africa," they also had their "own peculiarities" due to different stages of socioeconomic development. These differences called for "far different methods and means" in the revolutionary struggle and were deemed perfectly acceptable to "the general line of the international communist movement" as drafted and accepted at the 1957 and 1960 Moscow conferences. The experiences of both the orthodox Latin American communists and the guerrilla movements served to "refute the anti-Marxist theories of the leadership of the CCP" (Chinese Communist Party), which were said to be "aimed at the alienation of the national-liberation movement from the common struggle of the peoples . . . for socialism."[75] This last sentence is a significant reminder of the Soviet Union's concern that China might usurp the international revolutionary process if the Kremlin did not adopt a more flexible official doctrine.

An extrapolation of this new revolutionary policy appeared in another *Kommunist* article the following month. This piece specifically approved the utility of armed struggle and guerrilla operations in some Latin American countries while supporting peaceful means to power in others. However, this statement of policy warned that "armed struggle and the creation of partisan detachments" was "a completely justified course" only where dictators who were "the henchmen of foreign monopolies" were in power, and did not apply to liberal reformist regimes.[76]

Implementation of the "many roads to power" strategy did not take place until after the resignation of Nikita Khrushchev in October 1964. Acting upon Palmiro Togliatti's recommendation to convene regional meetings of communist parties,[77] the Soviet Union called a conference in Havana in December 1964 that ostensibly was to be attended by all Latin American and Caribbean communist parties but which excluded pro-Chinese splinter groups. Castro's willingness to allow the meeting to be held in Cuba further estranged the Chinese and thus was seen as another victory for the USSR in the worsening Sino–Soviet dispute. There is evidence that Castro had lobbied for the policy shift and saw it as a personal vindication for his Latin American strategy rather than as an indication of growing Soviet control over his regime.[78] At this stage, Castro naively believed that he could continue to use the Soviets for his own ends while maintaining his independence—a misconception later held by the Bishop regime in Grenada and the Sandinistas in Nicaragua.

The Soviet policy change was given official approval in a resolution adopted by the CPSU and the Latin American communist parties at the Havana meeting. Soviet policymakers achieved a surface unity among the Caribbean and Latin American communists by the Solomonic device of dividing nations between Castroite and orthodox strategies based on the degree of repression and the viability of insurgent forces in those countries. The resolution called for "support in an active form" for "fighters" in Venezuela, Colombia, Guatemala, Honduras, Paraguay, and Haiti. In all other countries, Castro and his followers were expected to work amicably with orthodox communist parties that followed traditional tactics. To maintain communist unity in Latin America, the Havana resolution called for further meetings of parties so that they could concert their activities or agree to pursue different policies in various areas.[79]

The apparently successful outcome of the Havana conference pleased the Kremlin's strategists, for it allowed them to exploit any revolutionary opportunity that occurred in Latin America and the Caribbean without undue risk to the USSR's international prestige or relations with the West. Fidel Castro would effectively serve as their proxy: if his insurrectionary tactics succeeded, the Soviet Union could eventually move in and take control of the new regime; if Castroite methods failed, the Kremlin could disavow support for violent revolution and self-righteously proclaim its enduring commitment to "peaceful coexistence." What was important, though, was that Soviet influence would prevail regardless of the road to power taken by communists in Latin America and the Caribbean.

Fidel Castro had other ideas. He thought that the time had come for him to wean his regime of what he perceived as a pretence of vassalage to the USSR so that he could emerge as the undisputed fountainhead of revolution in the Western Hemisphere.

The Taming of Fidel Castro

Fidel Castro's move to assert his independence came only days after the close of the Havana conference. In his traditional Anniversary of the Revolution speech on January 2, 1965, he told the Cuban people that they had come to take socialist aid against imperialist aggression too much for granted. This had created "a kind of obsequious [*acomodaticio*] attitude on the part of our people" toward their Soviet benefactors. This meant that "something is lacking in our revolutionary spirit," and thus there was a danger of "lowering our revolutionary dignity."[80] Castro's criticism of both the Soviet Union and China grew bolder during the year leading up to the Tricontinental Conference ("The First Conference of Solidarity of the Peoples of Africa, Asia, and Latin America") held in Havana in January 1966, which the Cuban leader intended to use as a pulpit for winning converts to his revolutionary strategy throughout the Third World.

The Tricontinental Conference was a success in building Soviet and Cuban ties with disparate revolutionary groups (including the founders of the Sandinistas), but proved a disappointment to Fidel Castro. The Soviet delegate, a candidate Politburo member, preempted Castro's plan to be recognized as grand master of Third World insurrectionary movements by unequivocal affirmation of the USSR's support for "people's liberation wars, the armed struggle of oppressed peoples."[81] The Chinese delegation attacked Castro, thereby nearly completing the PRC's estrangement from Cuba and rendering it almost impossible for Castro to continue his tactic of playing off the Russians against the Chinese. Castro deeply resented being perceived as a Soviet puppet by those Third World nations and organizations he had hoped to impress, and is reported to have remarked bitterly that "it is the USSR which has attached itself to the Cuban line."[82]

During the second half of 1966, Castro began to deliberately strain his relationship with Moscow. In addition to the increased stridency of his call for violent revolution in Latin America and Africa, he adopted an ideological line of "left revisionism," denouncing material incentives and proclaiming that Cuba was arriving at the stage of communism before the USSR. Castro's vendetta against bureacratism left the economy a shambles while he wasted Soviet aid on a variety of almost comically absurd ventures such as the giant Coppelia ice cream emporium. However, his worst heresy, in the eyes of fellow members of the Soviet bloc, was the assertion that he, and not the CPSU, was the real revolutionary.[83]

The Kremlin grew increasingly concerned that Castro's inept handling of the machinery of government might cost it the USSR's considerable investment in Cuba. Dissension had grown to epidemic proportions, leading to acts of sabotage and the formation of at least 179 "counterrevolutionary bands" which, Raúl Castro admitted in July 1967, cost the regime "precious lives and the equivalent of between 500 and 800 million U.S. dollars" to "liquidate."[84] In 1966, members of a "microfaction" (composed of old-line communist members of the PSP such as Aníbal Escalante) had begun regular meetings with Soviet and other Eastern bloc officials to warn them of impending disaster in Cuba if corrective measures were not taken against Fidel Castro. These microfaction members were convinced that the Cuban Revolution had become fundamentally anti-communist and anti-Soviet and was headed for political and economic bankruptcy. Fidel, whom they described as "crazy," was said to want to "rise to a higher stature . . . than Marx, Engels and Lenin."[85] Moscow's local agents concurred with this assessment, for Rudolf P. Shliapnikov, a senior KGB adviser attached to the Cuban Ministry of the Interior, told members of the microfaction that "in Cuba, conditions are present for a new Hungary . . . internal dissension is great." The KGB officer felt that Cuba's police apparatus was inadequate to deal effectively with a general uprising because it was filled with "petit bourgeois."[86] Such an insurrection could prove disastrous for Soviet strategic plans in Latin America and the Caribbean, for it would be an open invitation for U.S. intervention.

Following the meeting at which Shliapnikov expressed his views, another KGB operative identified as Vadim Lestov was sent from Moscow to contact Aníbal Escalante and take his written report directly to the CPSU Central Committee. Two groups of East Germans were also sent to Cuba to investigate the situation, while Dr. Emilio de Quesada, a member of the microfaction, traveled to Prague to confer with a senior member of the Czech Communist Party's Central Committee.[87] The internal situation in Cuba was deemed so serious that Soviet Prime Minister Aleksei Kosygin spent five days in Havana after his June 1967 meeting with President Johnson. During Kosygin's visit, Raúl Castro reportedly confronted Soviet Ambassador Alexandr Alexeiv with evidence that Shliapnikov and other Russian advisers had been conspiring with the microfaction. Shliapnikov was recalled to Moscow the next month, while Alexeiv, a rather easygoing KGB officer who had served in Cuba since 1959 and was considered to have "gone native," left Havana "to undergo medical treatment," leaving the Soviet embassy without an ambassador for nearly ten months.[88]

The Soviet Latin Americanists' exhaustive analysis of the Castro regime must have led the CPSU Central Committee to the conclusion that elimination of the charismatic Fidel Castro would have proved counterproductive insofar as such an act might provide the catalyst for a civil war and subsequent U.S. intervention. As will be seen, a remarkably similar situation developed during the last months of Grenada's People's Revolutionary Government, when unsuccessful attempts were made to maintain Castro's popular protégé Maurice Bishop as a ceremonial leader rather than depose him in favor of the pro-Moscow Coard faction.

The Kremlin decided to "tame" Fidel Castro by applying economic and political pressure on him. Economic figures corroborate the timing of this decision, for Soviet military aid to Cuba seems to have stopped at the end of 1966 and resumed three years later. A gradual reduction in oil shipments also began in the last part of 1966, leading to cutbacks in parades as early as January 1967 "to save oil."[89] One year later gasoline rationing was imposed as factories, sugar mills, and vehicles stopped running for lack of fuel and Cuba was gripped by its worst economic paralysis in history. The situation proved so critical that one-third of Cuba's military petroleum reserves had to be diverted to the civilian economy.

In retrospect, the Soviet Union was remarkably patient with Fidel Castro, perhaps because its policymakers realized that his continuance in power was as vital to their strategic ambitions in the Western Hemisphere as his own goals were dependent on their continuing goodwill. However, in addition to its curtailment of economic and military aid, the Kremlin demonstrated its power to Castro in other ways. It did so in the case of Che Guevara's final guerrilla adventure in Bolivia, which some of his men reached after a circuitous journey through the Soviet bloc where they were reportedly supplied with false passports to enable them to enter Argentina and Bolivia.[90] On the final day of the year 1966, the secretary general of the pro-Moscow Bolivian Communist Party arrived in Guevara's camp to discuss joint operations, but only on the condition that Guevara agree to follow "a line parallel to that of the Party" (that is, adhere to the dictates of the Kremlin) and that the secretary general be named political and military chief of the guerrillas. When Guevara refused to accept these conditions, he was abandoned by the orthodox Bolivian communists and subsequently captured and executed by Bolivian security forces. Speculation remains that Guevara was betrayed by a Soviet agent as a lesson to Castro.[91]

By the end of 1967, Castro's options had become severely restricted. Guevara's death symbolized the failure of independent Castroite guerrilla movements in Latin America and revealed the danger of trying to put pressure on the Soviet Union. The United States remained committed to denying Cuba any real access to Western markets, while the Chinese had virtually written off the Castro regime and even criticized Guevara after his death.[92] Cuba sank deeper into an economic morass as trade deficits with the USSR increased, goods grew scarce, and rationing became part of the status quo.

Fidel Castro's final fling of anti-Soviet behavior began in the last months of 1967. On November 6, he deliberately snubbed the Kremlin by ordering his ambassador to Moscow not to attend the heavily publicized ceremony honoring the 50th anniversary of the Bolshevik Revolution. This was a serious transgression, for the USSR intended the anniversary celebrations to inspire respect for its power and achievements among an array of Third World leaders who had been invited to Moscow for the event. Castro had succeeded in embarrassing the Soviet Union in front of Third World regimes (such as his own) that were being wooed into the Soviet camp. The Cuban leader's latest assertion of independence was also poorly timed in light of the Kremlin's concern over Romania's new independent stance vis-à-vis Soviet foreign policy. Only seven months previously Romania had defied Moscow by establishing diplomatic relations with West Germany and had subsequently developed strong "fraternal" relations with the notoriously nonconformist Castro regime.

The crisis in Soviet–Cuban relations reached a head in January 1968 with the trial of thirty-five members of the pro-Moscow microfaction, who were sentenced to lengthy prison terms for engaging in "clandestine propaganda against the line of the Party" and attempting to "undermine Cuba's international relations with other governments."[93] Simultaneously with news of the trial came the announcement that Cuba would not participate in the forthcoming meeting of communist parties to be held in Budapest. These actions could not have come at a worse time for the Kremlin which, troubled by Romania's defiance, had just witnessed the beginning of the "Prague Spring" with Alexander Dubček's accession to power in Czechoslovakia.

A decision to take a much sterner line with the Castro regime had already been made by the time of the microfaction trial, probably as a result of Aníbal Escalante's arrest on December 10, 1967. In mid-January, the Soviet Union announced that its new ambassador to Cuba was Alexandr Soldatov, a high-ranking professional diplomat who had recently completed a tour of duty as ambassador to Great Britain.[94] Several weeks later *Pravda* carried an article by the director of the Latin American Institute that openly criticized Castro's policies for the first time. However, the article ended with the customary affirmation that the Soviet Union "has helped and will continue to help Cuba in every way possible," a signal that Fidel, the prodigal son, still had the option of returning to the Soviet fold.[95]

Sometime during the spring of 1968, Fidel Castro came to the conclusion that accommodation with the Soviet Union was the only way his regime could survive. There is strong evidence that Raúl Castro, Fidel's younger brother, played the decisive role in influencing this policy shift. Raúl had always maintained close ties with Moscow and, although one of the main accusers at the trial of the microfaction, had made a point of exempting Soviet military advisers from any wrongdoing. It is also significant that Raúl Castro had taken a lengthy leave of absence from the Armed Forces Ministry in January 1967, ostensibly "to study." It seems likely that the younger Castro deliberately chose to distance himself from the quarrel with the USSR so as to protect his own communication lines with the Kremlin.[96] Whatever the exact scenario may have been, both Castro brothers must have become alarmed at the perilous state of their regime, manifested in the wave of sabotage that began to spread over the entire island in April. This was accompanied by acts of vandalism committed by roving bands of youthful dissenters in downtown Havana.[97]

It was Raúl Castro who gave the first public indication that a deal had been struck with the Soviet Union, choosing the traditional May Day celebration (an occasion marked by the conspicuous absence of Fidel) to make a speech that was totally devoid of his brother's now routine criticism of the USSR. Later that month, Fidel Castro emerged to receive a high-ranking Bulgarian trade mission, which advanced Cuba credit for the purchase of agro-industrial equipment. This apparently insignificant event is important as an indication that the Kremlin had accepted Castro's gesture of obeisance, for the state visit to Cuba of Todor Zhivkov, the Bulgarian premier, had been abruptly canceled in mid-January as a sign of Soviet displeasure.[98] A further sign of the thaw in Cuban–Soviet

relations is the speech given by Fidel on May 30 in which he effu-
sively praised the East Germans, conveniently forgetting that they
had been singled out as coconspirators with the microfaction only
five months earlier.[99]

According to the testimony of defectors, a secret agreement was
signed with the Soviet Union in the spring of 1968 that effectively
ceded Cuban sovereignity in exchange for Soviet economic aid. The
reported terms of the treaty were as follows.

First and foremost, the Russians demanded the institutionalization of the Soviet model; that is, a strict adherence to Moscow's
interpretation of the principles of democratic centralism and
proletarian internationalism. Although this was resisted by the en-
trenched Cuban bureaucracy, a number of orthodox Marxist-Leninists eventually were given positions of influence in the policy-
making apparatus.[100]

Secondly, the Castro government pledged not to make any public pronouncements against the USSR and to "accept the historic
role that the Communist Parties play in the world revolution and
especially in Latin America." Castro promised "not to discredit
these parties publicly so that there will not be anti-communist and
anti-Soviet belief in Latin America, etc."[101]

The Soviet part of the secret agreement was designed to serve
as a means of gaining direct control over every Cuban government
ministry. The Soviet negotiators stated that they would "increase
considerably their technical assistance through which they would
send an approximate number of five thousand technicians, who
would be distributed in the Armed Forces, mineralogy, industrial
processing and exploitation of mineral deposits, atomic reactor, agriculture, fishing, DGI, etc." The USSR would also increase its shipments of raw materials and agricultural machinery and enlarge its
volume of purchases from Cuba.[102]

Raúl Castro was officially reinstated as minister of the Revolutionary armed forces, first deputy prime minister, and second secretary of the Cuban Communist Party (PCC) only days before Soviet troops crushed the Dubček regime on August 21, 1968. Fidel
Castro refrained from passing judgment on the invasion for more
than two days, during which time Cubans were presented with the
extraordinary spectacle of Czech technical advisers, accompanied

by sympathetic Cubans, parading through Havana with banners reading "Russians Go Home From Czechoslovakia."[103] Given the prevalent Cuban mood of solidarity with the Czechs, Fidel Castro's public "analysis" of the Soviet invasion on the night of August 23 offers telling evidence of the USSR's achievement of hegemony over his nation. The Cuban leader's opening remarks were perhaps an indication of his own sympathies as well as his peoples', for he told his television and radio audience that "some of the things we are going to say here will be in contradiction with the emotions of many."[104]

Castro said that the Czech leadership had been "in camaraderie with pro-Yankee spies" and with "the agents of West Germany and all that fascist and reactionary rabble." There could be no other conclusion but that "Czechoslovakia was moving toward a counterrevolutionary situation, toward capitalism and into the arms of imperialism." At this point, Fidel launched into an extraordinarily faithful paraphrasing of the "Brezhnev Doctrine," which had been published in *Pravda* only the day before: "We consider that it was absolutely necessary, at all costs, in one way or another, to prevent this eventuality from taking place. . . . Our point of view is that . . . the socialist camp has a right to prevent this in one way or another. . . . We look upon this fact as an essential one."[105]

Cuban Vassalage

Cuba's incorporation into the Soviet system accelerated after Castro's historic endorsement of the Brezhnev Doctrine. Aside from the conversion of Cuba into a major military bastion, the two main objectives of the Kremlin were stabilization of the Cuban economy and the organization of a dependably pro-Soviet government.

Moscow was greatly concerned about Cuba's growing commercial debt, arising out of the island's chronic trade deficit with the Soviet bloc. The trade deficit, which amounted to 441.8 million rubles ($339 million) in 1968, represented only a part of Cuba's debt to the USSR and its satellites, which included hard currency loans, cumulative interest charged on credits, and the cost of supporting Soviet technical and military advisers. Without Che Guevara to guide his economic policies, Castro came under Soviet pressure to recant his grievous mismanagement of the Cuban economy. In the spring of 1970, he cryptically said that "a certain scepticism [has] developed concerning our economic plans" in Moscow.[106] Castro followed this statement on July 26 with an unusual public confession of errors in economic planning and management, warning his people that they faced a lengthy period of shortages and other economic problems.

During the remainder of the year, the Kremlin began the process of recasting the Cuban economy in the Soviet mold. In December 1970, the Soviet–Cuban Inter-Governmental Commission for Economic, Scientific, and Technological Cooperation was established to assist Cuba in undertaking long-range economic planning in coordination with the USSR's current five-year plan.[107] It is worth noting that at the same time the commission was formed, a member of the CPSU Central Committee was appointed ambassador to Cuba, signifying a determination on the part of the Kremlin to take a direct role in the management of the Cuban government.

The USSR continued to expand its presence in Cuba by increments, testing the United States' reaction at each step before continuing. The Cienfuegos affair and other military probes (discussed in the following chapter) left the Kremlin with few doubts that Washington had effectively ceded Cuba to the Soviet sphere of influence. In July 1972, the Soviet Union took the extraordinary step of granting Cuba full membership in the Council for Mutual Economic Assistance (CMEA or COMECON), thereby submitting the Cuban economy to the discipline of integration with the Soviet and Eastern European economies. Because the ruble is mandated as the standard currency for international transactions within COMECON, the Soviet Union automatically became the legal arbiter of Cuba's trade and controlled the peso's rate of exchange—a classic dependency feature of imperialism similar to America's colonial ties with Britain. Cuba's membership in COMECON also illustrates the strategic importance the USSR now officially attached to the island, for Cuba was, and remains, the only COMECON member in the world outside of the Soviet Eurasian landmass.

By the time of its admission to COMECON, Cuba already ranked sixth in order of major Soviet trading partners, ahead of Romania.[108] On December 23, 1972, the USSR signed five major trade, aid, and debt rescheduling agreements with Cuba while Fidel Castro was in Moscow to celebrate the fiftieth anniversary of the founding of the Soviet Union.[109] The terms of the agreements are unusual in light of the USSR's standard miserliness in administering economic aid to other Third World client states. These therefore serve as further evidence that the Kremlin was making a long-term investment in Cuba from which it hoped to reap substantial strategic gains. Essentially, the agreements deferred the liquidation of Cuba's accumulated debt to the Soviet Union since 1960, with payments on principal and interest to begin in 1986 and run until the year 2011. Moscow also granted massive new credits, with payments on the new debt also postponed to the twenty-five-year period between 1986 and 2011. In effect, this amounts to little more than a huge subsidy from the Soviet Union in consideration of the normal attrition in the value of the peso over such a long repayment period as well as the moratorium on interest payments during this time.[110]

By the end of 1975, Soviet and Eastern European advisers and technicians had largely taken over management of the ponderous Cuban economy and had inaugurated Cuba's first five-year plan, based directly on, and linked to, the Soviet model. This system, which remains in use today, seems designed to make Cuba permanently dependent on the Soviet Union, for it left sugar as the principal sector of the economy, subsidized by the USSR at a price well above the world market rate. Nickel, Cuba's second major export, is also heavily subsidized at prices pegged on occasion as high as 50 percent above the world market price. Even excluding military aid and other types of "hidden" expenditures, cumulative Soviet economic aid to Cuba totaled $16.6 billion by 1979, and has since increased to the point where it now averages $4 billion per year, equivalent to over one-quarter of Cuba's gross national product. The Kremlin considers Cuba to be such a valuable strategic asset that it gives the island more than half of the Soviet Union's total international economic assistance.[111]

The USSR has also gone to great lengths to structure a government in Cuba that is subservient to Soviet interests while maintaining a facade of independence or "nonalignment." This was formally initiated at the first congress of the Cuban Communist Party, held in December 1975, which approved a set of principles and statutes nearly identical to those regulating the functions of the Soviet and Soviet bloc parties. Fidel and Raúl Castro were elected first and second secretaries, respectively, of the PCC Central Committee. The congress also approved a new constitution that specifically recognized "the help and cooperation of the Soviet Union" in the preamble. The constitution provided for a legislative body closely resembling the Supreme Soviet (without the Soviet of Nationalities) but called the "National Assembly of People's Power." The Cuban version of the Presidium of the Supreme Soviet was designated the Council of State.[112]

At the first session of the National Assembly of People's Power in December 1976, Fidel Castro was unanimously elected president of the Council of State, thereby automatically becoming president of the Council of Ministers. Thus, Fidel was confirmed as both head of state and head of the government, although his actual degree of power is debatable.

The Soviet Union, never a power to place its reliance on a single faction or leader, has ensured its control over the Cuban government by seeing to it that surviving members of the PSP (as well as henchmen of Raúl Castro, Fidel's legal heir) have been placed in key decision-making positions. The notorious microfaction trial has been long buried by the Castro regime, and Ramiro Valdés, the official responsible for the investigation and arrest of the microfaction in his powerful position as minister of the interior, was suddenly removed from office in August 1968. Valdés was placed in official limbo for some time as a sign of Soviet displeasure before being exonerated in late 1972.[113]

Since 1968, members of Fidel Castro's old Twenty-sixth of July Movement have been quietly removed from important positions in the Cuban government and replaced by PSP factionalists and "Raúlists"—younger, Soviet-trained officers from the Armed Forces Ministry. Today, the Executive Committee of the Council of Ministers, the Cuban government supervisory body for all governmental activities and departments, contains only two Twenty-sixth of July veterans including Fidel (the other, Guillermo García Frías, is a relative nonentity). The remainder of the Executive Committee is divided between Raúl plus two other Raúlists, and four PSP factionalists led by Carlos Rafael Rodríguez, who is one of the most powerful men in Cuba today as a result of his adroitness in political survival. Rodríguez's role on the Executive Committee is supervision of all foreign agencies, thus giving him control of all lines of communication with Moscow. He was responsible for the replacement, in 1975, of a Castroite with a PSP man in the sensitive post of ambassador to the Soviet Union.[114]

The younger Castro and his PSP allies also appear to have won control of the PCC Party Secretariat, where they constitute a bloc of at least seven votes against Fidel's three. Fidel still maintains dominance of the PCC's Political Bureau, and thus appears to have control of the actual Cuban Communist Party apparatus through his role as first secretary of the party. He will probably be allowed to remain the leader of Cuba for life if he never again oversteps the bounds established by his overlords in Moscow.

In comparison to his early nonconformity, Fidel Castro has been remarkably obedient to the terms of his 1968 agreement with the USSR. Any analysis of his statements and actions since that time shows that his support for Soviet foreign policy has been almost total. One of the most glaring examples of Cuban loyalty to the dictates of Moscow took place in the UN General Assembly on January 14, 1980, when Cuba backed the USSR in the roll-call vote that condemned the Soviet invasion of Afghanistan. The only other Western Hemisphere nation to support the USSR was Grenada, itself well on the road to Soviet vassalage thanks to the surrogate efforts of Cuba.

The Soviet Union's economic and political reorganization of Cuba was designed to provide a stable foundation for its main strategic interest in the island: its use as a Western Hemisphere bastion for the export of revolution and the ultimate projection of Soviet power.

SAN ANTONIO DE LOS BANOS AIRFIELD, CUBA

SOVIET NAVAL RECONNAISSANCE AIRCRAFT

3
Cuba: A Base for
Soviet Power Projection

Espionage and Subversion

Although the Soviet Union considers the intelligence services of its Eastern European satellites to be of great value, the four Cuban intelligence agencies—the *Dirección General de Inteligencia* (DGI), the *Dirección de Operaciones Especiales* (DOE), the *Departamento América* (DA), and the *Departamento General de Relaciones Exteriores* (DGRE)—have a role that is second only to the KGB in furthering Soviet global ambitions.[1]

In 1962, senior KGB officer Alexandr Alexeiv was named as Soviet ambassador to Cuba. Alexeiv, a personal friend of Fidel Castro, offered to organize and train the DGI (established in 1961) in the basic tradecraft of espionage and subversion. In 1963, the KGB started training DGI officers in Moscow, recruiting as many as it could as direct Soviet agents. As recounted in chapter 2, a few KGB officers who were niños—sons of Spanish communists who took refuge in the Soviet Union during and after the Spanish Civil War—posed as Cubans and actually joined the DGI.[2] However, until 1968, the DGI was overwhelmingly nationalistic and loyal to Fidel Castro. Under the direction of Ramiro Valdés and Manuel Piñeiro Losado, the DGI was largely responsible for the investigation and indictment of the PSP microfaction. In fact, as a result of the microfaction trial, all KGB advisers attached to the DGI had been summarily deported from Cuba.[3]

After the "taming" of Fidel Castro, the Soviet Union moved quickly to gain control of the DGI. During the winter of 1968–69,

---

Facing page: Soviet reconnaissance aircraft operate out of Cuba to fly missions along the U.S. Atlantic Coast. Nicaragua's Punta Huete runway is long enough to accommodate this type of aircraft, giving the Soviets a potential facility for reconnaissance flights along the U.S. Pacific Coast. *Department of Defense photo*

all chiefs of DGI centers overseas were recalled to Havana to receive orders from Manuel Piñeiro Losado concerning Cuba's new relationship with the Soviet Union. Aside from being informed that there had been a "lessening of contradictions between both countries," the DGI station chiefs were told that there was to be a new emphasis on industrial espionage to acquire scientific and technical information for the USSR.[4]

Following Raúl Castro's return from Moscow in the spring of 1970, the DGI was purged of all anti-Soviet officers and subjected to a fundamental reorganization. Between five and eight KGB advisers were attached to the executive office of the DGI, among them a KGB general who was given an office next door to the DGI chief. The KGB advisers were responsible for monitoring operations and communications involving all DGI divisions; the intelligence service's annual operations plan had to be submitted to the KGB general for his approval.[5] The DGI began expanding toward a goal of two thousand staff officers, twenty-five of whom were sent to Moscow each year for advanced training and indoctrination that the Kremlin hoped would instill loyalty to the USSR.[6] In addition, the reorganized DGI was ordered to recruit four hundred operatives into a "national liberation" department whose sole purpose was coordinating revolutionary activities. As Fidel Castro considered the latter to be his personal bailiwick, he set up a new organization called the Directorate of National Liberation (DLN) and largely staffed it with the anti-Soviet officers dismissed from the DGI.[7] Although the USSR allowed the DLN to exist—probably as a sop to Fidel's ego—the agency was cut off from all Soviet funds and shared intelligence, causing a severe restriction in its activities. Reportedly, many of the DLN's Castroite officers were later recruited into the DA (a branch of the Cuban Communist Party).[8]

The DGI and the DOE, together with an internal security branch called the *Departamento de Seguridad de Estado* (DSE), come under the jurisdiction of the Ministry of the Interior, now headed by the KGB-trained, former DSE chief General José Abrahantes.[9] The DGI has six divisions, equally divided between operations and support services. The three operations divisions consist of the Political/Economic Intelligence Division, the External Counterintelligence Division, and the Military Intelligence Division.[10]

The DGI's Political/Economic Intelligence Division consists of four sections: United States (including Mexico and Canada); Africa–Asia–Latin America; Western Europe; and Eastern Europe. The External Counterintelligence Division conducts operations against foreign intelligence services and Cuban exiles; the Military Intelligence Division mainly serves as a branch of the KGB in collecting information on the U.S. armed forces.[11] The DGI's military Intelligence Division also uses Cuban diplomatic cover in Western Europe to collect information on NATO forces.[12]

Today the DGI's overseas operations are so closely coordinated with the KGB that it effectively functions as an arm of Soviet intelligence. For example, at the end of 1971, the Cuban intelligence agency began operating an espionage network in Great Britain for the benefit of the KGB as a result of the British government's expulsion of 105 Soviet agents in September of that year. Due to the USSR's inability to replace these agents with new operatives, the seven DGI officers at Cuba's London embassy (a post where the entire Cuban staff numbered only ten) were assigned some of the KGB's tasks in the British Isles, including intelligence collection and supervising the espionage activities of Moscow's Warsaw pact satellites.[13]

More recently, two DGI agents posing as UN delegates were expelled from the United States in July 1982 for attempting to set up a telecommunications monitoring system for eavesdropping on U.S. satellite relays.[14] The DGI is also extensively involved in international narcotics trafficking, and coordinates drug smuggling operations into the United States with both Marxist revolutionaries and international criminal organizations.[15]

The DOE (English translation: Directorate of Special Operations) is an elite special forces detachment used for highly skilled services such as the tactical and logistical support of guerrilla operations and the training of Latin American, Caribbean, and African revolutionaries. DOE commandos are first believed to have been employed abroad in Angola in November 1975, and subsequently had what may have been decisive roles in the Grenada coup d'état of 1979 and the final Sandinista offensive against the Somoza government in Nicaragua.[16] The DOE also protects Fidel Castro on both internal excursions and visits abroad and has been used to storm diplomatic missions in Havana occupied by Cubans seeking asylum.[17] With the exception of the Angolan operation, DOE troops normally serve in six- to ten-man teams and undergo training based on that used by the Soviet Union's *Spetznaz* special forces.[18]

Copying the system in effect in the Soviet Union, the PCC established its own intelligence branches in 1974. These took the form of the DA and the DGRE. DGI chief Manuel Piñeiro Losado, never trusted by the USSR since the microfaction trial, was given command of the DA, whose mission was subversion and covert contacts with leftist groups in the Western Hemisphere. DGRE was given this responsibility for the rest of the world.[19]

Though the DA and DGRE lack the generous funding of the DGI and compete with it in certain operations, they nonetheless serve the overall strategic interests of the USSR under the terms of Fidel Castro's 1968 agreement. In the fall of 1983, there were two or three DA officers at every Cuban diplomatic post in the Western Hemisphere, including the United Nations and the Cuban Interest Section in Washington, D.C. At the DA post in Panama, which also has responsibility for Colombia, there are currently about half a dozen DA agents. Several recent Cuban ambassadors have been identified as DA personnel, including Julián Enrique Torres Rizo in Grenada, Julián López Díaz in Nicaragua, and Oswaldo Cardenas Junquera (together with his wife, Ida Borja Paz Escalante de Gomez, also a DA agent) in Suriname. Other DA officers holding senior diplomatic positions are Damian Arteaga Hernandez, first secretary at the Cuban Embassy in Buenos Aires, Argentina; Pedro Silvio Gonzalez Perez, minister-counselor in Georgetown, Guyana; Jorge Luis Joa Campos, consul general in Mexico City; and Jose Francisco Ross Paz, chargé d'affaires in Quito, Ecuador.[20]

Cuban intelligence personnel selected for clandestine operations in Latin America and the Caribbean go through an elaborate training program conducted by Cuban, Soviet, East German, and Czech instructors in Havana, with special sessions in surrounding cities. Cuba's extensive cultural exchange and propaganda activities are designed to support covert operations and elicit support for armed struggle. *Prensa Latina,* the Cuban government's press agency, is reported to be completely under DGI control, as is the Institute for Friendship with the Peoples (ICAP).[21]

Prensa Latina has field offices in thirty-five countries, including eleven Latin American and Caribbean nations. The agency combines news gathering and propaganda dissemination with intelligence operations. Radio Havana, Cuba's shortwave broadcasting service, transmits more than 350 program hours per week in eight languages to all parts of the world. Prensa Latina and Radio Havana, in close coordination with Tass and Radio Moscow, regularly use disinformation to distort news reports transmitted to the Caribbean region, especially those concerning areas such as Central America, where Soviet–Cuban covert operations are most intense.[22]

Since 1964, the Soviet Union has generally backed Cuban efforts to incorporate nondoctrinaire revolutionary groups into broad politico-military fronts dedicated to armed struggle. However, it was not until Fidel Castro's successful unification of the three Nicaraguan Sandinista factions in 1978—the insurgency's turning point—that Moscow began to take a more active role in coordinating Latin American and Caribbean revolutionary movements. For example, a senior CPSU functionary traveled to Panama in August 1981 to discuss strategy for Central America with Manuel Piñeiro and leaders of various Marxist-Leninist fronts in Latin America.[23] The Soviet Union has also used its extensive propaganda network to selectively discredit anticommunist governments and organizations such as the Nicaraguan "contras," while building international support for revolutionaries such as the FMLN of El Salvador and the Chilean FPMR (Manual Rodríguez Patriotic Front).[24]

That the Soviet Union is more selective in its support of armed revolutionary groups than Cuba is due to its caution in becoming openly identified with insurgents seeking to overthrow Latin American governments with which Moscow maintains "normal" diplomatic relations. During 1985, the Soviet media largely refrained from public support of the Colombian M-19 and FARC (Revolutionary Armed Forces of Colombia)—both of which are actively supported by Cuba and Nicaragua—yet devoted attention to Chilean and Salvadoran revolutionaries.[25] Moscow finances only those DGI operations that have its approval, such as the training of the Bolivian Army of National Liberation (ELN) in Chile during the Allende regime. Controlling the source of funds for revolutionaries has proven to be an effective means of bringing them under Soviet influence.[26]

Cuba has several military camps devoted to expatriate training in subversive operations and revolutionary tactics. Guerrilla warfare and urban terrorism, as well as Marxist-Leninist doctrine, are taught at these special schools where young revolutionaries acquire knowledge of weaponry, explosives, combat engineering, demolition, sabotage, and jungle warfare tactics.[27] Two of the main camps, which can accommodate several hundred trainees each, are located in Pinar del Río province and in Guanabo, to the east of Havana. Guerrillas from El Salvador, Nicaragua, Guatemala, Costa Rica, Honduras, Colombia, the Dominican Republic, Chile, Uruguay, Haiti, Jamaica, Grenada, and other Caribbean islands have undergone training in these facilities over the past decade. Recruits for guerrilla training are often provided with false documentation (such as Cuban passports) and are flown to Cuba in civil aircraft under cover as students or other occupations. Panama was used as a regular transit point for Latin American guerrilla trainees until March 1981, when public exposure and U.S. pressures forced the Panamanian government to impose stricter controls on exiled Central and South Americans.[28]

Each year, Cuba also offers hundreds of scholarships to students from Latin America and the Caribbean. Every Cuban mass organization operates schools in organizational work and indoctrination. These schools are open to a limited number of carefully chosen foreign students. Courses in agitation and propaganda, which are open to foreigners, are offered at the Central Union of Cuban Workers' Lázaro Peña Trade Union Cadre School. The Cuban Communist Party also offers special courses for non-Cubans at provincial party schools and at the Ñico López National Training School, its most elite educational institution.[29]

At graduation ceremonies in July 1981, there were seventy Cuban and sixty-nine foreign graduates of the Ñico López school. The foreign students represented political organizations from Venezuela, Costa Rica, Panama, Peru, Colombia, Ecuador, Jamaica, the Dominican Republic, Guatemala, Nicaragua, Chile, Grenada, Angola, Namibia, South Africa, South Yemen, and São Tomé e Príncipe. Their presence was called "a beautiful example of proletarian internationalism."[30]

In addition to training at the advanced level, Cuba offers scholarships to secondary school students. In 1980, nearly eleven thousand non-Cuban teenagers were enrolled in fifteen schools on the Isle of Youth (formerly the Isle of Pines). During Grenada's four-and-a-half-year relationship with Cuba several hundred youths from the island received training and indoctrination in Cuba on special scholarships. Remarkably, young Grenadians continued to be sent to Cuba on these "scholarships" as late as the beginning of 1985, more than a year after the island's Marxist regime was ousted.[31]

Evidently, the infrastructure for Cuba's revolutionary agitation in Latin America and the Caribbean is a multifaceted yet carefully coordinated mechanism. The Soviet Union, through its KGB and GRU (Soviet Military Intelligence), provides cohesion and direction to a complex network that consists of Cuban intelligence officers, members of Cuba's foreign ministry, the armed forces, mass organizations, and various commercial and cultural entities. This extensive apparatus is designed to support both subversion and revolutionary armed struggle. The latter is a cherished mission of Fidel Castro, and is now the objective of the USSR's strategic policy of military assistance to the "peripheral theatres" of the Third World.

Although the Soviet Union has used military assistance to advance its strategic goals throughout the world for much of its history,[32] a clear policy for employing military aid in areas such as Latin American and the Caribbean emerged after the publication of a theoretical article in 1975 written by General I. Ye. Shavrov, who was then commandant of the Soviet General Staff Academy.[33]

Noting a distinct relationship between the strategic nuclear balance and the incidence of local wars, Shavrov stated that regional conflicts in the developing world were "epicenters" of the global struggle between East and West. The Vietnam War experience had demonstrated the tactical and strategic importance of irregular warfare in initiating a crisis in the foreign and defense policies of the United States, and had awakened the USSR to the cost benefits of surrogate military forces. General Shavrov suggested that Soviet military aid was now the most important factor in determining the outcome of regional conflicts, and predicted that the Soviet Union's bluewater navy and growing airlift capability would permit it to inhibit Western influence in regional conflicts while at the same time supporting forces and regimes allied with the USSR.[34]

Soviet economic ties with the Third World—never of any lasting benefit in "building socialism"—were subordinated to exporting military and political influence. A 1976 book of essays on Soviet policy toward Africa said that "material aid on the part of the socialist states has ceased to be a factor directly promoting the transition to a non-capitalist path." Today, the essay continued, "the main factors, favoring such an orientation, are the political, military–strategic and moral influence of the states of the socialist community."[35] The following year, Karen Brutents, deputy chief of the CPSU Central Committee's International Department, called for active Soviet support for national liberation movements, saying ". . . today it is a question of carrying on the offensive against imperialism and world capitalism as a whole to do away with them."[36]

General Shavrov's strategic analysis was based on the results of the USSR's probes into traditional Western spheres of influence during the late 1960s and early 1970s—the period of détente with the West. The Soviet Union entered into détente because it was strategically expedient—part of a strategy enunciated as early as 1925 by Josef Stalin, who announced a policy of peaceful coexistence based on his perception that the revolutionary movement was ebbing while capitalism was achieving a temporary stabilization. For Stalin, as well as subsequent Soviet leaders, peaceful coexistence was nothing more than a convenient tactic that did not prohibit international communists from continuing the struggle against the capitalist West.[37]

The Soviet leadership concluded that East–West détente could only serve to benefit their global objectives. By 1970, Soviet strategic nuclear forces were approaching parity with the United States, and arms control talks were therefore seen as a means of restraining any attempt by the United States to regain strategic superiority while allowing the Soviet military buildup to continue. Détente would also give the Soviet Union greater access to Western credits and technology, allowing it to improve the domestic economy without shifting resources from the military sector.

In the view of the Soviet hierarchy, a continuing military buildup did not contradict détente because the West had sought rapprochement due to its realization that the correlation of forces had decisively shifted in favor of socialism. Détente therefore resulted from an acceptance of Soviet power by the United States and its allies. Strategically, the relaxation of East–West tensions reduced the possibility of a nuclear confrontation, leaving enormous scope for the buildup of Soviet conventional and proxy forces and new opportunities for employing them for power projection on an international scale.

A Military Bastion

Cuba has two primary values as a Soviet client state: its highly strategic location and its willingness to serve Moscow as an international proxy.

Following the consolidation of the USSR's influence over Cuba in 1968, the Soviet navy extended its forward deployment on a global scale. This new arc embraced more distant waters new to Soviet warships, such as the Arabian Sea, the Horn of Africa, and areas of the Indian Ocean, in addition to the Caribbean. To cover such an area and maintain even a minimum presence and patrol required a new direction to be taken in maritime strategy. Overseas bases therefore acquired a new and urgent focus. A major set of problems for the new bluewater Soviet navy concerned the transit times to the American seaboard. The construction of base facilities to provide logistic support for Soviet submarines at Cienfuegos in Cuba was therefore compelled by strategic necessity, for it placed the main U.S. naval bases of Norfolk and Charleston within a two-day transit time.[38]

The Soviet reappearance in the Caribbean came as preparations were being made for the opening round of Strategic Arms Limitation Talks (SALT I). In July 1969, a nine-ship Soviet navy task force, including a Kynda-class guided missile cruiser, a destroyer, a frigate, one nuclear-powered and two diesel-powered submarines, visited Cuba and conducted maneuvers in the Gulf of Mexico. This exercise was described by the Soviet army's official newspaper, *Krasnia zvezda,* as a "graphic illustration of the combat unity between Soviet and Cuban armed forces."s3[39] The naval force left the Caribbean after visiting the islands of Martinique and Guadeloupe. Simultaneously, a new Soviet Yankee-class ballistic missile submarine (SSBN) began its first patrol in the North Atlantic.[40]

There can be no question that this Soviet naval exercise was designed as a direct challenge to the Monroe Doctrine. In 1960, Nikita Khrushchev had tested the United States by declaring that the Monroe Doctrine, having "outlived its time," had died "a natural death."[41] Although it took the U.S. government more than two years to realize that Khrushchev's statement was not empty rhetoric, it did enact legislation to reaffirm the Monroe Doctrine via Public Law 87–733, passed by a joint resolution of Congress on October 3, 1962—two weeks before the beginning of the Cuban missile crisis. Yet even Public Law 87–733 must have been seen by the USSR as an indication of U.S. weakness, for the joint resolution acknowledged and, ipso facto, accepted the existence of a Soviet-sponsored, Marxist-Leninist regime in the Western Hemisphere. The underlying message of Public Law 87–733 was clear: The United States did not wish to expel "extracontinental Communist powers" from the Americas, but only to contain the "Marxist-Leninist regime in Cuba" to prevent it from extending "its aggressive or subversive activities to any part of the hemisphere."[42]

The July 1969 visit of the Soviet naval task force was the first time since the destruction of the Spanish fleet off Santiago de Cuba in July 1898 that the naval force of a rival extrahemispheric power had entered the Caribbean. (With the exception of submarines, Soviet warships had not been deployed in the area during the 1962 missile crisis.) In retrospect, Soviet actions during the cruise appear unusually provocative in the context of the major U.S.–USSR confrontation in Caribbean waters less than seven years previously. Shadowed by the U.S. Navy, the Soviet warships were replenished by their support vessels forty miles off Dry Tortugas—a small group of islands at the entrance to the Gulf of Mexico, part of Monroe County, Florida—before sailing directly into Havana for a week-long visit. Leaving Cuba, the flotilla conducted antisubmarine warfare (ASW) exercises in the Gulf of Mexico, then sailed directly across the Caribbean, skirting Jamaica and Grenada. The *Grozny,* a Kynda-class guided missile cruiser, paid a port call to the French island of Martinique, while the *Bedovyi,* a Kilden-class guided missile destroyer, and the *Lena,* a naval oiler, visited Barbados. These ships rendezvoused with the remainder of the fleet off Barbados on August 12, 1969, and left the Caribbean.[43]

The composition of this Soviet task force is also significant vis-à-vis its use as a means of testing U.S. reaction to Soviet deployment of both conventional and nuclear weapons within a traditional U.S. sphere of influence. The U.S. government was fully aware that the guided missile cruiser *Grozny* normally carried Shaddock SS-N-3 surface-to-surface missiles with nuclear warheads. A November-class attack submarine accompanying the flotilla was also believed to be carrying nuclear weapons.[44]

Preoccupied with Vietnam and preparations for SALT I, the new Nixon administration chose to ignore the Soviet Union's exploratory move into an area that had low priority on the policy agenda. The threshold of U.S. reaction had therefore been raised once again, prompting the Kremlin to continue its Caribbean probes, each one incrementally bolder than its predecessor.

On November 17, 1969—three months after the Soviet flotilla's Caribbean cruise—the first session of SALT began in Helsinki, Finland, amid widespread Western hopes for détente with the USSR. Coinciding with the Helsinki meeting, the Soviet minister of defense, Marshal Andrei Grechko, paid a highly publicized visit to Cuba, accompanied by the deputy chief of the Soviet Naval Staff.[45] In the months following Grechko's visit, Soviet military activities in and around Cuba gradually increased. In April 1970, Raúl Castro spent five weeks in the Soviet Union where he met with Leonid Brezhnev "to discuss the further development of Soviet–Cuba relations."[46] During Raúl's Moscow visit, a pair of Soviet Tu-20/95 Bear D naval reconnaissance aircraft flew nonstop from a Northern Fleet base near the White Sea to Havana—the first time that such aircraft had landed outside the Soviet bloc nations. This was strategically important for the USSR, demonstrating the capability of the Bear D—the naval variant of the mainstay Tupolev long-range, turboprop bomber—to fly regular C^3I (command, control, communications, and intelligence) missions to and from Cuba. Soviet-supported, Cuban-flown MiG fighter aircraft already based in Cuba practiced flying defensive escort for the Bears under simulated combat conditions.[47]

In a Lenin Day speech on April 22, four days after the historic Bear flight, Fidel Castro proclaimed his readiness to establish closer military ties with the Soviet Union.[48] A series of two more Tu-20/

95 flights followed, apparently as part of the major "Okean" Soviet naval exercises taking place in the North Atlantic. A seven-ship naval task force from these exercises put in at the Cuban port of Cienfuegos on May 14, 1970. The flotilla included a guided missile cruiser, a submarine tender, and a nuclear-powered Echo-II-class submarine armed with short-range cruise missiles designed for use against shipping, thus marking a further escalation in the introduction of Soviet offensive weapons into the Caribbean.[49]

National Security Adviser Dr. Henry Kissinger felt sufficiently concerned about the growing Soviet air and sea activity in the region to summarize it for President Nixon on June 1, 1970:

> While the Soviet naval visits may be part of the overall trend in recent years toward increased Soviet naval activity ever further from Soviet home ports, they may also be an effort to "accustom" Washington to greater Soviet use of Cuba by establishing gradually the precedent of visits and bunkering of active Soviet fleet and air units. The Soviets could conceivably wish to maintain Soviet naval units in the Caribbean–South Atlantic on a more or less permanent basis, refueling and resupplying out of Cuba.[50]

On September 2, 1970, the Pentagon announced that another Soviet naval task force was approaching Cuba. On September 9, a naval squadron of six ships, including a submarine tender, arrived in Cienfuegos. On September 25, a Pentagon spokesman announced that two heavy barges and a large tug had gone into Cienfuegos and that construction of a base for Soviet Yankee-class SSBNs "could not be ruled out."[51] On the same day, the White House issued its first warning to the Soviet Union not to build a strategic submarine base in Cuba, emphasizing that it would view any such effort "with the utmost seriousness."[52] Though the warning seemed to stress the servicing of submarines in Cienfuegos itself, the message as to what was expected of the USSR was expanded by a White House source in December to preclude servicing "in or from bases in Cuba."[53] President Nixon personally affirmed this interpretation in a television interview on January 4, 1971, when he said: "Now, in the event that nuclear submarines were serviced either in Cuba or from Cuba, that would be violation of the understanding."[54]

The exact nature of this "understanding" remains ambiguous. However, Nixon also stated that the original Kennedy–Khrushchev "agreement" of 1962, under which the United States promised not to invade Cuba in return for a Soviet pledge to keep its offensive strategic weapons off the island, was expanded in October 1970 to bar a Soviet naval base in Cuba.[55]

The Cienfuegos affair was allowed to slip into obscurity, largely so as not to jeopardize the main round of SALT negotiations, which opened in Vienna in April 1970. Ironically, these were taking place as yet another Soviet naval flotilla, which included a nuclear-powered cruise missile submarine and a tender, made a "brief rest visit" to Cienfuegos.[56] Henry Kissinger said that "it was a measure of the times that, while Jordan was blowing up and the Soviets were building a submarine base in Cuba, the Senate was debating ABM from the premise that defensive American strategic deployments were somehow provocative."[57]

To this day, the Soviet Union asserts that it has not built its own military bases in Cuba and that it has always fully adhered to the Kennedy–Khrushchev understanding of 1962. However, the USSR did not specifically comment on or agree to President Nixon's "understanding" that ostensibly prohibited the servicing of nuclear submarines at sea by tenders based in Cuba, nor did it concede the right of Soviet naval vessels to use "Cuban" military bases.

Although the Nixon administration announced that, through forceful diplomacy, it had won a victory in Cuba, [58] subsequent events demonstrated that the Cienfuegos affair was perceived by Moscow as U.S. acquiescence to an escalation of Soviet power in the Caribbean. In May 1972, shortly before the summit meeting between Nixon and Brezhnev the same month, a Soviet Golf-II SSBN was deployed to Cuba along with a submarine tender. The deployment was timed to make a U.S. response as difficult as possible, taking place during the final sessions of the bilateral negotiations to prevent unintentional confrontations between warships at sea. During this period, U.S. naval commanders were under orders to avoid any serious confrontation with Soviet naval vessels that might jeopardize the negotiations. Further evidence that the deployment was a calculated test is that the place chosen for the six-day rendezvous of the Soviet warships was Bahía de Nipe on the northeast coast of Cuba, more than a hundred kilometers from the controversial port of Cienfuegos.[59]

U.S. publicity on the deployment was negligible at the time, and there is no evidence that the U.S. government lodged a formal protest accusing Moscow of violating the Cienfuegos "understanding" by servicing a ballistic missile submarine at a Cuban port.[60] The Soviet Union learned a valuable strategic lesson from this tactical probe: The Moscow summit and SALT I were of such importance to Washington that they would simply not be risked in another confrontation over Cuba.[61]

Four months after the signing of SALT I—amid renewed Western enthusiasm for détente as well as Richard Nixon's 1972 presidential campaign as the "Peace President"[62]—the Kremlin took its next step of incremental power projection in the Caribbean. In September, Soviet Tu-95 Bear D reconnaissance flights off the U.S. eastern seaboard began regular use of Cuban airfields. Again, the U.S. government failed to make any protest to the Soviet Union, saying that "only the movement of large numbers of such planes into Cuba on a permanent basis would be a problem."[63] By the following year, twelve Tu-95 deployments to Cuba had been made, while Soviet submarines had completed twenty-two port calls to the island—the largest number of such visits to any country outside the USSR.[64]

One year later, in April 1974, a Golf-II SSBN cruised openly into Havana and received an official Cuban welcome. By 1975, Cienfuegos was being routinely used by Soviet surface vessels and submarines, while a Soviet submarine rescue ship was now stationed on a more or less permanent basis in the Caribbean. In 1976, the Soviet and Cuban navies began the first of what have now become annual exercises together in the Caribbean. The following year, one of the Cuban-based Soviet Tu-95s flew closer to the U.S. mainland than ever before, overflying a U.S. Navy task force off Charleston, South Carolina, before conducting surveillance of the new USS *Spruance* (DD-963), off Boston. In December of 1977, a Soviet naval squadron, including an attack submarine, patrolled off the Florida coast, skirting the U.S. territorial limit.[65]

After six years of incremental power projection in the Caribbean without protest from the United states, the Soviet Union began construction of a new naval base in Cuba, ostensibly for use by the Cuban Navy.[66] In February and May 1979, Cuba received its first two Foxtrot-class attack submarines from the USSR. The official pronouncement from the Carter administration on these deliveries was that they represented "no serious threat to U.S. interests."[67]

The SALT II negotiations during the early part of 1979 as well as preparations for President Carter's summit meeting with Leonid Brezhnev that June must have appeared to the Kremlin as a suitable atmosphere in which to accelerate Soviet influence in the Caribbean region. Grenada fell to a DOE-assisted Marxist coup d'état in March 1979 and Nicaragua was taken over by another Cuban-supported, pro-Soviet revolutionary movement in July. While Carter and Brezhnev were meeting at Vienna in June, the Soviet Union was delivering two squadrons of twenty-four An-26 Curl transport aircraft to Cuba. The An-26 is a tactical transport capable of carrying thirty-eight combat troops or five tons of cargo for a distance of six hundred miles. These aircraft were almost immediately put to use ferrying military supplies to Costa Rica for delivery to the Sandinistas during their final offensive, demonstrating the direct application of military support to "epicenters" of the global struggle as an element of Soviet Caribbean strategy.[68]

In August 1979, Senator Frank Church, chairman of the Senate Foreign Relations Committee, disclosed that U.S. intelligence had "discovered" a 2,600-man Soviet "combat brigade" in Cuba. This revelation embarrassed the Carter administration because only the previous month Secretary of Defense Harold Brown had told the Senate Foreign Relations Committee that "there was no evidence of any great increase in the Soviet military presence in Cuba in the past few years" and that there were no "significant Soviet military forces in Cuba."[69] Brown's statements were correct insofar as Soviet forces had been deployed in Cuba for nearly twenty years, and elements of the "combat brigade" had been on the island since 1976, the year of Carter's election. President Carter had suspended U.S. aerial surveillance of Cuba as a gesture of goodwill towards the Castro regime, and the "brigade" had been photographed on maneuvers only after surveillance resumed in mid-1979.[70]

The Soviet "combat brigade" was reportedly a unit that had been transferred from Eastern Europe to guard and handle tactical nuclear weapons as well as to protect other sensitive Soviet installations in Cuba. Elements of this force came from East Germany and Czechoslovakia, where they reportedly guarded nuclear weapons depots and mobile missile launchers. The force is based near the Punta Movida complex, a Soviet-built facility linked by rail to the Cienfuegos naval installation, which is now off limits to the Cuban population. The Punta Movida facility is believed to be used to store and service nuclear weapons from Soviet submarines, although there have been reports that tactical nuclear weapons for the MiG-23BN Flogger F squadrons based in Cuba may also be stored there.[71] Soviet pilots are regularly assigned to the Cuban Air Force, and probably fly the MiG-23 because it is the most advanced aircraft in the Cuban inventory.[72]

The "combat brigade" incident was also quickly downplayed by the Carter administration. Fearing that controversy over Soviet activities in Cuba would affect SALT II's ratification by the U.S. Senate, President Carter said there was "no need to panic" because the Soviet troops represented "no direct threat to the United States" and "had no visible means of crossing the sea to operate anywhere but in Cuba."[73] By these words, the president of the United States had effectively sanctioned the stationing of Soviet combat forces in Cuba.

Although discovery of the Soviet force was an accident and not the result of a deliberate tactical probe, the incident must have served to reinforce Moscow's theory that U.S. policymakers would seek the most expedient resolution to any potential U.S.–USSR "crisis" rather than risk a high-priority item on both the domestic and international political agenda such as arms control. By obtaining de facto recognition of its right to maintain combat forces in Cuba, Soviet strategists may have decided that the deployment of Soviet and Soviet proxy forces elsewhere in the Caribbean would also come to be accepted by Washington.

Soviet naval and air activities in and around Cuba continued an incremental expansion during the early 1980s. For example, from November 25, 1982, until February 2, 1983, a four-ship Soviet Navy task force operated from Cienfuegos, conducting ASW exercises in the Caribbean and Gulf of Mexico with a Cuban frigate and submarine chasers. At one point, two of these ships—the 7,600-ton guided missile cruiser *Admiral Isakov* and the frigate *Rezvy*—sailed to within 50 miles of the Mississippi Delta.[74] From March to April 1985, a flotilla including the helicopter carrier *Leningrad,* a new Udaloy-class destroyer, and support ships conducted exercises in the Caribbean with elements of the Soviet-supplied Cuban Navy. Another Soviet naval task force arrived at Havana at the end of December 1984—the twenty-fourth such flotilla to enter the Caribbean since 1969.[75] Soviet strategic offensive Golf- and Echo-class submarines have been using the Cienfuegos naval base for years with few protests from the U.S. government and little attention from the U.S. media. This base now has a new nuclear warhead handling facility, new quays, and new submarine pens.[76]

In 1981, the Soviet Union began using Cuba's San Antonio de los Baños military airfield as a permanent facility for Tu-95 Bear Ds; since early 1983, Tu-142 Bear Fs have been based there.[77] The Bear F is an ASW aircraft used to track U.S. submarines in the northeastern and central Atlantic. In January 1982, a pair of Tu-95 Ds penetrated into the U.S. air and defense zone, which extends two hundred miles from the U.S. coast, and inspected a new U.S. aircraft carrier undergoing sea trials only forty-two miles off the coast of Virginia.[78] In March 1983, ten Tu-95s were detected in Cuba, at least two of which were confirmed by the chief of naval operations as having operable bomb bays.[79] Unconfirmed intelligence reports in 1985 indicated that four of the Bear D aircraft deployed at San Antonio de los Baños had been acquired by the Cuban Air Force to justify their permanent basing in Cuba.[80]

Soviet air and naval bases in Cuba are vital strategic assets. The naval logistics base at Cienfuegos permits Soviet SSBNs and cruise-missile-carrying submarines (SSGNs and SSGs) to double their on-station time off the U.S. eastern seaboard by allowing their tenders to draw supplies easily from a secure, deep-water port. In addition, mechanically disabled Soviet submarines deployed off the United States can be quickly towed to Cuba without the risk of foundering that would be incurred during the long voyage across the North Atlantic and the Barents Sea. Facilitating and extending the deployment of SSBNs, SSGNs, and SSGs accords with the Soviet strategic nuclear doctrine of maximizing first-strike capability and ensuring the survival of its strategic forces in the event of an escalating conflict.[81] The use of Cuban ports and airbases also greatly benefits Soviet ASW efforts. Soviet naval air reconnaissance aircraft work in tandem with surface ships and attack submarines (SSNs) to monitor U.S. SSBN and SSN movements to and from East Coast home ports.

At the political level, Soviet naval deployments in the Caribbean—almost always in coordination with the Cuban Navy—serve to reassure the Castro regime of Moscow's willingness to defend it, regardless of the fact that a formal defense pact (long coveted by Fidel Castro) has never been made. Other leftist forces in the Caribbean are also bolstered by regular traversing of "America's Lake" by the Soviet Navy—a cost-effective means of reinforcing the beleaguered Sandinistas' belief that the "correlation of forces" had indeed shifted in favor of socialism.

Lying only ninety miles from the United States, Cuba is also an ideal location for strategic intelligence gathering operations. In the mid-1960s, the USSR established a major electronic intelligence collection facility at Lourdes, outside of Havana, which is today the largest and most sophisticated non-U.S. installation of its type in the Western Hemisphere. The Lourdes complex is operated by about two thousand Soviet personnel and consists of a headquarters complex, an antenna field, a satellite receiver, and more than fifty buildings that contain monitoring, processing, and analysis equipment.[82] From Lourdes, Soviet technicians monitor NASA space program activities at Cape Canaveral, and U.S. military and shipping communications including transatlantic communications. The facility allows the USSR to eavesdrop on telephone communications throughout the United States. Lourdes also targets signals transmitted by U.S. B-1 and B-52 bombers during practice flights from Florida to Louisiana and Virginia, radio traffic to and from Atlantic Fleet Headquarters in Norfolk, Virginia, and signals transmitted by U.S. Army units on manuevers at Fort Benning, Georgia.[83]

The Lourdes facility, along with a similar facility in the Soviet Union, allows complete coverage of the global beams of all U.S. geosynchronous communications satellites.[84] Lourdes and a Soviet laser tracking station located near Santiago de Cuba are also used to support the USSR's space surveillance program. Cuba's almost year-round clear skies make the island a valuable site for space-related activities.[85]

Lourdes and other Soviet facilities in Cuba, including nuclear warhead storage bunkers, are staffed and guarded by many of the approximately sixteen thousand Soviet personnel based on the island.[86] These include the "combat brigade" of some twenty-nine hundred men, including a battalion of forty T-72 tanks, three five-hundred-man battalions of mechanized infantry in armored personnel carriers, a battalion of eighteen 122-mm guns, a company of helicopters, plus 150-man companies of engineers and support troops.[87] A small KGB commando company, a *Vysotniki* company, and sixty-man *Raydoviki* unit have also appeared in Cuba. These special forces are equivalent to the U.S. Green Berets or the British Special Air Service. The Soviet forces joined Cuban troops in carrying out amphibious and air defense exercises during the months of May and June, 1983.[88]

Recent intelligence reports also indicate that the Soviet Union may be engaged in chemical and biological warfare activities in Cuba that violate the 1925 Chemical Warfare Convention and the 1975 Biological Warfare Convention. The reported violations include biological and chemical warfare production, storage, and training assistance to Third World revolutionaries, including the Nicaraguan Sandinistas, the FDR-FMLN Salvadoran guerrillas, the Palestine Liberation Organization (PLO), and the South West Africa People's Organization (SWAPO) in Namibia.[89] In 1981, a "Yellow Rain" manufacturing plant was reportedly constructed at Kiminor, Limones township, in the province of Matanzas. This is allegedly operated by about seventeen Soviet scientists, and shipments are reported to have been made to Poland, East Germany, and to Soviet forces in Afghanistan. A second plant for the manufacture of biological toxins designed for use in water supplies has also reportedly been identified. This is protected by a new air defense missile system located in the region of Santa Cruz del Norte.[90]

A Soviet Military Surrogate

After the Soviet leadership concluded that Fidel Castro had genuinely accepted Moscow's domination, the USSR revived its program of building Cuba into a formidable military power in its own right. In January 1969, the Soviet Union announced that it was initiating a comprehensive reequipment of the Cuban armed forces.[91] Between 1970 and 1976, Soviet military deliveries to Cuba averaged 13,228 metric tons per annum. After Cuba's intervention in Angola had demonstrated its effectiveness as a Soviet military surrogate, arms deliveries abruptly doubled, before falling back to pre-1977 levels in 1980. However, over the next four years the metric tonnage of Soviet military deliveries to Cuba more than tripled, a factor that can be traced to the large quantities of materiel being supplied to Grenada and Nicaragua via Cuba.[92]

By 1986, Cuba had amassed a powerful inventory of war materiel from the Soviet bloc. The Cuban Army alone (not counting the one-million-strong People's Militia) is composed of nine active and eighteen reserve divisions. The regular armed forces include an army of 160,000 (with 135,000 reserves), a navy of 12,000, and an air force of 16,000 (including air defense forces). In all, Cuba has over 2.3 percent of its population in the regular armed forces. Cuba also has some 285 fighter and training aircraft,[93] 950 tanks, nearly 100 helicopters, three Foxtrot-class attack submarines, a pair of Polnocny-class amphibious assault ships, two Koni-class frigates, eleven corvettes, and approximately 70 torpedo and missile attack boats (including the modern Turya torpedo boat, exported only to Cuba).[94]

The USSR's steady buildup of Cuba's offensive air and sea capabilities could prove a serious threat to U.S. shipping during wartime. In any NATO–Warsaw Pact confrontation, more than half of all NATO resupply materiel would be shipped from U.S. Gulf Coast ports via SLOCs that pass within easy striking distance of Cuba. Furthermore, some 45 percent of all U.S. seaborne trade and 55 percent of all U.S. imported oil currently traverses vulnerable Caribbean shipping routes.[95] The now permanent Soviet and/or Soviet surrogate naval and air presence in the Caribbean means that, at the outbreak of hostilities between the United States and the USSR, Soviet and/or Soviet surrogate military assets would already be in place for Caribbean basin SLOC interdiction. The U.S. Navy would be faced with the mission of dealing with Soviet, Cuban and, eventually, Nicaraguan submarines, causing significant diversion of U.S.

ASW assets from vital NATO operating areas in the North and Central Atlantic.[96]

The Cuban Navy's surface fleet would also present a major threat to U.S. and allied shipping during a conflict. Since 1978, the offensive and defensive mine warfare capability of the Cuban Navy has been greatly augmented by the Soviet Union. Cuba's ten plastic-hulled Yevgenya-class minesweepers and two *Sonya*-class minesweepers/minehunters would provide a viable counter to U.S. attempts to quarantine Cuba by laying mines.[97]

Cuba's relatively large fleet of missile and torpedo craft also represent a dangerous anti-SLOC force. Although these craft, as well as the Cuban Navy's frigates and corvettes, could not survive a direct confrontation with U.S. or NATO forces, they would waste critical NATO time and assets during a general war. Cuba's Osa- and Komar-class missile boats would be even more dangerous when operating with Koni-class frigates, which can provide limited anti-air coverage with their SA-N-4 missiles and cannon.[98]

Soviet and Cuban air assets could also prove highly effective in Caribbean-wide anti-SLOC operations. Tu-95 and Tu-142 aircraft based in Cuba are equipped for follow-up guidance of sea-targeted missiles launched from submarines or surface craft.[99] With a combat radius of over five-hundred nautical miles, the nuclear-capable MiG-23BN could also cause major damage in the early stages of a major conflict. Even without refueling, the MiG-23BN could command much of the Caribbean basin. Using bases in Nicaragua and elsewhere for refueling would greatly expand the capability of these aircraft for SLOC interdiction even if the prevailing U.S. political climate does not allow for the prepositioning of such assets in Central and South America prior to the outbreak of hostilities.[100]

The Cuban air defense system, coupled with Cuba's large number of combat interceptor aircraft, would make neutralization of the Cuban armed forces a costly operation for the United States. In addition to some twenty-eight surface-to-air missile (SAM) battalions equipped with Soviet SA-2, SA-3, SA-6, and SA-7 missiles, the Cuban armed forces deploy 50 Frog-4 surface-to-surface missiles, each of which is capable of carrying a two-hundred kiloton nuclear warhead.[101] The batteries of modified SA-2 antiaircraft missiles and mobile SA-6 launchers, supplied by the USSR in 1979, are largely controlled by some of the twenty-eight hundred Soviet military advisers in Cuba, who provide technical advice in support of the air force, the air defense system, and the navy.[102]

Since 1975, the Cuban military has served as a successful Soviet military proxy, playing a decisive role in installing pro-Soviet regimes in Angola, Ethiopia, Grenada, and Nicaragua. At the end of 1985, more than fifty thousand uniformed Cuban military personnel were serving in sixteen identified countries on four continents, with a large number of militarily trained "construction workers" and "internationalists."[103] Intensive training and combat experience, coupled with first-class air and sea-lift capabilities furnished by the Soviet Union, would enable Cuba to place an initial assault force of one thousand men, accompanied by either tanks or artillery support, almost anywhere in the Caribbean in less than six hours. This unit could hold a bridgehead until a division-sized invasion force could reinforce it using Cuba's large air force, civil air, or merchant shipping fleets.[104]

Soviet use of Cuban proxy forces internationally illustrates the adaptability of the USSR's strategic planning by making use of the ideologically approved Leninist tactic of opportunism. In his memoirs, senior Soviet defector Arkady N. Shevchenko relates that the idea for the large-scale Cuban military operation in Angola during 1975 had originated in Havana rather than in Moscow. Growing Soviet military strength during the early 1970s had prompted the Kremlin to exploit "opportunities to expand Moscow's" influence in Africa, yet Soviet strategists wished to expand the USSR's "zone of control without incurring high costs."[105] The "high costs" Shevchenko referred to would have been the risk of confrontation with the United States, a deterioration of détente, and the type of international outcry over Soviet imperialism engendered by the invasion of Afghanistan four years later. The Soviet Union took advantage of Castro's need to maintain the idea of himself as a great international figure as well as his desire to boost revolutionary fervor in Cuba by a foreign adventure. As the following chapters illustrate, similar Soviet initiatives in the Caribbean and Central America were also usurped by Kremlin strategists.

The Cuban military's surrogate role in projecting Soviet influence throughout the Caribbean has been largely covert, although this may be changing as growing numbers of Cuban troops are committed to combat in Nicaragua.[106] Fidel Castro's revolutionary zeal, melded with the discipline and sophistication of Soviet strategists such as Boris Ponomarev, have created an ideal vehicle for subverting the Caribbean's "seemingly quite reliable rear lines of American imperialism."[107] After the restructuring and equipping of Cuba as a secure Soviet base, it was used as a springboard for the projection of Soviet power in this strategically vital region.

"GRENADA, NICARAGUA, CUBA.

Three giants rising up
to defend their rights to independence,
sovereignty and justice on the very threshold
of imperialism."

This People's Revolutionary Government of Grenada poster, which appeared in the *Free West Indian* on March 23, 1983, shows Moscow's Caribbean triumvirate in the early 1980s: (*left to right*) Fidel Castro, Maurice Bishop, and Daniel Ortega.

4
Grenada

Background to a Revolution

The invasion of Grenada on October 25, 1983, by a multinational force from the United States and six Caribbean island nations led to the discovery of a priceless collection of documents detailing the internal politics and international activities of Grenada's People's Revolutionary Government (PRG). These records, stored in the National Archives in Washington, D.C., serve as important evidence of Soviet strategic policy toward Grenada and other Caribbean countries.

The Grenada documents contain material on the most intimate details of the PRG, from secret military treaties with the Soviet Union to reports of internal surveillance on "enemies of the state." Although this large horde of invaluable material will provide a source of primary research for generations of scholars, it has already been the subject of scholarly works by Jiri Valenta, Uri Ra'anan, Robert Pfaltzgraff, Jr., Richard Shultz, Sidney Hook, and other authorities on Soviet foreign policy.

Soviet and Cuban involvement with Grenada antedated the March 13, 1979, coup d'état that brought Maurice Bishop's and Bernard Coard's New Jewel Movement (NJM)—vanguard party of the PRG—to power. In August 1969, a Soviet trawler, possibly part of the Soviet naval task force whose warships were then calling at the neighboring islands of Barbados and Martinique, visited Grenada for several days. While this vessel was docked in the island's capital city of St. George's, members of its crew were observed photographing and measuring a remote peninsula called Calivigny

Point—a site that subsequently became one of Grenada's main military bases.[1]

Grenada's highly strategic location was obvious to the Kremlin's geostrategists. It is located less than one hundred miles off the coast of Venezuela which is an important Organization of Petroleum Exporting Countries (OPEC) member. Grenada forms part of what General Wallace H. Nutting, former U.S. Southern Commander, Central and South America, called a "triangular base complex," incorporating Cuba, Nicaragua, and Grenada, which would allow Soviet–Cuban forces to project tactical air power over the entire Caribbean basin.[2] Within a five-hundred-mile radius of Grenada are oilfields, refineries, and tanker lanes that supply the United States with approximately 55 percent of its imported oil. More than two-and-a-half million barrels of refined oil are produced per day in countries falling within this five-hundred-mile radius.[3] Grenada's proximity to vulnerable, newly independent Caribbean nations, as well as to the South American continent, also made it an ideal site for the export of subversion.

Beginning in 1963, Maurice Bishop spent seven years studying law in London, during which time he also traveled to East Germany and Czechoslovakia.[4] Although the future Grenadian revolutionary leader became a Marxist-Leninist during this period, he was not a follower of the Soviet road to communism, considering himself a disciple of Julius Nyrere, C. L. R. James (a West Indian Trotskyite) and Fidel Castro.[5] After Bishop returned to Grenada to practice law in early 1970, he attended an important meeting of Caribbean radicals held at Rat Island, St. Lucia, to discuss future strategy for the region. In 1972, Bishop helped organize a secret conference in Martinique to discuss the establishment of "a new Caribbean Society" based on socialist principles. Conference participants hoped to develop a "clearing house" to coordinate revolutionary activities throughout the Caribbean.[6]

Also in 1972, Bishop and another Grenadian lawyer, Kenrick Radix, founded a political organization called the Movement for the Assemblies of the People (MAP), which generally favored parliamentary means to power until several MAP candidates were defeated in the island's 1972 elections. Thereafter, the MAP declared that its "single aim" was "the organization of a mass movement to seize political power," and that "the strategy and tactics" to achieve this was "the mass uprising."[7] At the beginning of 1973, the little-known MAP united with the popular, moderately socialist Joint Endeavour for Welfare, Education, and Liberation (JEWEL) to form the New Jewel Movement, thereby assuming both JEWEL's strength and moderate facade—a necessary tactic for communists in a conservative and deeply religious country like Grenada. As a lecturer in law at the University of the West Indies' (UWI) campus in Kingston, Jamaica, Coard had developed strong ties with the network of young radicals from across the Caribbean who received indoctrination in Marxist-Leninist theory at UWI. Coard insisted on a doctrinaire approach to party organization, and by the spring of 1974, the NJM had decided "in theory and in principle that we should build a Leninist party."[8]

Almost from its inception, the NJM had two wings: a Castroite one led by Maurice Bishop, and an orthodox or "Leninist" wing headed by Bernard Coard, who favored strict adherence to the Soviet model. In 1975, Coard founded OREL, a radical student organization that was amalgamated with the NJM the following year to strengthen Coard's power base within the party. Significantly, many of Coard's young OREL disciples subsequently became officers in Grenada's People's Revolutionary Army (PRA).

The activities of Bishop and his comrades aroused the interest of the Cubans, who presumably relayed reports on the NJM's progress to Moscow via the DGI. Like the Sandinistas, the NJM was a Cuban discovery and therefore the responsibility of Havana to nurture until such time as it has proved itself worthy of direct Soviet attention. Oswaldo Cardenas, a DA officer who later became Cuban ambassador to Suriname, was assigned to work with the NJM in Grenada prior to the 1979 coup.[9]

In 1976, a Grenada–Cuba Association was founded to involve Cuba more closely in Grenadian affairs. Bishop and other NJM members openly traveled to Havana in the years preceding the coup d'état and had guerrilla warfare manuals and revolutionary literature confiscated from them on their return to Grenada. Hudson Austin, future commander of the PRA, received military training in Cuba and Guyana along with half a dozen other Grenadians.[10]

The overthrow itself was carried out with the aid of a team of black Cuban commandos from the Directorate of Special Operations who had reportedly been infiltrated into the island several days prior to March 13, 1979.[11] Given the subsequent history of Grenada's relations with the USSR, it seems more than coincidental that a Soviet cruise ship, the *Taras Shevchenko,* had paid a rare visit to St. George's the previous night and remained in port throughout the day of the "revolution." Soviet crewmen were observed at Point Salines, Richmond Hill, and St. George's reporting on the coup's progress via hand-held radios. Because the Cuban military involvement in the overthrow was obviously preplanned, it seems possible that the *Taras Shevchenko* was routed to Grenada to allow Soviet officers to observe a "national liberation" venture coordinated by their Cuban surrogates.[12]

A Strategy of Deception

Maurice Bishop utilized the classic Castroite ploy of saying that he had been "forced" to turn to the Cubans for military aid because the United States and other Western nations had turned him down. The newly appointed Grenadian prime minister had indeed made a very ambiguous request for arms to U.S. diplomatic officers on April 7, 1979. However, the next day, before a formal response could come from Washington, Bishop told a rally that he "planned" to ask Cuba for arms (a quantity of which were already enroute), and that Grenada would soon receive Cuban diplomatic recognition followed by technical and material assistance.[13]

On April 13—exactly one month after the coup—Bishop made a speech that seems deliberately designed to ostracize his regime from the United States. Accusing U.S. Ambassador to the Eastern Caribbean Frank Ortiz of making "veiled threats" and ignoring his pleas for aid, Bishop angrily said that "we are not in anybody's backyard, and we are definitely not for sale."[14] This speech was picked up by a variety of international news agencies and became the basis for the widely disseminated disinformation about Grenada being pushed into the Soviet camp by U.S. insensitivity.

The famous "backyard" speech set the stage for next day's official announcement that Cuba had established formal diplomatic relations with Grenada, assigning Julián Enrique Torres Rizo as chargé d'affaires. Torres Rizo, a senior DA intelligence officer and former member of the Cuban mission to the United Nations,[15] was promoted to full ambassador on October 10. The large Cuban diplomatic staff occupied a heavily guarded villa and promptly began infiltrating Grenada's British-style government ministries, the police force, media, public health, and educational systems. Torres Rizo was invited to be an observer at high-level government policy meetings, where his suggestions were listened to with respect by PRG cabinet ministers.

An important part of the NJM's doctrine was the belief that the United States was the "No. 1 enemy" that would not allow another openly Marxist-Leninist regime to be established in its sphere of influence. Like Bishop's mentor, Fidel Castro, the PRG entered into the international political arena under the cloak of moderate, reformist socialism. Because it considered itself to be a true Leninist vanguard party, the NJM believed that its right to rule Grenada was based on the dialectical forces of history rather than the mandate of the "politically underdeveloped" working class and "National Bourgeoisie."[16] Prior to seizing power, the NJM leadership had formulated guidelines for the facade their regime would exhibit to the world. Although they hated and feared the United States, it was necessary for the PRG's survival to reassure Washington that the "revolution" was not communist and that they would preserve "private property . . . individual rights [and] hemispheric solidarity." It was decided that the new government should proclaim that it would hold "free and fair elections" under a new constitution "at the earliest possible opportunity."[17] Helped by a generally supportive Western media, the PRG was soon able to persuade many governments to extend diplomatic recognition based on its ostensible moderation and democratic pledges.

Considering what was then a close interrelationship between Grenada, Cuba, and Jamaica, it is worth noting that Jamaican Prime Minister Michael Manley served as the PRG's strongest lobbiest for U.S. recognition, telling a State Department official that "the NJM was like his own party, engaged in the difficult task of instituting new policies while keeping the Communists out." Praising the Carter administration's Caribbean policies, Manley said that "the NJM wanted America as a friend."[18]

The NJM party elite, most of whom were from upper-middle- or middle-class backgrounds, found it easy to induce political moderates and even conservatives among their relatives and friends to accept positions in the government or provide vocal support for its policies during the PRG's first months in office. Regardless of their ideology, the majority of non-working-class Grenadians were united in their opposition to Sir Eric Gairy, the prime minister deposed by the coup d'état. Although Bishop's leftist political beliefs were well-known throughout Grenada's tightly knit society, even his close relatives refused to believe that he was a true communist, thus lending great weight to the PRG's "moderate socialist" image.

The relationship with moderate elements of Grenadian society was only a tactical device, an ex post facto variation of the popular front designed to deceive the West and prevent military intervention. Maurice Bishop summarized this approach during his secret 1982 "Line of March for the Party" speech, which revealed the NJM's strategy:

> From the start too, comrades, we had an alliance with sections of the upper petty bourgeoisie and national bourgeoisie. . . . [T]his was done deliberately so that imperialism won't get too excited and would say "well they have some nice fellas in the thing; everything alright." That was the mistake, for example, the comrades in Gambia made a few months ago. Remember the Gambia coup d'etat a few months ago? What was the first thing those comrades did? They say, "we are Marxist-Leninists and we just had a Marxist-Leninist revolution and we go wipe out the bourgeoisie." The same day they overthrow them. . . . So fortunately, the NJM had a little more sense than that.[19]

Beyond a doubt, this strategy was closely coordinated with the Soviet Union and Cuba. As Grenada's relationship with the USSR grew, Soviet officials repeatedly counseled the PRG to present a moderate face to the world. During a PRG delegation's visit to Moscow in 1981, Soviet trade officials told the Grenadians that the USSR's assistance "must never be provocative from the point of view of the international situation."[20] The Soviet Army's chief of staff, Marshal Nikolai Ogarkov, gave his Grenadian counterpart, Major Einstein Louison, a similar warning in March 1983, saying that because "Grenada was located close to U.S. imperialism," it was necessary for the "Grenada Revolution to be specifically vigilant at all times."[21] The following month, Soviet Foreign Minister Andrei Gromyko commended Maurice Bishop for Grenada's "low-key" dealings with other "radical Caribbean parties," remarking that the NJM and other leftist groups should "exercise great care and flexibility so as not to provoke the imperialist forces to smash the progressive forces."[22]

The same concern for secrecy was observed in the military aid agreements Grenada signed with the Soviet Union and its client states. An example of this can be found in article 6 of the treaty signed with the USSR in Havana on October 27, 1980:

> The Government of Grenada and the Government of the Union of SSR shall take all the necessary measures to ensure keeping in secret the terms and conditions of the deliveries, all the correspondence and information connected with the implementation of the present Agreement.[23]

The PRG developed a remarkably sophisticated propaganda network in North America and Western Europe to positively influence public opinion about the Grenadian "Revolution." This public relations campaign was largely coordinated by the Cuban DA, particularly by Venceremos Brigade veteran Gail Reed, the U.S.-born mistress of Ambassador Torres Rizo. Reed served as a liaison between the PRG and Sánchez Parodi of the Cuban Interest Section in Washington, as well as DA agents at the United Nations.[24] The PRG also cultivated friendships with Washington-based lobbying organizations such as Randall Robinson's Transafrica and with members of the Congressional Black Caucus. U.S. Representative Ronald Dellums (D–Calif.), chairman of the House Subcommittee on Military Construction, visited Grenada in April 1982 on a fact-finding trip to ostensibly judge whether Cuban construction projects on the island had any military significance.[25] One of Dellums's assistants visited Grenada later that year, bringing with her a draft of the congressman's report for the NJM Political Bureau:

> 2.2. *Ron Dellums:* His assistant Barbara Lee is here presently and she has brought with her a report on the International Airporg

[*sic*] that was done by Ron Dellums. They have suggested that we look at the document and suggest any changes [*sic*] we deem necessary—they will be willing to make the changes. Cde. Layne was assigned the task.[26]

Ewart Layne, the Political Bureau member assigned to edit Dellums's report, was a lieutenant colonel in the PRA and deputy secretary of defense. He was sent to the Soviet Union for "studies" together with fellow PRA officers.[27]

The PRG also used deception to maintain the flow of funds from international lending organizations to subsidize Grenada's seriously mismanaged economy. During a Political/Economic Bureau discussion on IMF assistance in August 1983, Maurice Bishop suggested using "the Surinamese and Cuban experience in keeping two sets of records." The bureau decided that "the Comrades from Nicaragua and Cuba must visit Grenada to train Comrades in the readjustment of the books."[28]

Cuban Militarization

Unlike the cautious USSR, Cuba was precipitous in establishing an overt presence in Grenada. Only three days after the coup, the Cuban ship *Matanzas* arrived in St. George's with a cargo of weapons and ammunition.[29] Significantly, the voyage from Cuba for a freighter similar to the *Matanzas* would normally require at least seven days. Shortly afterwards, a nonscheduled Cubana flight from St. Lucia to Trinidad made an "emergency" landing on Grenada, leaving eight Cuban DA officers and military instructors behind. On April 9, the Guyanese ship *Maimito* docked in St. George's after dark and unloaded tons of Soviet weapons and ammunition concealed in a shipment of rice.[30] These armaments included one thousand AK-47, two thousand M-52, and four hundred M-16 rifles; two hundred submachines guns, one hundred pistols, one hundred RPG-2 grenade launchers, twelve 82-mm mortars, a dozen 75-mm cannons, and twelve antiaircraft guns. The shipment also included nearly three million rounds of 7.62-mm ammunition, a half-million rounds of 5.56-mm ammunition, and four thousand RPG-2 grenades.[31]

The Cuban military and technical presence increased during the following months as Cuban advisers organized and trained the native People's Revolutionary Army and People's Militia. Grenadian soldiers dressed in Cuban-style uniforms and carrying AK-47 assault rifles soon became a common sight on the island, along with Soviet Niva jeeps, Lada police cars, and ZU-23 antiaircraft artillery.

The Cubans took early advantage of Grenada's strategic southeastern Caribbean location by establishing a training school on the island for revolutionaries from neighboring countries. This was initially located in a restricted zone at La Sagesse Estate before being moved to the more secure camp at Calivigny Point.[32]

Grenada's neighbors soon became alarmed over the island's militarization, close ties with Cuba, and active involvement in the export of revolution. Only two months after the NJM's coup d'état, the island of St. Vincent protested an attempt by sixteen armed Grenadian soldiers to land on one of its dependency islands,[33] and in January 1980, the government of Trinidad and Tobago charged that more than two hundred of its citizens had undergone training in terrorism, sabotage, and guerrilla warfare by Cubans in Grenada. A number of Cuban-inspired terrorist incidents had occurred in Trinidad, which the oil-rich island termed "a serious threat to the country."[34] Kenrick Radix, Grenada's minister of justice, was deported from Antigua for allegedly trying to foment revolution, and dissidents from St. Vincent also reportedly underwent terrorist training at the DGI/DA school on Grenada.[35]

Growing Soviet Influence

Grenada took on increased importance to Moscow and Havana after the electoral defeat of Jamaica's ardently pro-Cuban Prime Minister Michael Manley in October 1980. Prior to the NJM coup in Grenada, Jamaica had represented the Soviet bloc's most important initiative in the English-speaking Caribbean because of its traditional role as a leader and trendsetter for the smaller former British islands. Grenada was now the most promising entrepôt for the diffusion of Soviet influence through the English-speaking West Indies.

The loss of Jamaica to the U.S. sphere of influence closely preceded the decision by Moscow to increase its influence in Grenada and accelerate the island's militarization via its Cuban surrogate. On November 18, 1979, Prime Minister Bishop announced that Fidel Castro had personally authorized Cuban aid to construct a new "international airport" in Grenada.[36] Although the airport project had been a centerpiece of the PRG's domestic economic development program for some months, neither the Grenadians nor the Cubans had the funds to proceed with it. The PRG was fully aware that the bulk of the airport construction funds and materials came from Moscow via Havana by means of a complicated arrangement whereby the CPSU reimbursed the PCC for outlays.[37] Wary of provoking a U.S. reaction, Soviet officials repeatedly turned down Grenadian requests for direct financial assistance to complete the airport. It is also likely that the USSR, having dealt with the spendthrift Castro regime during the 1960s, was reluctant to entrust large cash transfers to the PRG.[38] An additional $12 million worth of financing for the airport was provided by Libya, Syria, Iraq, and Algeria.[39]

In December 1979, a Cuban "gift" of eighty-five pieces of Soviet heavy construction equipment, four thousand tons of cement, and fifteen hundred tons of steel, together with the vanguard of a two-hundred-fifty-man Cuban construction brigade, arrived on the island to begin work on the new airfield, to be built at Point Salines, a peninsula on Grenada's southwest coast. The Cubans constructed a camp on the airport site consisting of twenty-two prefabricated wooden barracks designed to house forty men each. A large plantation house expropriated from former Prime Minister Sir Eric Gairy was remodeled to provide offices for Cuban and East German engineers.[40] On December 7, the PRG established diplomatic relations with the USSR via a communiqué signed in Havana.

In the case of Grenada, no Soviet subversion or covert political maneuvering was necessary to win influence with the PRG. Exhorted by Deputy Prime Minister Bernard Coard, the NJM worked hard to win the approval of the USSR. The PRG was based on the Soviet model, with an NJM Central Committee, a Politburo, and organizations such as the People's Militia and Pioneers. The NJM pressured Cuba to champion Grenada's "cause" with the Kremlin,[41] a policy that was supported as strongly by Maurice Bishop as it was by Bernard Coard. Survivors of the regime report that Bishop was easily intimidated by Coard's intellect and ideological discipline, and allowed the deputy prime minister to gradually dominate the policy process.

Grenada followed Cuba's example by voting against the UN resolution calling for the withdrawal of foreign troops from Afghanistan after the Soviet Union's invasion of that nation in December 1979. Staunchly defending the USSR, Maurice Bishop declared that "we certainly support fully the right of Afghanistan to call on any country, including the Soviet Union . . . in circumstances such as these, where external aggression is being faced."[42]

The USSR's relationship with Grenada became more overt after the UN vote. In May 1980, Bernard Coard paid his first official visit to the Soviet Union and Eastern Europe. In Moscow, he met with Boris Ponomarev, secretary of the CPSU Central Committee, and A. S. Chernyayev, deputy chief of the CPSU Central Committee's International Department.[43] Following this meeting, Coard signed treaties with the USSR, Czechoslovakia, and Bulgaria that granted Grenada several million dollars' worth of trade credits and machinery, plus scholarships for Grenadian students.[44]

For nearly a year after Coard's visit the Soviet–Grenadian relationship was kept low-key. Diplomatic business was mainly conducted in Havana, where the first of three known top-secret military assistance treaties was signed on October 27, 1980. During the summer and fall of 1980, the USSR seems to have followed a policy of keeping its distance from the PRG as well as from the Nicaraguan Sandinistas for fear that exposure of its Caribbean activities would benefit Ronald Reagan during that year's U.S. presidential campaign. Maurice Bishop's increasingly radical statements concerned Soviet policymakers, particularly when the Western media began using them to implicate the USSR in Grenada's militarization. In a March 1980 interview with *Newsweek,* Bishop said that his new "international airport" might be used for Soviet and Cuban airlifts to trouble spots, and further alarmed the government of Trinidad by declaring: "Suppose there's a war next door in Trinidad, where the forces of Fascism are about to take control, and the Trinidadians need assistance. Why should we oppose anybody passing through Grenada to assist them?"[45]

Shortly after making this statement, Bishop announced that he would send five hundred Grenadian soldiers to Namibia to fight alongside SWAPO forces.[46] Grenadian *brigadistas* were also sent to Nicaragua in October 1980,[47] where some were reported to have been killed in counterinsurgency operations against the Miskito Indians.[48] Such actions and rhetoric must have appeared disturbingly reminiscent of the young Fidel Castro to the CPSU Central Committee's International Department.

Throughout 1981, Cuba continued to serve as an intermediary with Grenada for both the Soviet Union and its Eastern European satellites. Soviet and Czech military aid was extensive during this period: by the end of June 1981, more than six thousand rifles and submachine guns, two dozen 82-mm mortars, and an equal number of artillery pieces, plus more than 5.3 million rounds of various types of ammunition had been transshipped to Grenada from Cuba.[49] This quantity of armaments was far more than needed to equip the PRA and People's Militia, and there is evidence that Grenada was itself beginning to serve as a weapons transshipment depot for other Soviet-sponsored revolutionary forces in the Caribbean region. Several RPG-2 (Chinese Type 56) grenade launchers captured by security forces in El Salvador during 1984 were found to closely fit the same serial number sequence of RPG-2s discovered in Grenada, one hundred of which were delivered to the island in April 1979 together with four hundred U.S.-made M-16 rifles left behind in Vietnam. Some of these rifles were also unaccounted for and believed to have been reexported from Grenada.[50]

This large inventory of armaments did not appear to satisfy the PRG's defense needs, perhaps a further indication that the Grenadians knew that a certain percentage of the shipments were not designated for their use. In mid-November 1981, Maurice Bishop sent a letter to Raúl Castro via Colonel Alfredo Luaces Delgado—head of the Cuban military mission in Grenada—seeking his help on soliciting further military aid from the USSR. Bishop enclosed a copy of the PRG's request for aid, asking "Comrade Raúl" to offer his "advice and suggestions on the best ways to present this document to the Soviets."[51] Bishop was apparently knowledgeable enough about the Soviet–Cuban relationship to know that Raúl was a far better choice for a conduit to Moscow that his brother Fidel.

Grenada's Role in Soviet Caribbean Strategy

Soviet–Grenadian relations reached a major turning point in 1982. In July, Maurice Bishop visited Moscow where he was officially welcomed as "chairman of the Politburo of the Central Committee of the New Jewel Party."[52] At a press conference held after his arrival, Bishop said that Grenada's "strategic aim . . . is to further develop relations with the socialist countries . . . and we want to follow our own way, the way of close relations with the socialist community, the Soviet Union in particular."[53]

Amid extensive coverage by *Pravda* and Moscow Domestic Television Service, Bishop met with Nikolai Tikhonov, chairman of the USSR's Council of Ministers, and Mikhail Gorbachev, who was then a member of the CPSU Central Committee and a confidant of the dying Brezhnev's political heir, Yuri Andropov. Emerging from the meetings, Bishop announced that he had "concluded substantial economic and political agreements with the Soviet Union to cut his country's dependence on the West."[54] The Kremlin had granted him $1.4 million to buy "500 tonnes of steel, 400 tonnes of flour and other essential goods," in addition to a ten-year credit of $7.7 million to finance the construction of a satellite earth station, the purpose of which, according to Bishop, was to "give us the opportunity of receiving directly in Grenada [*an English-speaking country*] all the programs that are taking place on television, on radio and whatnot in the Soviet Union."[55] The USSR further agreed to fund and construct a new deep-water port on Grenada's east coast, in exchange for which Soviet ships would be granted "recreational calls" at the facility.[56]

The Grenadian leader also said that the USSR had agreed to buy Grenada's two main crops, nutmegs and cocoa, at "stable prices," and stated that the NJM had signed an interparty agreement with the CPSU, the goals of which were "to promote cooperation in the training of government and party cadres" and the development of "contacts between the party press and the mass communication media, to inform the public of their countries about the activity of the two countries and of their home and foreign policy. . . ." This agreement was signed on behalf of the CPSU by Boris Ponomarev, chief of the International Department and secretary for nonruling communist party liaison, rather than K. V. Rusakov, secretary for ruling communist party liaison, who would have been the expected signatory if the CPSU seriously accepted the NJM as a Marxist-Leninist party.[57]

Bishop did not divulge the existence of several secret treaties signed with the USSR during his visit, most of which had a clear military application. Foremost among these was a Soviet–Grenadian agreement in which the Soviet Union promised to deliver to the island over a three-year period some fifty armored personnel carriers, sixty mortars, sixty antitank and other heavy guns, fifty portable rocket launchers, fifty RPG-7 grenade launchers, two thousand submachine guns, and tons of other military equipment. The agreement also provided for "Soviet specialists and interpreters" to be sent to Grenada in exchange for "Grenadian servicemen's training, upkeep, meals in the Soviet military educational establishment," the expenses for which were "borne by the Soviet Party."[58] Apparently, an agreement was also reached at this time to furnish Grenada with two Soviet military transport aircraft.[59]

The July 1982 secret treaties also provided for special equipment to be supplied to Grenada's Ministry of the Interior for state security and intelligence collection purposes. This was probably in response to a Grenadian "request" made directly to Yuri Andropov, then KGB chairman, following a meeting in Grenada between Maurice Bishop, Liam James (a Soviet-trained PRA officer and Coard protégé), General Hudson Austin, and Vladimir Klimentov, a KGB officer attached to the Soviet embassy in Kingston, Jamaica.[60]

A 1982 report to Maurice Bishop from the PRG's minister-counselor in Moscow, Bernard Bourne, offers some clues to the USSR's decision to embrace Grenada more openly as well as the Soviet Union's existing degree of influence on the PRG. Bourne reported that at a meeting with CPSU representatives on April 22, 1982, he was told that the Kremlin regarded the NJM as a communist party and therefore seemed to disapprove of its membership in the Socialist International (SI). This appears to have been a cause of some concern to the CPSU, which was why "the Soviet comrades" had been "dealing with us cautiously and sometimes sceptically."[61] This apparently genuine reason for Soviet wariness was extrapolated by Grenada's ambassador to Moscow, W. Richard Jacobs:

> The Soviets have been burnt quite often in the past by giving support to Governments which have either squandered that support, or turned around and become agents of imperialism, or lost power. One is reminded of Egypt, Samolia [*sic*], Ghana and Peru. They are therefore very careful, and for us sometimes maddingly slow, in making up their minds about who to support.[62]

Apparently satisfied with the NJM's allegiance to Moscow, the Soviet Union decided that it could safely utilize Grenada as its chief proxy in the English-speaking Caribbean. Playing on the vanity of Grenadian leaders as deftly as they had manipulated Fidel Castro's egotism, the "Soviet comrades" invited the NJM to the USSR's six-tieth anniversary celebrations while informing the Grenadians that other leftist Caribbean parties had "asked for invitations." The Bishop regime was told that the "final decision on these invitations will be taken by the CPSU after consultation with the NJM via the Embassy." The CPSU also invited Grenadian "Central Committee comrades" and "leading members of our mass organizations" to the Soviet Union for "rest and familiarization."[63]

Grenada's embassy in Moscow was designated to "serve as a bridge between the CPSU and the Left Parties in the English-Speaking Caribbean." This work was deemed "decisive" for the Soviet policy-making process because Grenada was "able to give details of the situations in each of these countries," based on ". . . analyses and assessments by the CC NJM and information on developments at home and in the region."[64]

The NJM leadership *wanted* to serve the strategic interests of the USSR, believing that this would enable them to "develop good working relations and become a trustworthy ally of the CPSU." Unlike Cuba and Nicaragua, Grenada's leaders seemed almost anxious to subjugate their nation to Soviet imperialism. They viewed their "revolution" as "a world-wide process with its original roots in the Great October Revolution." The PRG was worried about "Grenada's distance from the USSR and its small size" and believed that for the island to "assume a position of increasingly greater importance" it was necessary "to be seen as influencing at least regional events." To enhance Grenada's "importance in the Soviet scheme of things,"[65] the PRG was determined to establish itself "as the authority on events in at least the English-speaking Caribbean, and be the sponsor of revolutionary activity and progressive developments in this region at least."[66]

Bernard Bourne's 1982 report also provides information on the Soviet officials responsible for policy toward Grenada. Arrangements for Maurice Bishop's July 1982 visit to the USSR were handled by a "Comrade Nikolai" who was identified as "Chief of the Department for North-America and the English-Speaking Caribbean" within the International Department of the CPSU Secretariat. During Bishop's visit, the International Department's head, Boris Ponomarev, was present during party-to-party discussions, as was, apparently, Mikhail Gorbachev.[67] The International Department has a decisive influence on Soviet foreign policy, disseminating Politburo decisions to lower CPSU levels and implementing CPSU policy.[68]

There is evidence that, beginning in 1982, the strong Cuban influence on the PRG was gradually displaced by the Soviet Union. Moscow's policy decisions were relayed directly to the NJM Central Committee via the Soviet ambassadors in Havana and Kingston, often without the knowledge of the Cubans.[69] In September of that year, Soviet Ambassador Gennadiy I. Sazhenev arrived in Grenada with an initial staff of eight (which had grown to nearly thirty by October 1983). The Soviet diplomats' arrival reportedly coincided with Cuban Ambassador Torres Rizo's prohibition from further attendance at NJM Politburo and Central Committee meetings—an indication of the NJM's internal power struggle that would lead to the PRG's demise.[70]

The USSR's involvement with Grenada intensified over the course of the twelve months following Sazhenev's arrival. The Soviet news agency Tass opened an office in Butler House, the main PRG office complex, "to inform Grenadians of world events."[71] Selected Grenadian students were sent to the Lenin School in Moscow, the most important CPSU training institution for foreign communists. Grenadian youths were also sent to the GDR Higher Party School in East Germany. It is interesting to note that a high percentage of those students sent to study in Eastern Europe were the children or relatives of the NJM party elite, while those educated in Cuba were almost exclusively second echelon.[72]

In May 1983, the PRG accepted a Soviet invitation to send nine mid-level economic officials to Moscow to attend a two-month course offered by Gosplan, the Soviet economic planning entity.[73] This seems to have been part of a plan to begin collectivizing the Grenadian agricultural sector.[74] That same month, a ten-man delegation from Grenada's Ministry of Construction went to the Soviet Union for a training course in planning.[75] This followed a visit by a Soviet surveying team in March, which concluded that the USSR would build a new port and a cement plant producing fifty thousand tons of cement per year on the island of Carriacou, an isolated, thirteen-square-mile dependency of Grenada with a population of seven thousand farmers and fishermen. The Soviet officials said that the cement plant would require a new power facility capable of generating seventy-five hundred kilowatts of electricity, and that the site chosen for the new harbor would be Tyrrel Bay, a commodious and sheltered anchorage used by the British fleet in the eighteenth century. As part of this development package, the USSR "also offered to supply Grenada with 2,000 tons of steel as a gift for building roads, buildings, bridges and so on."[76] The Soviet visit occurred during a Cuban construction project to extend the runway of Carriacou's airfield, located less than a mile from Tyrrel Bay.

In June 1983, Grenada hosted a regional "Conference on Peace," during which Foreign Minister Unison Whiteman advised his youthful audience to "follow the courageous lead of the USSR," adding that "the policies of the United States were undermining the universally accepted doctrine of peaceful co-existence."[77] The following day, Grenada's Ministry of Planning signed a series of contracts "in the areas of education, communications, water supply and seaport development" with Boris Nikolayev, economic counselor at the Soviet embassy. Under the terms of these agreements, sixteen Soviet teachers arrived with their families in Grenada in September 1983 to teach "science and mathematics."[78] Residents of the island, which had been a quiet British possession only nine years earlier, were now treated to the spectacle of teenaged members of the Grenada–Soviet Friendship Society giving clench-fisted salutes while chanting: "Long live the Soviet Union! Long live Proletarian Internationalism!"[79]

These and other Soviet-sponsored developments in Grenada offer dramatic testimony of the island's rapid incorporation into the Soviet system. However, the USSR's strategic plans for the island were abruptly terminated by the power struggle between the two wings of the NJM, an unforeseen occurrence that it was powerless to control.

Dissolution of the People's Revolutionary Government

The bitter infighting between the Coard and Bishop factions of the NJM is too complex to be adequately dealt with here. In essence, Maurice Bishop had come under growing criticism from Coard and his Soviet-trained supporters for the deteriorating state of the Grenadian economy and the prime minister's inability to deal with his nation's numerous other problems. Bishop was also under suspicion for his 1983 meeting in Washington, D.C., with U.S. National Security Adviser William Clark and two other senior U.S. officials. The Soviet officials responsible for Grenadian affairs were highly displeased that Bishop had not informed them of the meeting beforehand and that he had ordered the PRG's ambassador in Moscow to keep its details confidential.[80] The Coard faction proposed that "Joint Leadership" be shared between Bishop and Coard, with Bishop's specific responsibilities largely reduced to ceremonial functions. By this time Bernard Coard already controlled the Political Bureau (the NJM's chief policy-making element) and the Organizing Committee (the NJM's chief administrative organ), thereby negating Maurice Bishop's theoretical power as chairman of the NJM Central Committee.

When Bishop refused to accept the rival faction's demands, he was deposed, ejected from the party and placed under house arrest. Island-wide demonstrations and strikes followed, causing the PRA to disarm the pro-Bishop People's Militia to prevent a civil war. On October 19, 1983, Bishop was freed by a large crowd led by Foreign Minister Unison Whiteman and taken to Fort Rupert, where the garrison was persuaded to lay down its arms.

Several hours later a PRA armored assault unit in Soviet-supplied BTR-60 armored personnel carriers attacked Fort Rupert, killing more than a hundred civilians and capturing Bishop, Whiteman, and others, who were summarily executed. The formation of a Revolutionary Military Council (RMC) was announced and the island was placed under martial law. These circumstances lead to the joint U.S.–OECS intervention on October 25 to protect U.S. lives and stabilize an anarchic situation.

The role of the sixty-two Soviet and Soviet bloc officials on the island during this episode can only be surmised. It is now known that Bernard Coard and his Soviet-trained PRA officers were responsible for Bishop's execution, and Hudson Austin, the RMC chairman, was captured following the allied intervention at a house leased to East German security advisers. The Soviet media was supportive of the coup against Bishop, a fact for which the RMC was deeply grateful.[81] Fidel Castro, on the other hand, was quick to denounce the killing of his friend and protégé, demanding that those responsible be "punished in an exemplary way."[82]

Despite Fidel's disapproval, the Cuban government (probably on orders from Raúl Castro) assured the RMC that Cuban aid to Grenada would continue, and reaffirmed its support for the "revolutionary process" on the island. After a delay of five days, and probably at Soviet instigation, an An-26 transport aircraft carrying Carlos Diaz Larranga, the PCC official responsible for Grenadian affairs, and Colonel Pedro Tortolo Comas, chief of staff of the Cuban Army of the Center, was dispatched to Grenada. Tortolo, a graduate of the Frunze Military Academy and the Voroshilov Staff College in the USSR, commanded the Cuban defense of the Point Salines international airport during the allied invasion, subsequently finding refuge in the Soviet embassy when his forces surrendered. Fidel Castro appears to have vented his anger and frustration over Grenada on this Soviet-trained officer, for he ordered Tortolo demoted to private and sent to Angola.[83]

Grenada's Military Potential

The Soviet Union's primary interest in Grenada, as demonstrated by its military aid, was the island's potential as a base for various means of power projection. As in the case of Cuba, economic and technical assistance was of secondary importance, designed to provide a stable political environment for the basing of Soviet tactical and strategic assets.

The most visible Soviet-subsidized construction project in Grenada was the ninety-eight-hundred-foot all-weather "international airport" being built by some six hundred Cubans at Point Salines. Although ostensibly constructed for Grenada's moribund tourist industry, a sufficient body of evidence has emerged to support the theory that the airfield was to have a military application.

The PRG was aware that its Soviet and Cuban benefactors had other plans for the airport besides tourism. In a speech to Jamaica's official communist party, the Workers' Party of Jamaica (WPJ), in December 1981, Grenadian Minister of National Mobilization Selwyn Strachan stated that Cuba would eventually use the new airport to supply troops to Africa, and that the USSR would also find it useful because of its "strategic location" astride vital sea lanes and oil transport routes.[84] Liam James, the Soviet-trained deputy defense secretary, recorded in his notebook that during an NJM meeting on March 22, 1980, one of the agenda items was "Airport will be used for Cubans and Soviets."[85] Another NJM member who had received training in Moscow wrote in his diary in October 1983 that rumors were being spread that "the Party wanted Bishop to sign for the Airport to be a Military Base and he did do that."[86] Another tantalizing clue is offered by the minutes of a Political Bureau meeting on June 22, 1983, at which one of the decision items—unfortunately not discussed—was "Soviet Pilots and Planes."[87]

The documents found in Grenada indicate that the USSR was planning to provide the PRG with its own air force—possibly as a pretext for permanently stationing Soviet aircraft and pilots on the island, if Cuba is used as a precedent. On May 24, 1983, Soviet Ambassador Sazhenev told Maurice Bishop that a Soviet military aircraft (an An-26) capable of carrying "39 paratroopers" would be supplied to Grenada but was being sent to Cuba for assembly. Sazhenev stated that his superiors preferred that Cuban pilots fly the aircraft, and pressed Bishop to decide what colors and emblems should be painted on it. From the transcript of the conversation, it appears that other such aircraft were to be supplied to Grenada in the future, for the Soviet ambassador said: "Fifteen specialists will travel from Moscow to work on the aircrafts. An additional engine and spare parts enough for five planes will be attached. All spare parts will be left in Cuba under supervision of Specialists from the U.S.S.R."[88]

Only a month prior to this meeting, the NJM's Organizing Committee had discussed a Soviet offer to send four "physically fit" Grenadians to the Soviet Union to be trained as pilots.[89]

Other Soviet military construction projects were planned for Grenada. In March 1983, Marshal Nikolai Ogarkov told Grenadian officials that Soviet specialists were being sent to Grenada "to conduct studies related to the construction of military projects."[90] These probably included the "sea port" planned for the island's east coast, the Intersputnik satellite station (which probably would have had an electronic C^3I function), and a maritime facility on the dependency island of Carriacou.

The USSR may also have been considering the employment of Grenadian soldiers as Soviet proxies in Africa or Central America. Plans had been drawn up to build the People's Revolutionary Army into an eighteen-battalion force by the end of 1985, giving it a strength of between 7,200 and 10,000 personnel. In proportion to its population of less than 100,000, this would have given Grenada the largest military force of any country in the world.[91] In addition to training courses in the USSR, East Germany, and Cuba, PRA personnel were scheduled for training in Vietnam in "(a) anti-chemical warfare, (b) anti-radioactivity warfare, (c) reeducation of antisocial and counterrevolutionary elements, (d) Yankee tactics and the weapons used in Vietnam."[92]

The loss of Grenada was a major setback to Soviet strategic plans for the Caribbean. The U.S.–OECS intervention served as a warning that the United States was still committed to the defense of its national security interests in the region, thus generating renewed confidence in the United States among democratic governments throughout the Caribbean basin. However, a far more important Soviet strategic asset was still being actively developed on the Central American isthmus—the Sandinista stronghold of Nicaragua.

PUNTA HUETE AIRFIELD

M-1939 ANTIAIRCRAFT ARTILLERY SITE

M-1939 ANTIAIRCRAFT ARTILLERY SITE

M-1939 ANTIAIRCRAFT ARTILLERY SITE

ALERT REVETMENTS

FUELING APRON

AIRCRAFT DISPERSAL AREA

PUNTA HUETE

MANAGUA

5
The Role of Nicaragua in Soviet Strategy for the Caribbean

A Revolution Betrayed

The Sandinista (FSLN) victory in Nicaragua on July 19, 1979—following closely on the Marxist coup d'état in Grenada—was the first successful social revolution in Latin America since the Cuban Revolution of 1959. It now seems clear that there were really two revolutions in Nicaragua: one, broadly based, to establish a Western-style democracy; the other, narrowly based, to establish a Marxist-Leninist state. The success of the latter demonstrated the application of V. I. Lenin's classic "two-stage" revolutionary strategy: a nationalist-Bourgeois coup d'état following by Marxist usurpation of power.

The Sandinistas trace their party's origins to Nicaragua's original Moscow-oriented communist party, the Nicaraguan Socialist Party (PSN), founded in 1937.[1] Outlawed by the Somoza regime in 1950 in response to Washington's anticommunist "Truman Doctrine" (a measure adopted by the Batista regime in Cuba three years later), the PSN went underground and began recruiting party members among the students at the National Autonomous University of Nicaragua (UNAN) as well as the business community. The father of Daniel and Humberto Ortega Saavedra—now, respectively, president and defense minister of the Sandinista regime—was a secret PSN member who owned an import–export business specializing in

Facing page: Nicaragua's Punta Huete airfield has a 10,000-foot runway—the longest of any military airfield in Central America—that can accommodate any aircraft in the Soviet inventory. *Department of Defense photo*

trade with the Soviet bloc.[2] Both Ortega brothers were members of the PSN youth, and Humberto Ortega attended Patrice Lumumba University in Moscow together with Henry Ruiz, another member of the FSLN's current National Directorate, under PSN auspices.[3]

Carlos Fonseca Amador, Silvio Mayorga, and Tomás Borge— the three founding members of the FSLN—were also PSN Youth members who formed a Marxist cell while students at UNAN. Fonseca was sent to Moscow in 1956 as the PSN's delegate to the Sixth World Youth and Student Festival and was so impressed by the Soviet system that he wrote a book upon his return to Nicaragua titled *A Nicaraguan in Moscow*. The book was a statement of Fonseca's profound belief in Marxism-Leninism as interpreted by the Kremlin, and formed the basis for his role as the FSLN's chief ideologue and theoretician until his death in 1976.[4]

After the Cuban Revolution of 1958, Fonseca, Mayorga, and Borge broke with the PSN over their support for the Castroite model of revolution. In 1959, the Castro regime armed and trained a group of fifty-five Nicaraguans and Cubans who, under Fonseca's command, attempted to enter Nicaragua for the purpose of overthrowing the Somoza government. However, the revolutionaries were crushed by the Honduran Army. Fonseca and other survivors fled to Cuba, where they were joined by Tomás Borge. Under the direction of Che Guevara, the young revolutionaries developed a plan for another Cuban-style armed insurrection in Nicaragua.[5]

Following an almost identical policy to that of the 1950s-era Cuban Communist Party, the Nicaraguan PSN began actively opposing Fonseca and his young, middle-class revolutionaries, accusing them of "military opportunism" that endangered the "legitimate" party.[6] When Fonseca again tried to enter Nicaragua in the summer of 1960, the PSN betrayed him to Somoza's security forces, leading to his arrest and eventual deportation.[7]

In 1961, Fonseca, Mayorga, and Borge founded the National Liberation Front (FLN) as an autonomous political–military organization dedicated to achieving a Cuban-style revolution in Nicaragua. However, the FLN's lack of success in recruiting anyone besides a handful of idealistic, middle and upper-class young Nicaraguans led Fonseca to conceal the organization's Marxist-Leninist ideology behind a facade of nationalism. This was accomplished by adopting General Augusto César Sandino (see chapter 1) as the patron saint of the revolution. In 1962, the FLN's name was officially changed to the Sandinista National Liberation Front (FSLN).[8] After the Sandinistas' third attempt to launch an armed rebellion failed the following year, they returned to the tactic of civic organizing and university recruitment and were immediately accepted as allies of the PSN.[9]

Sandinista Ideology and Strategy

The FSLN's ideological orientation was clearly delineated long before taking power. Tomás Borge has stated that he has been "a Communist" since "his youth."[10] Sandinista defectors such as Humberto Belli have testified to the Marxist-Leninist indoctrination given to FSLN cadra in the USSR, Cuba, Jordan, Lebanon, North Korea, Libya, Algeria, and South Yemen in the years preceding the Sandinista victory of 1979.[11] Like its prerevolutionary colleagues in Grenada, the movement considered itself a Leninist vanguard party, as the FSLN's May 1977 Political–Military Platform made clear:

> The national liberation process will come about by breaking the chains that bind our country to the foreign imperialist yoke. The social liberation process . . . will come about as long as we have our Marxist-Leninist cause and a solid vanguard to provide leadership in the struggle. . . .
>
> It is a revolutionary war because, using the worker–peasant alliance with the guidance of a Marxist-Leninist vanguard, it will . . . create the conditions to enable the Sandinista process to progress through the democratic revolutionary phase toward socialism.[12]

In a communiqué issued less than a year before the FSLN assumption of power, strict conformity to Leninist tactics was emphasized:

> This Sandinista nuclear vanguard must occupy and direct the governing organs. . . . This nucleus must base itself in the scientific doctrine of the proletariat, in Marxism-Leninism, as a sure guide for the transformation of society.[13]

On September 21, 1979—two months after assuming power in
Managua—the FSLN National Directorate convened a top secret
seventy-two-hour meeting to discuss strategy for consolidating the
revolution and transforming Nicaragua into a Marxist-Leninist
state. The report on this meeting, titled "Analysis of the Situation
and Tasks of the Sandinista People's Revolution," bears an extraordinary resemblance to Maurice Bishop's "Line of March for the
Party" speech, which revealed nearly identical revolutionary strategy for Grenada.[14] Calling the "imperialist power of the United
States" Nicaragua's "true enemy," the FSLN said that one of the
most important tasks facing it in its early days was to make certain
"political arrangements . . . to thwart Yankee imperialism." These
"arrangements" followed the same pattern adopted by the NJM almost simultaneously, including a temporary "alliance of conve-
nience . . . with the bourgeoisie, just to give some representation to
people with a patriotic reputation." Stressing "the expectation of
financial help from the Western bloc" to help rebuild Nicaragua's
shattered economy, the Sandinistas decided that it was necessary "to
appear reasonable during this 'intermediate' period" by maintaining "at the present moment . . . a neutral position with respect to
the imperialists. . . ."[15]

Bluntly stating that the FSLN was "an organization whose
greatest aspiration is to retain revolutionary power," the Sandinista
leadership outlined the tasks necessary to achieve what subsequently became a de facto dictatorship under the guise of "democratic socialism." The "enemies of the revolution" were identified
as "the bourgeoisie betrayers of the fatherland" (*vendepatria*), the
"residue of Somocism," and "the ultra left." These three groups
were to be "isolated . . . from the democratic sectors of the Revolution" and brought under the FSLN's control. The "most revolutionary classes" were to be educated, organized, and given leadership to "convert them into the motor that moves the revolutionary
process," while leftist parties "such as the MAP [a Maoist organi-
zation] and the Trotskyites" were to be treated as enemies. It was
decided that "small political parties" (*micropartidos*) had to be tolerated "because of international opinion," although FSLN agents
were "to work within them to get them to support the revolution."[16]

Subversion of religion already constituted a Sandinista tactic.

The FSLN National Directorate decided to treat the Catholic Church cordially, "following a cautious policy designed to neutralize conservative elements, develop close ties to sympathetic elements, and stimulate the revolutionary sectors." Protestant churches and missionaries, which were "generally made up of North American religious groups," had to be restricted and watched by the Sandinistas' internal security apparatus (*una labor de inteligencia*). Political commissars were to be assigned to the army to "purify" it by "eliminating incompatible elements."[17]

Because Sandinista foreign policy was founded on "the principle of revolutionary internationalism," the "consolidation of the Nicaragua revolution" would inevitably "strengthen revolutionary feeling in Central America, Latin America, and in the world."[18] Remarkably, although the Carter administration was completely cognizant of the Sandinistas' policy of deceit, by means of a copy of the FSLN Directorate report sent to Washington by U.S. Ambassador Lawrence Pezzullo in December 1979, the U.S. government knowingly allowed itself to be used by the FSLN. Between mid-1979 and early 1981, almost $120 million in aid was sent to Nicaragua, a period during which more than a thousand metric tons of Soviet bloc military equipment was supplied to the Sandinistas.[19]

Further evidence of the FSLN's policy of deceit is provided by a speech made in May 1984 by Bayardo Arce, one of the nine Sandinista *comandantes* and then director of the government political commission established to prepare for Nicaragua's upcoming "elections".[20] Arce's speech was delivered to the Central Committee of the Nicaraguan Socialist Party (PSN), the orthodox, pro-Moscow communist party that was both the FSLN's ideological parent and a strong Sandinista ally. Responding to a question from a member of his audience about the need to hold elections in Nicaragua, Arce explained "the perspectives that we Communists must have on the electoral process." Acknowledging that "the elections are bothersome to us," he said that nevertheless "from the point of view of the reality we have, the elections are a tool of the revolution and a way of advancing the building of socialism." Because the Sandinistas would control the elections, they would be used as a tactical device to "disarm the international bourgeoisie" and "remove one of the United States' policy justifications for aggression against Nicaragua." Arce promised his sceptical comrades that a Sandinista electoral victory would result in a "Red constitution," the removal of the "facade of pluralism," and the establishment of "the party of the revolution, the single party."[21]

Like Maurice Bishop, his deceased Grenadian counterpart, Bayardo Arce placed a strong emphasis on his country's "strategic relations with the USSR" and its commitment to "revolutionary internationalism"—a reference to FLSN support for Marxist guerrillas in other parts of Central America. The PSN Central Committee members were told that the assured Sandinista victory in the November 4 elections would make it appear to the world that the people of Nicaragua "are in favor of Soviet–Cuban advance, are in favor of totalitarianism, are in favor of Marxism-Leninism, are in favor of Soviet–Cuban military advisers, are in favor of revolutionary internationalism."[22]

The removal of the "facade of pluralism" in Nicaragua is now nearly complete, and with it has come open admission by other Sandinista leaders that their regime is of a Marxist-Leninist nature. Speaking at a conference in East Berlin honoring the centennial of Karl Marx's birth, Comandante Víctor Tirado declared: "We, the founders and organizers of the FSLN, prepared our strategy, our tactics and our program on the basis of Marx' teachings. . . ."[23] Humberto Ortega, Sandinista defense minister and brother of Nicaraguan President Daniel Ortega, told the Sandinista army (EPS) that "Marxism-Leninism is the scientific doctrine that guides our revolution, the instrument of analysis of our vanguard to understand the historical process and to create the revolution. . . ."[24]

The Sandinistas' tactic of deceit is one of the most important elements of Soviet strategy toward the Caribbean. Known to Latin American revolutionaries as *el manto* (the "cloak" or "mantle"), the tactic is Leninist in origin, but exhibits a growing sophistication based on the recent revolutionary experiences of regimes such as Grenada's PRG in addition to the classic deception techniques practiced by the USSR (for example, the "abolition" of the Comintern in 1943).[25] A successful manto must also take into account the shifting political and social moods of the Western democracies, who are the primary targets of the tactic of deceit. The secondary targets are the common people of the Caribbean and other Third World Marxist-Leninist regimes, who are continually warned about the "imperialist aggression" that threatens their "democratic socialist" and "peace-loving"nations.[26]

Cuban Assistance

Cuban support for the FSLN was generally meager during the 1960s and early 1970s, largely due to the Sandinistas' failed efforts to maintain an effective guerrilla movement or to generate popular support. FSLN delegates attended major Cuban-sponsored leftist meetings such as the Organization of Latin American Solidarity (OLAS) conference in 1967 as well as the Tricontinental Conference held the previous year.[27] The Castro regime also coordinated revolutionary training programs for the FSLN both in Cuba and in other radical Third World states. For example, Tomás Borge, who is now Nicaraguan interior minister, was one of between fifty and seventy Sandinistas sent to Lebanon for joint Cuban–Palestine Liberation Organization (PLO) training in 1969, while other Nicaraguans received military and subversive training at PLO camps in Libya. PLO-trained Sandinistas took part in several terrorist operations in the Middle East during the early 1970s, including an attempt to overthrow the government of Jordan's King Hussein.[28]

Following the successful Sandinista raid on the Castillo Quant residence in December 1974 (an operation which, however, failed in its goal of taking the U.S. ambassador hostage), Cuba took an active interest in the insurgents.[29]

The raid followed the return to Nicaragua of an elite group of highly trained revolutionaries led by Humberto Ortega. This group had first undergone an indoctrination course in Cuba before proceeding to Czechoslovakia for a highly structured political–military training program. After being joined by a group of Nicaraguan students from Patrice Lumumba University in Moscow, the combined group was sent to North Korea for an additional six months of military instruction. These young men and women were infiltrated back into Nicaragua, where they subsequently formed the officer corps of the dominant "insurrectionalist tendency" military wing of the FSLN under Humberto Ortega's command.[30]

The sophisticated military training provided to the Sandinistas—and their subsequent success in carrying out the Castillo Quant operation—appears to have been a by-product of the Soviet Union's innovative strategic doctrine of military assistance to peripheral theatres of the developing world, which made its public appearance almost concurrently.[31] Having demonstrated their newly acquired military prowess during the operation, as well as receiving international attention from the raid, the Sandinistas were perceived by the Kremlin as a viable insurgent force, and the USSR awakened to the invaluable strategic possibilities to be gained by securing a foothold on the Central American isthmus if the FSLN could conquer Nicaragua.

In 1977 and early 1978, Armando Ulises Estrada Fernandez, deputy director of Cuba's DA, worked to unify three FSLN factions or "tendencies": the *Insurrectionalists* (also called the *Terceristas*), the *Prolonged Popular War* (GPP), and the *Proletarian* (TP). The latter was led by Jaime Wheelock (now Sandinista minister of agriculture), who had been influenced by his orthodox Marxist education in East Berlin and the University of Leipzig and believed that organization of the urban masses was a major precondition of revolution.[32]

Unification of the Sandinista factions was given priority by Havana. A united revolutionary front was necessary to convince the world that the FSLN was a serious challenger to the Somoza regime. However, it was also necessary, as part of the manto or tactic of deceit, to draw moderate elements of the Nicaraguan opposition into the front to lend it legitimacy and the support of the West, especially the United States, members of the Organization of American States (OAS), and European social democratic parties.[33] This was largely accomplished by creating, in 1977, a political support organization called *Grupe de los Doce* ("Group of the Twelve") composed of a dozen ostensibly moderate, socially prominent members of the opposition to Somoza. Although Grupo de los Doce included genuine democrats such as Arturo Cruz (currently a leader of the anti-Sandinista United Nicaraguan Opposition or UNO), the group was dominated by closet Marxists such as Sergio Ramirez (currently Nicaraguan vice president) and the Catholic priests Miguel D'Escoto (foreign minister) and Fernando Cardenal (minister of education).[34]

Leaders of the three Sandinista factions were brought to Havana and told that military and financial assistance from Cuba was contingent upon the FSLN achieving effective unity.[35] During the Eleventh World Youth Festival held in Havana in July 1978, Fidel Castro betrayed his eagerness to promote a Marxist victory in Nicaragua when he prematurely announced the unification of the FSLN factions and urged other Latin American revolutionaries to demonstrate solidarity with the Sandinistas by staging operations in their own countries. In reality, continued disagreement about tactics and division of power delayed the official FSLN announcement of unification until December 26, 1978, when Tomás Borge was also named coordinator of the front.[36]

By the end of 1978, Cuban advisers had been sent to northern Costa Rica to train and equip FSLN battalions with arms flown in from Cuba on Soviet An-26 transports—two squadrons of which had recently been supplied to the Castro regime. The six-hundred-mile range of the An-26 indicates that these aircraft were supplied by the Soviet Union specifically for providing tactical airlift support to Caribbean theater operations such as the insurgency in Nicaragua, rather than for Cuba's African campaigns, which required long-range Il-76 and An-12 aircraft.[37] The Cubans were careful not to jeopardize international sympathy for the guerrillas by giving them Soviet-made weapons; instead, U.S. M-16s captured in Vietnam were supplied, along with West German G3s and Israeli UZIs purchased from international arms dealers. This tactic worked so well that it became a model for supplying other Marxists insurgents, such as the guerrilla forces in El Salvador.[38] When the FSLN's final offensive was launched in the summer of 1979, Cuban military advisers from the DOE, the elite commando unit that had recently assisted in the March 13, 1979, coup d'état in Grenada, accompanied Sandinista columns and maintained direct radio communications with Havana.[39] An operations center run by the DA in San José, Costa Rica, was the focal point for coordinating Cuba's support to the insurgents. After the fall of President Anastasio Somoza, the chief of the DA's San José center, Julián López Díaz, became Cuban ambassador to Nicaragua, and one of his assistants, Andres Barahona, was redocumented as a Nicaraguan citizen to become the de factor, although not titular, head of the country's new intelligence service, the Sandinista General Directorate of State Security (DGSE).[40]

As with the Grenada coup d'état four months earlier, the Cuban role in directing the Sandinista regime began within hours of the FSLN's assumption of power. Within a week of President Somoza's departure, approximately one hundred Cuban security and military advisers were in Managua, with this figure doubling by October 1979.[41]

Cuban, East German, and Bulgarian advisers quickly began organizing the DGSE along textbook KGB lines using Cuban intelligence manuals containing Russian technical words with a Spanish translation.[42] Nearly all DGSE personnel were sent on training courses in Cuba where they, along with Grenadians and Angolans, studied enemy activities, counterintelligence, operative psychology, and Marxism. Key officers also took part in advanced training course in the Soviet Union and Bulgaria for periods of one to five years. Such programs led to advanced professional degrees with specialties in the field of intelligence, and were intended to thoroughly Sovietize the students.[43]

The DGSE is basically a copy of the Cuban DGI, with an identical number of sections. Although the Cuban Communist Party's DA works with the DGSE, the KGB-controlled DGI actually controls the Nicaraguan intelligence service.[44] The approximately three thousand Nicaraguans working under Lenin Cerna, de jure chief of the DGSE, are now assisted and directed by four hundred Cubans, forty to fifty East Germans, about twenty-five Bulgarians, and seventy Soviet officers. There is one experienced Cuban or Soviet bloc case officer for every six Nicaraguan security men.[45] Although Cuban advisers are assigned to each DGSE section, KGB personnel mainly work in the DGSE's intelligence division, leaving counterintelligence work to the Cubans and Nicaraguans. East German advisers are mainly involved in electronic surveillance; the Bulgarians staff the DGSE's Center for Information and Analysis.[46]

Soviet–Nicaraguan Relations

Unlike the Soviet experience in Cuba and Grenada, the USSR's presence in Nicaragua in the immediate postrevolutionary period was considerably overt. This was probably due primarily to Nicaragua's greater importance to Moscow's strategy than Grenada, where so-vietization was largely left to the Cubans during the first two years after the NJM coup d'état. As discussed in chapter 3, another contributing factor may have been the Carter administration's acquiescence to Soviet adventurism in the Caribbean.

Soviet military advisers arrived in Nicaragua almost immediately after the FSLN victory. For example, Sandinista Army Chief of Staff Joaquín Cuadra was advised by a group of five Soviet generals and vice generals as early as August 1979. This group was the vanguard of Soviet personnel who were sent to Nicaragua to advise on defense for both the short and the long term. Soviet military personnel made all major decisions regarding the supply of military aid to the Sandinistas and were reportedly engaged in preparing both offensive and defensive scenarios for future Central American conflicts.[47]

In November 1979, Henry Ruiz—a Sandinista National Directorate member who is currently Nicaraguan minister of planning—visited the Soviet Union for a series of meetings with Soviet officials, including Boris Ponomarev, who, as has been shown in earlier chapters, was one of the leading architects of the USSR's Latin American policy.[48] Ruiz had received training in both Cuba and the Soviet Union prior to the overthrow of Somoza and was considered to be one of the most pro-Soviet members of the Executive Committee of the FSLN National Directorate. Coinciding with Ruiz's visit, a large rally was held in Managua to commemorate the anniversary of the Russian Revolution.[49]

In January 1980, Soviet embassy personnel began arriving in Managua, along with various Soviet planning and trade missions. Simultaneously, an announcement was made of Nicaraguan coffee sales to the USSR.[50] From March 12–22, 1980, a large Sandinista delegation headed by Humberto Ortega and Tomás Borge visited Moscow for a series of meetings with CPSU and Soviet government officials. A party-to-party agreement between the CPSU and the FSLN was signed at this time, preceding by more than two years a nearly identical treaty made with Grenada's NJM.[51] On March 19, Politburo member Andrei Kirlenko told the Sandinista delegation that "the Soviet people warmly hailed the victory of the Nicaraguan revolution, which occupies a worthy place in the development of the world national liberation movement." In his official reply, Tomás Borge said the Leonid Brezhnev was "widely known as a tireless fighter for peace, security and progress." Borge also declared the FSLN's support for Soviet foreign policy by saying that his government and party "deeply support the policy of relaxation of international tension pursued by the Soviet Union."[52] A joint communiqué issued at the conclusion of the Sandinistas' visit confirmed Nicaraguan alignment with the main tenets of Soviet foreign policy.[53]

The FSLN delegation also signed a variety of economic and technical assistance agreements during the Moscow visit, some of which were virtual duplicates of treaties made less than two months later by Grenadian Deputy Prime Minister Bernard Coard. The Sandinistas received Soviet promises for help in developing Nicaraguan mining and agricultural enterprises, power engineering, transport, and communications. The USSR also agreed to send Soviet "experts" to Nicaragua and to accept Nicaraguan personnel for training in the Soviet Union—again, almost identical wording to article 3 of the top-secret USSR–Grenada agreement of July 27, 1982.[54] As discussed in chapter 7, both Grenadian and Nicaraguan agreements with the USSR have significant parallels to Soviet–Guyanese treaties made during the Forbes Burnham regime.[55]

Again paralleling Moscow's development of relations with Grenada, the first secret Nicaragua–USSR arms agreement was signed in the Soviet capital in May 1980. The protocol included the provision of T-54/55 tanks and other armored vehicles to the FSLN together with small arms, artillery, and antiaircraft weapons.[56] According to Sandinista Vice Minister of the Interior Comandante Edén Pastora, a member of the secret delegation, Soviet officials in Managua had pressured the FSLN leadership into accepting the tanks against the advice of Fidel Castro and several comandantes who feared that such an early escalation in Nicaraguan military capability might prove provocative to the United States.[57] In light of the subsequent incremental buildup of the Sandinista armed forces by the Kremlin, it seems that the introduction of apparently outmoded tanks into Nicaragua was designed to test U.S. reaction which, by now predictable to Soviet strategists, proved to be negligible.[58]

Less than three weeks after the FSLN delegation returned from Moscow, Soviet Ambassador German Shlyapnikov was received in Managua with great fanfare by the Sandinistas, who heralded his arrival as the beginning of an important increase in ties between Nicaragua and the USSR.[59] The Soviet envoy's arrival indicated Moscow's official approval for the FSLN's policies, and closely followed other signs that the Kremlin was pleased both with the tactics of the Sandinistas as well as their ideological orientation.

The important Soviet Latin American affairs journal, *Latinskaia Amerika*, had featured several articles on Nicaragua in its first three issues of 1980. The most significant of these articles was a report of a roundtable discussion by experts from Moscow's Institute of Latin America, including Sergo Mikoyan, editor of *Latinskaia America*. This essentially new generation of Soviet Latin Americanists repudiated its predecessors' criticism of the guerrilla warfare strategy and tactics of Che Guevara, saying that

[T]he experience of Nicaragua refuted previously existing distorted treatment of partisan actions, confirmed the correctness of the strategic directives of Che Guevara, embodied his idea of a powerful people's partisan movement.[60]

The dramatic success of the Nicaraguan insurgency in installing a pro-Soviet regime in a highly strategic location demonstrated that low-intensity warfare could be a major factor in attaining Soviet geostrategic goals if the tactics of deceit, proxy assistance, and military aid were employed effectively. Such a conclusion by highly influential Soviet strategists and theoreticians indicates that insurgencies in other parts of Latin America and the Caribbean are viewed as important means of implementing Soviet strategy in the region.

Throughout 1980, the Soviet presence in Nicaragua increased subtly yet steadily. Nicaraguan students were sent to Hungary and the Soviet Union in the fall, coinciding with an announcement of Soviet assistance for an "Adult Education Program."[61] In August, a Soviet oceanographic vessel arrived off Nicaragua's Caribbean coast to "appraise East Coat Marine wealth," spending several weeks surveying the sleepy port of El Bluff, which subsequently became the site of a major Bulgarian harbor development project.[62] A cooperation agreement was also signed with Soviet television and

Tass, and several *Barricada* reporters were sent to Moscow on a journalism training course.[63]

Soviet influence became more pronounced in 1981 as Soviet bloc weaponry began appearing in Sandinista People's Army and People's Militia units. In June, the FSLN admitted the existence of Soviet Mi-8 helicopters, but said that these had been "lent" to Nicaragua for a six-month period.[64] The same month, a Society for Friendship with Socialist Countries (*Asociación de Amistad con los Paises Socialistas*) was inaugurated by USSR Ambassador Shlyapnikov. A few days later, the Soviet ambassador donated several vehicles to the Sandinista Workers' Federation (CST) in an impressive ceremony, during which he said that "the triumph of the Sandinist people's revolution opened the doors for broad cooperation between the workers of the USSR and Nicaragua." CST Secretary General Lucio Jiminez, a self-proclaimed Marxist, answered in kind, saying that "the experiences of the victorious Soviet people are the guiding light and the path taken by all the oppressed and exploited peoples of the world to achieve their liberation."[65] Also in June, it was announced that over two thousand tons of Nicaraguan coffee were to be shipped to the USSR, East Germany, Czechoslovakia, Hungary, and Bulgaria in exchange for trade credits.[66]

By 1982, the Soviet presence in Nicaragua had become considerably more overt. Military assistance increased substantially, and materiel began arriving directly from the Soviet bloc. In February 1982, a Soviet ship delivered about 270 military trucks to the port of Corinto, bringing the total Soviet bloc truck inventory in Nicaragua to more than eight hundred. In April, another Eastern bloc ship delivered four Soviet heavy tank ferries, one small patrol boat, and twelve BM-21 mobile multiple rocket launchers. The tank ferries provide the Sandinista army with an offensive water crossing capability, while the mobile rocket launchers—which have already been used to bombard Honduran territory—give the EPS a mass firepower weapon unmatched in the region.[67]

Significantly, in mid-1982, Cuban Defense Minister Raúl Castro visited Managua with a high-level military delegation, supposedly to "offer aid for flood damage." Afterward, it was announced that two thousand additional Cuban construction workers were being sent to Nicaragua, engendering an increase in military construction activity.[68]

In November 1982, an additional group of twenty-five Soviet T-54/55 tanks was delivered, bringing the total of such weapons at that time to approximately fifty. This delivery followed a visit by Daniel Ortega to Moscow earlier in the year, which in many ways paralleled the visit of his Grenadian counterpart Maurice Bishop. In all probability, Ortega, like Bishop, had signed another secret arms agreement with the USSR during his Eastern European tour. To enhance the mobility of Sandinista ground forces, the Soviet Union also delivered more Mi-8 helicopters, An-2 aircraft, and BTR-60 armored personnel carriers. Several weeks later, eight new 122-mm howitzers were delivered, supplementing the twelve 152-mm guns delivered in 1981.[69] In later December 1982, the first delivery was made of sophisticated Soviet electronic equipment: a high frequency/direction-finder intercept facility of a type seen previously in Cuba. This type of equipment is able to intercept signals from throughout Central America, and is especially useful in pinpointing military communications sites of the anti-Sandinista forces as well as Honduran army bases.[70]

Pursuing a classic dependency policy seen in its relations with Cuba, Grenada, and other Soviet client states, the USSR signed a bilateral trade agreement with Nicaragua in May 1982. Worth some $2 billion, the agreement allows Nicaragua to exchange fourteen thousand tons of coffee, cotton, and sugar for Soviet manufactured goods and "aid" projects—a contract that insures that the Nicaraguans receive no hard currency to use in international trading or in erasing their $400 million trade deficit.[71]

Strategic Implications

Possibly the most significant Soviet–Nicaraguan action of 1982 was Leonid Brezhnev's speech before the Congress of Soviet Trade Unions on March 16, when he warned that NATO's deployment of Pershing II missiles in Europe "would compel us to take retaliatory steps that would put the other side, including the United States itself, its own territory, in an analogous position." When asked where such threatened Soviet missile deployments would occur, a member of the Soviet Intermediate-range Nuclear Forces (INF) negotiating team in Geneva told the Spanish news agency EFE that the site could be either Cuba or Nicaragua.[72]

Although such statements—if interpreted as referring to the deployment of Soviet intermediate-range ballistic missiles in the Western Hemisphere—are almost certainly bluff, they nonetheless imply that a prime strategic goal of the USSR is to create a threat to the United States along its southern border. In light of the Kremlin's officially stated acknowledgment of the "correctness" of Guevarist–Castroite armed insurgencies, it seems more likely that such a low-risk, insidious method is the preferred means of placing "the United States itself" in "an analogous position."

Soviet involvement in Nicaragua in 1983 escalated. As part of the "bilateral trade agreement" signed by Daniel Ortega in Moscow in May 1982, the USSR was leased the Pacific coast harbor of San Juan del Sur as "a port of call for Soviet fishing boats." Since the USSR acquired legal access to this port, Soviet engineers and technicians have descended on San Juan del Sur, taking over a hotel as their headquarters.[73]

Strategically, acquisition of port facilities with major servicing capabilities on the Pacific side of Nicaragua may be one of the most important Soviet military achievements in the Western Hemisphere since the construction of the Cienfuegos submarine base in Cuba. San Juan del Sur lies within easy striking distance of the major SLOCs running to and from the Panama Canal. Some two hundred Bulgarian engineers are involved in developing another major port facility at El Bluff, on the Caribbean coast near Bluefields, as part of a $140 million "trade" agreement.[74] Scheduled for completion in 1987, the facility will feature a one-thousand-foot pier and the ability to handle ships up to twenty-five thousand tons; that is, all Soviet naval vessels up to and including the Kirov-class nuclear-powered, guided missile cruiser, which displaces twenty-three thousand tons. Nicaraguan officials have openly stated that "the port will turn El Bluff into a citadel."[75] In December 1983, the Sandinistas announced that twenty-two workers of the El Bluff port project would leave for Bulgaria that month for "training," while another five thousand Nicaraguan construction workers were sent to Bulgaria in 1984 for an unspecified purpose.[76] Cuban technicians have also begun work on a new $200 million railway that will connect El Bluff with the Pacific port of Corinto "with the purpose of linking the Pacific and Atlantic Oceans in ten years."[77]

In the spring of 1983, both UN Ambassador Jeane Kirkpatrick and Costa Rican Foreign Minister Fernando Volio Jimenez reported that the Sandinista government had signed a secret agreement with the Soviet Union for construction of a sea-level, interoceanic canal with its terminus at the port of San Juan del Sur.[78] Although denied by Nicaraguan officials, Comandante Sergio Ramirez, at a July 19, 1983, speech to inaugurate the El Bluff–Corinto railroad, said ". . . we are today starting no less than the construction of the Nicaraguan canal. It is not a waterway, as the imperialists have always imagined it, but a dry canal, a railway canal that will allow us to transport cargo and passengers from the Atlantic to the Pacific Coast of Nicaragua."[79] Regardless of whether a second waterway is ever constructed across Nicaragua, the Cuban-built railway is itself of strategic significance. In the event of a major regional military conflict, the railway would play an important logistics role, quickly moving troops and equipment from coast to coast while resupplying forces that may be otherwise cut off by the closing of a port such as Corinto.

Of further strategic importance was the contract signed on June 13, 1983, between Nicaragua and the USSR for the construction of a ground satellite station in Nicaragua as part of the Soviet Intersputnik satellite communications system.[80] The next day, an identical agreement was signed in Grenada, lending further evidence of coordinated planning for the Caribbean region at the highest levels of the Soviet government.[81]

Today, Nicaragua "hosts" some seventy-five hundred Cubans, including approximately three thousand military and security advisers attached to the armed forces and the DGSE. The remaining forty-five hundred personnel are technical advisers, teachers, doctors, and construction workers.[82] Cuban construction workers in Nicaragua must also be considered a potential military force as, by their own admission, all construction "brigade members belong to the Territorial Troops Militia in Cuba or to the reserve, and that if necessary, all of them are willing to fight on the side of the militiamen here who are as daring as we are."[83] Many of the so-called "teachers" in Nicaragua are also reportedly Cuban military personnel.[84]

Although Cuban military advisers have served with the Sandinista armed forces since 1978, regular Cuban troops were not committed to combat operations against anti-Sandinista guerrillas until the second half of 1985. Today, company-sized formations of Cuban soldiers are deployed in the field, and there have been reports that entire Cuban battalions may be employed in counterinsurgency operations in the event that anti-Sandinista forces increase in strength.[85] Cuban and Soviet crews also fly daily combat missions in Soviet-supplied helicopters, which are believed to be under the direct tactical command of one of the two Cuban generals stationed in Nicaragua, rather than the Sandinistas.[86]

Official Soviet support for the Sandinista regime became public in late July 1983, during a visit to Moscow by Comandante Jaime Wheelock, minister of agrarian reform. Following Wheelock's meeting with Boris Ponomarev and the deputy head of the CPSU's International Department, the Soviet government announced its consistent solidarity "with the Nicaraguan people in the defense of the country's sovereignity and national independence, in defense of its revolutionary gains and its sacred right to shape its own destiny."[87] The meeting with Ponomarev and Chernyayev offers another parallel to the Soviet Union's first official show of support for the PRG in Grenada, for these same two senior Soviet officials met with Bernard Coard under almost identical circumstances two years earlier. Two days after Wheelock's meeting, Yuriy Fokin, secretary general of the Soviet Foreign Ministry, announced during an official visit to Managua that his government would support Nicaragua, politically or otherwise, should possible U.S. aggression occur.[88] Such statements are strikingly reminiscent of Soviet rhetorical support for the Castro regime during the USSR's incremental extension of influence into Cuba. By the spring of 1985, Soviet–Nicaraguan relations were so close that the Sandinistas, like their Cuban mentors, declared an official three-day mourning period following the death of Soviet leader Konstantin Chernenko.[89]

In May 1983, General Arnaldo Ochoa Sánchez, Cuban vice minister of defense, arrived in Nicaragua on a secret fact-finding mission. Ochoa's presence was of great interest to Western intelligence agencies, for he, along with Soviet Generals Petrov and Borisov, had been responsible for the successful Ogaden counteroffensive in Ethiopia from January to March, 1978.[90] Considered a brilliant tactical innovator and a seasoned combat veteran from his earlier service in Angola, Ochoa had also made a secret fact-finding mission to Ethiopia in February 1977—one year before the Ogaden counteroffensive. General Ochoa was probably sent to Nicaragua to assess the military situation in the context of the U.S.-backed, anti-Sandinista insurgency and to determine whether increased Cuban or Soviet military involvement would be advisable.[91]

In the first six months of 1983, eleven shiploads of heavy Soviet weapons were unloaded in Nicaragua, compared with fourteen in all of 1982.[92] Ten other Soviet bloc ships carrying military supplies arrived in Nicaragua over the course of the summer. For example, during the week of July 30, more than two hundred Soviet-built military vehicles, including two tank transporters, eighty jeeps and five field ambulances, were unloaded from freighters at the port of Corinto.[93] On June 3, a Bulgarian ship unloaded Soviet T-54/55 tanks at El Bluff, followed by a shipment of twenty BTR-152 armored personnel carriers, five BRDM (BTR-40) vehicles, four BM-21 multiple rocket launchers, and other vehicles of lower tonnage. On June 5, an East German ship unloaded one hundred military trucks and several tons of weapons and other military materiel at Corinto; on June 8, authorities at Puerto Limon, Costa Rica, searched the hold of the Soviet ship *Nadezhda Krupskaya* and found that it was carrying several Mi-8 helicopters intended for Nicaragua.[94]

Taken in context with developments in Cuba and Grenada, it would appear that the Soviet Union is stockpiling equipment in Nicaragua both to provide supplies to insurgent forces in neighboring countries and to assure sufficient materiel in the event that trans-oceanic supply lines are interrupted by a protracted regional conflict. The Sandinistas have increased their military forces to some sixty-two thousand regular troops on active duty, with another fifty-seven thousand in active reserve. In October 1983, military registration for an additional two hundred thousand men was decreed.[95]

By the end of 1986, the Sandinista military machine had become the largest armed force in Central America. The Nicaraguan armored capability of some 350 main battle tanks, light amphibious tanks, armored personnel carriers, and other vehicles exceeds that of even much larger Latin American countries, such as Mexico and Colombia. Although the approximately 110 Soviet-made T-54/55 tanks forming the core of this force would be considered obsolete by NATO or Warsaw Pact standards, they still represent a powerful weapon in Central America, and are currently capable of invading Honduras through the Choluteca Gap with relative impunity.[96] Honduran border towns have already experienced attacks by the Sandinistas, including a heavy bombardment by Soviet-supplied BM-21 rockets in July 1985.[97]

The EPS is also equipped with fifty-seven helicopters, including at least twelve Mi-24 Hind D gunships, which are described by the authoritative *Jane's All the World's Aircraft* as a "flying tank."[98] The Mi-24 has proven its lethality in Soviet counterinsurgency operations in Afghanistan, and is far more effective against anti-Sandinista guerrilla forces than fixed-wing aircraft such as MiGs or L39s.

In addition to a massive increase in military forces, the Sandinistas have added thirty-six new military bases built to Cuban specifications. Airfields are being constructed or improved that could serve military jet aircraft. For example, construction of a new dual-runway airfield at Punta Huete, near Managua, is proceeding at a rapid pace. Most of the ten-thousand-foot runway has been paved and work has begun on a parallel runway–taxiway. In August 1984, the commander of the Nicaraguan Air Force admitted that Punta Huete will be used for military purposes, indicating that, when completed, it will be Nicaragua's main military air base as well as the largest military airfield in Central America.[99]

Punta Huete's length of nearly two miles and thickness of more than three feet will enable it to receive any aircraft in the Soviet inventory. Revetments to handle more than a squadron of MiGs have already been built, placing the Panama Canal within four hundred miles of a base for ground attack aircraft.[100] However, Punta Huete offers disturbing possibilities beyond the tactical level. As with the Cuban-built airfield on Grenada, Punta Huete is designed for more than one purpose. Although it will be able to handle Soviet strategic bombers such as the Backfire, a more likely possibility in the not-too-distant future is that Punta Huete will serve Tu-142s—the Soviet naval reconnaissance version of the Tu-95s that have been flying regular patrols along the U.S. eastern seaboard for some years, using Cuban bases.

From Punta Huete, Soviet long-range reconnaissance aircraft could monitor all important U.S. West Coast military installations. The five-thousand-mile flying radius of the Tu-142 could easily allow it to spy on the new Trident submarine base in Puget Sound without violating U.S. airspace. This would place one of the United States' most vital strategic assets in jeopardy, for Soviet aircraft operating from Nicaragua could also track Trident SSBNs as they are in transit to their Pacific stations. The sensitive missile-testing facility at Vandenberg Air Force Base in California would also become vulnerable to Soviet electronic surveillance.[101]

Since 1981, more than a hundred Nicaraguans have been sent to Bulgaria for training as pilots and mechanics; the first class completed its training in December 1982, and the mechanics returned to Nicaragua.[102] The fifty pilots (trained to fly Soviet MiG aircraft) are currently in Cuba maintaining their flying proficiency while they wait for a suitable time to ferry their warplanes to Nicaragua. Reliable intelligence sources indicate that South Yemen has sold the Sandinistas ten MiG-17 fighters which, although antiquated, would still be capable of neutralizing neighboring Honduras's present air superiority, especially when operating with a squadron of more advanced MiG-21s, which Nicaraguan pilots have been training on in Cuba.[103] Soviet advisers are now deeply involved in upgrading the Nicaraguan Air Force, assisted by about twenty Libyan and as many as fifty PLO pilots and mechanics. The Palestinians are also flying and servicing both the Sandinista Air Force and Aeronica, the Nicaraguan civilian airline. In November 1983, nine Bulgarian pilots arrived in Managua via Madrid and Havana.[104]

Moscow's tactical probing of Washington's reaction to Nicaragua's military buildup has apparently convinced Soviet policymakers that the introduction of high-performance, fixed-wing Soviet combat aircraft into Nicaragua will not be tolerated during the remainder of the Reagan administration. The bellicose reaction of even some liberal members of the U.S. Congress to news of a possible delivery of such aircraft to Nicaragua in the fall of 1984 indicated that there would be strong bipartisan support for U.S. military action against Nicaragua if the "MiG threshold" were crossed.[105]

The Export of Revolution

The record of Nicaragua's use as a base for subverting neighboring countries is well established. Although the Sandinistas adhere to their deceit that they are not exporting revolution, their remarks at unguarded moments indicate otherwise. On the second anniversary of the FSLN victory, Interior Minister Tomás Borge declared: "This Revolution goes beyond our own borders."[106] More than a year earlier, Nicaraguan Foreign Minister Miguel D'Escoto had said:

> You [*the U.S.*] may look at us as five countries, six now with Panama, but we regard ourselves as six different states of a single nation, in the process of reunification.[107]

Other FSLN National Directorate members, who have expressed impatience with the cautious subterfuge of their fellow comandantes, have been more vocal in their admission of support for Marxist insurgents in El Salvador. Bayardo Arce has said: "We will never give up supporting our brothers in El Salvador"; Defense Minister Humberto Ortega bluntly stated: "Of course we are not ashamed to be helping El Salvador."[108] In May 1985, Arce openly met in Managua with the leader of the Salvadoran guerrilla movement FMLN's political front "as part of the exchange of contacts that Nicaragua maintains with the Salvadoran revolutionaries."[109]

In 1983, Tomás Borge was asked by a reporter to respond to the remark that since the revolution triumphed in Nicaragua, "it will be exported to El Salvador, then Guatemala, then Honduras, then Mexico?" Borge replied: "That is one historical prophecy of Ronald Reagan's that is absolutely true!"[110]

The Sandinistas believe that they must expand their revolution to the rest of Central America or it will be defeated—a dynamic application of Leninist doctrine that fits hand-in-glove with Soviet global strategy. In 1980, Tomás Borge told a North Korean audience that Nicaraguan revolutionaries would not be content until the imperialists had been overthrown in all parts of the world. Needless to say, the "imperialists" he referred to were not the world's only true ones in Moscow, but the United States and its allies.[111]

Training of foreign revolutionaries is conducted by a mix of Cubans, Nicaraguans, and international specialists in terror and subversion from countries as diverse as Libya and North Korea. The Cuban DOE is in overall charge of training, and recent Nicaraguan-sponsored operations, such as the Colombian M-19's attack on the Palace of Justice in Bogotá, exhibit DOE tactical characteristics.

The FSLN and the M-19 have been allies since 1976, and Colombian guerrillas fought in the Sandinista ranks during the Nicaraguan Revolution. Since 1979, the Sandinistas have provided training, arms, and financial assistance to the M-19. For example, in 1984, at least sixty M-19 guerrillas were trained in Nicaragua. One member of the M-19 currently works at DGSE headquarters in Managua as a liaison with other Latin American revolutionary groups; another M-19 operative, also employed by the DGSE, is "on loan" to the Salvadoran guerrillas.[112]

On November 6, 1985, about seventy M-19 terrorists seized Bogotá's Palace of Justice, taking hostage many of Colombia's supreme court justices along with other civilians. During the two-day seige that followed, 120 people were killed, including the president of the Colombian Supreme Court and all the guerrillas.

An investigation into the incident revealed that a five-man Sandinista commando unit—structured almost exactly like Cuban DOE units—coordinated the operation and gave tactical instructions to the M-19 guerrillas. Using false passports, the FSLN team had entered Colombia one month before the assault on the Palace of Justice, establishing an operations center in a Bogotá safe house from which they communicated with Havana and Managua via codes and radio frequencies smuggled into the country with them. For two weeks, the Sandinistas drilled the M-19 assault group using a scale model of the Palace of Justice constructed in the yard of the safe house.[113]

Of the forty weapons found in Palace of Justice at the end of the siege, twenty were identified as having been supplied directly by Nicaragua, as were all the ammunition and explosives used in the attack. The remainder of the weapons originated in the United States, where they were reportedly traded for a shipment of Colombian drugs.[114] The weapons supplied by the Sandinistas included U.S. M-16 and AR-15 rifles left behind after U.S. forces withdrew from Vietnam. These rifles were sold by Vietnam to Libya, and were shipped by the Qaddafi regime to Nicaragua. The weapons were then smuggled into Colombia by a terrorist named Rosenberg Pabon, who had received training in Libya during the preceding months.[115]

The Sandinistas demonstrated both their contempt for international law and their overt support for terrorism by holding a special service for the slain M-19 guerrillas at a church in Managua only two days after the end of the siege. During the service, an M-19 flag was displayed on the altar while a Sandinista official delivered a homily praising the terrorists. The ceremony was attended by Tomás Borge, the terrorist "tsar" of the Nicaraguan Interior Ministry.[116]

Nicaraguan participation in such operations is proof that the Sandinistas are already functioning as Soviet military proxies. Whether this role is expanded depends on the FSLN's success in consolidating its Marxist-Leninist revolution and eradicating the forces that threaten the regime. Worried Sandinista officials have reportedly been reminded by Soviet advisers that the USSR also faced major counterrevolutionary threats during its early days, but was able to survive and defeat its enemies through perserverance and heeding the dicta of Lenin.[117]

History has shown that no Marxist-Leninist regime has ever been overthrown except through internal coups d'état (as in Allende's Chile) or external military action (as in Grenada). The Marxist-Leninist leaders of Nicaragua will never succumb to economic or diplomatic pressure. The Sandinista threat has reached the point where only the application of force will halt its steady growth. If U.S. policy allows the FSLN to consolidate and dispose of its enemies, the revolution may, indeed, prove irreversible.

Nicaragua's Future

As the preceding pages indicate, Nicaragua is moving rapidly toward becoming another Cuba on the American mainland. Once the consolidation of the Marxist-Leninist Sandinista regime is complete, the Soviet Union will possess another strategic asset in the Caribbean rivaling, or surpassing, Cuba in importance. As yet, however, the process of revolutionary consolidation in Nicaragua has not reached its final stage and will not do so as long as the antiSandinista democratic resistance, or contra, forces remain a viable military opposition.

Now numbering nearly twenty-one thousand insurgents, the democratic resistance forces are a diverse mix of former Somoza-era National Guardsmen; noncommunist former Sandinistas; disaffected peasants; and oppressed racial minorities such as Caribbean coast Indians and blacks.[118] Antagonisms between the ruling Sandinistas and the prodemocratic insurgents are so profound that no possibility for a negotiated settlement of the conflict is considered possible by either side. Both sides therefore see the total destruction of the other as the only possible solution. If the Sandinistas succeed in decisively defeating the democratic resistance fighters, only direct U.S. military intervention will prevent the consolidation of Nicaragua into a secure Soviet base on the American mainland. However, as discussed in chapter 9, the anti-Sandinista forces represent a legitimate alternative to Sandinista rule, and can prevent the consolidation of Marxism-Leninism in Nicaragua if given sufficient U.S. military and economic assistance.

6

The Cases of El Salvador and Honduras

El Salvador

Within weeks of taking power in Nicaragua, the Sandinistas began training guerrillas from El Salvador and other Central American countries, including Guatemala, Costa Rica, and Panama. This marked the beginning of a strategy for exporting subversion throughout Central America, using Nicaragua as a base.

In December 1979, Fidel Castro invited the leaders of the Salvadoran Communist Party (PCS) and various leftist revolutionary groups to a meeting in Havana. This resulted in an agreement to form a committee for coordinating strategy among the groups. Castro reportedly devised this strategy himself and received Soviet approval for its implementation. The plan targeted El Salvador and Guatemala as the next "dominoes" to fall into the Soviet camp, with Honduras to be used as a corridor for the transit of guerrillas and supplies until it too fell to a revolutionary uprising.[1]

Three small noncommunist groups in El Salvador formed the "Democratic Front" in April 1980. Shortly afterwards, and under Cuban direction, Salvadoran Marxists united with the Democratic Front to form the Revolutionary Democratic Front (FDR), thereby establishing the "broad coalition" that has subsequently been used to give the impression that the guerrillas are democratic and not led by Marxist-Leninists. An almost identical strategy of deception was used by the Sandinistas in the years leading up to their revolutionary victory in Nicaragua.

Facing page: Soviet Bear-D long-range reconnaissance aircraft deployed to Cuba. These aircraft collect intelligence on U.S. military installations on the East Coast and U.S. naval activities in the Atlantic and Caribbean. *Department of Defense photo*

In June 1980, another meeting in Cuba amalgamated the military and political components of El Salvador's communist factions under a United Revolutionary Directorate (DRU). In November of the same year, a military alliance of the five Salvadoran insurgent groups, the Farabundo Martí Liberation Front (FMLN), was created.[2]

The DRU became the command structure for the Marxist-Leninist organizations and also the directing authority for the Democratic Front, for which the representatives of the three small noncommunist groups often act as ostensible spokesmen. The result of this well-planned coalition is that Marxist-Leninist groups control the guerrilla units, weapons, intelligence, and covert support from the Soviet bloc, Cuba, and Nicaragua; the noncommunist element provides a useful facade for maintaining international respectability—much as the FSLN did in Nicaragua.

Having achieved a unified command for the insurgent groups, Cuba moved to increase the military strength of the guerrillas with full, but discreet, support from the Soviet Union. In April 1980, Salvadoran guerrilla leaders met in the Hungarian embassy in Mexico City with representatives of Cuba, the USSR, Bulgaria, East Germany, Poland, and Vietnam. In June and July 1980, the Salvadoran insurgent chiefs went to Moscow, and then with the Kremlin's endorsement visited East Germany, Bulgaria, Vietnam, and Ethiopia—all of which promised them military assistance totaling nearly eight hundred tons of weapons and equipment.[3]

This Soviet-sponsored supply operation used mainly Western weapons, many of which came from U.S. arsenals abandoned in Vietnam. This was done to create the fiction that the insurgents were able to supply themselves primarily by capturing similar armaments from the largely U.S.-equipped Salvadoran armed forces. Some two hundred tons of these weapons and other military material were transshipped via Cuba, Grenada, and Nicaragua to arm the Salvadoran guerrillas for their unsuccessful "final offensive" in January 1981.[4]

Throughout 1981, Cuba, Nicaragua, and the Soviet bloc aided in rearming and reorganizing the Salvadoran guerrilla forces. By 1982, the FMLN had between four and six thousand full-time combatants, and an estimated five to ten thousand part-time supporters who provided political and logistical support as well as occasional combat operational services. The FMLN headquarters in Managua was developed into an extremely sophisticated C³I center. Tactical planning and daily operations were guided from this headquarters by Cuban, Nicaraguan, and East German officers working closely with their fledgling Salvadoran proxies.[5]

After El Salvador scheduled elections for March 28, 1982, to elect a Constituent Assembly, the Salvadoran government invited the Social Democrats (MNR) and the National Democratic Union (UND), the political arm of the Communist Party of El Salvador, to compete openly in the elections. Both of these parties, which support the FMLN, rejected the offer, and the tactical priority of the guerrillas became the disruption or prevention of the elections. After holding several meetings with FMLN leaders in Havana during December 1981, Fidel Castro ordered an increase in arms shipments to the Salvadoran insurgents so that an offensive could be launched to coincide with the elections.[6]

During the first three months of 1982, arms shipments into El Salvador surged. Supplies flowed into El Salvador through Honduras and Belize, using sea, air and overland routes. In February, for example, the guerrillas picked up a large shipment on the Salvadoran coast, near Usulután, after the cargo arrived by sea from Nicaragua. These supply operations now included larger quantities of more sophisticated heavy weapons. Deliveries in 1982 included U.S. M-60 machine guns, M-79 grenade launchers, and M-72 antitank weapons. One insurgent unit received several thousand sticks of TNT and detonators from Nicaragua. Individual units regularly were sent tens of thousands of U.S. dollars in cash for routine purchases of supplies from commercial markets and for payments (including bribes) to enable the clandestine supply pipeline to function. With this support, several thousand Salvadoran guerrillas attempted to prevent the March 1982 elections by destroying public buses, blocking highways, and attacking villages, towns, and voting places. Nonetheless, with several hundred official election observers from democratic countries and about seven hundred foreign journalists as witnesses, the people of El Salvador repudiated the extreme left by voting in overwhelming numbers. More than 80 percent of the eligible voters participated in the elections.[7]

Although Fidel Castro has often denied responsibility for shipping weapons to the Salvadoran guerrillas, West German Social Democratic leader Hans-Jürgen Wischnewski stated publicly in 1981 that Castro had admitted to him the Cuban role in the insurgency. Cuban Vice President Carlos Rafael Rodríguez confirmed that his country had trained Salvadoran insurgents during several interviews he gave during the fall of 1981. In an article published in the *Toronto Globe and Mail* on February 12, 1982, a Salvadoran guerrilla trainee described courses he had been given by Cuban instructors in various aspects of insurgency operations.[8] FMLN documents captured by Salvadoran security forces in April 1985 contain evidence that Cuba, the Soviet Union, Vietnam, Bulgaria, and East Germany have trained a steady stream of guerrilla leaders in military and political work over the past five years. These papers also indicated that Cuba and Nicaragua cut back assistance to the insurgents after the U.S. intervention in Grenada in October 1983, probably for fear that their export of Marxist-Leninist revolution might provoke a similar action.[9]

Concrete evidence of Sandinista support for Salvadoran insurgents emerged in December 1985 following an automobile crash in Honduras involving a Soviet-made Lada registered in Costa Rica. Honduran authorities investigating the accident discovered six hidden compartments in the wrecked vehicle filled with $27,400 in U.S. currency, plus 450 pounds of military equipment including 7,000 rounds of ammunition, 21 grenades, 12 radios, and 82 blasting caps for bombs. The Lada also contained sophisticated one-time code books and encrypting material, as well as letters. One letter carried tactical instructions for FMLN field commanders. Personal letters to Salvadoran guerrillas were also found, including one from Cuba and another from the Soviet Union written in Russian. The injured driver of the automobile confessed that he had come from Managua, had been trained in Cuba, and had made a similar run earlier in 1985.[10] The driver, a Costa Rican national, was a member of Costa Rica's communist Popular Vanguard Party. He stated that he was acting as a courier for the Salvadoran Armed Forces of Liberation (FAL).[11]

In August 1983, Honduran authorities captured Alejandro Montenegro, the second-in-command of the Salvadoran People's Revolutionary Army (ERP), one of the five insurgent groups forming the FMLN. Montenegro was responsible for guerrilla operations in the central front, an area including Guasapo and San Salvador. After accepting a political amnesty from the Salvadoran government (which led to his being sentenced to death in absentia by his former comrades), Montenegro revealed numerous details about the insurgents' strategy and tactics, as well as their coordination by the Cubans.

In July 1981, Montenegro traveled to Managua, whence he was sent to Havana with other guerrilla leaders to brief Cuban DA, DGI, and Department of Special Operations officers. "The Cubans first asked us to give them reports from each field commander," Montenegro said, "on how we were fighting the war, how many troops we had under our command, and what our plans and tactics were. After listening, then the Cubans gave us instructions on what to do." Later that year, Montenegro returned to Managua from El Salvador, where he met with his four Cuban "controllers" who had been introduced to him in Havana. This meeting was held in the FMLN's command and control center, from which all field operations are directed.[12]

When asked by an interviewer what the FMLN's objectives were, Montenegro replied: "Let's not fool ourselves. There is going to be no pluralistic, democratic government. A Marxist government is going to be imposed."[13] Commenting on U.S. policy for El Salvador, the former insurgent said:

> The Salvadoran people need moral and material support to bring about the political and social changes which will lead us to a stable democracy in which freedom and justice will reign. . . . In my personal opinion, I think that, yes, [*aid to the anti-Sandinista forces*] must continue. Because one must pressure Nicaragua politically and militarily as much as possible so they won't be an influential factor with other countries. . . . It is important to stop the Nicaraguans from continuing to help the guerrilla forces in El Salvador, Guatemala and Honduras. Only with political and military pressure can this be made to happen. . . . I don't think there's another method.[14]

El Salvador is perceived by the Kremlin as the next "epicenter" in Latin America for the global struggle between East and West. It would be greatly to the USSR's strategic advantage to actually provoke U.S. intervention in El Salvador, drawing U.S. ground forces into a conflict which the U.S. media, people, and Congress—provided with a steady flow of disinformation—would decry, thus dealing another demoralizing blow to the national psyche of the United States.

Honduras

Honduras's economic and social problems make it increasingly vulnerable to subversion and political intimidation by the Soviet-backed Sandinistas in neighboring Nicaragua. Both Honduras and El Salvador became targets for Marxist-Leninist revolution after the FSLN victory in July 1979.

One of the most active guerrilla movements in Honduras is the *Cinchoneros,* nickname of the Movement for Popular Liberation (MPL). The MPL is the military wing of the People's Revolutionary Union (URP), formed in 1978 as an offshoot of the Honduran Communist Party (PCH). Duplicating the insurgency tactics of the Sandinistas, the Cinchoneros kidnapped a U.S. oil company executive in April 1980, but were captured by Honduran authorities before their ransom demands could be issued. The guerrilla leader, Antonio Reyes Mata, was released as part of the amnesty declared by newly elected Honduran President Roberto Suazo Cordova, and promptly made his way to Cuba via Nicaragua. Reyes Mata returned to Honduras in July 1983 with a band of ninety-six guerrillas, some of whom deserted and alerted Honduran authorities. Reyes Mata was tracked down and killed before he could organize a rural insurgent base (the classic *foco* of Che Guevara). The deserters reported that they had been lured to Nicaragua in October 1981 by promises of agricultural and mechanical training, but had instead been sent to Cuba for a nine-month guerrilla training course run by the Cuban Ministry of the Interior's Directorate of Special Operations (the same unit that participated in the Grenada coup d'état in March 1979). Sent back to Nicaragua in September 1982, the Honduran guerrillas were quartered at a safe house in Managua prior to their infiltration into Honduras. This group was the advance element of a larger force designed to operate in four Honduran provinces, using a network of logistical bases in the rural highlands that were to have been supplied by Nicaraguan airdrops.[15]

Further evidence of Cuban–Nicaraguan support for Honduran insurgents was made public after a police raid in November 1981 on a safe house used by the Morazan Front for the Liberation of Honduras (FMLH) in Tegucigalpa. The captured Marxist revolutionaries included a Honduran, several Nicaraguans, and a native of Uruguay. Among the documents found were classroom notebooks from a one-year guerrilla training course held in Cuba in 1980 and a letter revealing that guerrillas at another FMLH safe house were responsible for transporting arms and ammunition into Honduras from Estelí, Nicaragua.[16]

Numerous other terrorist incidents have occurred in Honduras since 1980, including an aircraft hijacking and kidnapping incidents involving President Suazo's daughter and a leading Honduran banker. Such actions have clear parallels to guerrilla tactics employed in Nicaragua and El Salvador, as does the Cuban effort to unite the various Honduran guerrilla factions into one movement. This was achieved in March 1983, when the FMLH, the Cinchoneros, and the Central American Workers' Revolutionary Party (PRTCH) announced that they had merged into the National Unity Directorate of the Revolutionary Movement of Honduras (DNU–MRH).[17]

A stable Honduran government allied with the United States presents a major obstacle to Soviet expansionist designs in Central America. The neutralization of Honduras is therefore an important strategic objective, and Soviet proxies are actively seeking to achieve this through both subversive operations and politico-military intimidation.

Following the inauguration of President Suazo, the Cubans and Nicaraguans sought to persuade the new government to declare neutrality by promising that they would "spare" Honduras from the insurgency and terrorism plaguing El Salvador and Guatemala. When their overtures were rejected, these Soviet surrogates began an active campaign to intimidate Honduras into passivity through acts of terrorism and by implanting seeds of doubt about the reliability of the United States as an ally.

Aside from the subversive danger posed by Cuban and Nicaraguan support for indigenous Marxist-Leninist insurgents, Honduras faces a growing military threat from Nicaragua, as detailed in the preceding chapter. The Sandinista military machine already dwarfs the armed forces of Honduras, augmented on a monthly basis by infusions of advanced Soviet military hardware. Although the Sandinistas have not yet taken delivery of high-performance aircraft such as the MiG-21s their pilots have been training with, the former air superiority of the aging Honduran Air Force has been rendered nearly worthless by Nicaraguan acquisition of sophisticated mobile antiaircraft missiles, including at least seven hundred SA-7s.[18] Nicaragua has almost achieved the logistical and material capabilities needed to mount a successful invasion of Honduras.

Nicaragua has begun a gradual escalation of harassment against Honduras. In May 1984, the Honduran ambassador to Managua was recalled after Sandinista forces shot down a Honduran helicopter, killing all eight men aboard. This followed a similar incident in which a U.S. helicopter was destroyed after accidently straying across the border. Nicaraguan naval vessels have also attacked Honduran fishing boats. Beginning in 1983, a powerful Nicaraguan-based radio transmitter began interfering with broadcasts from Honduras's main radio station, hinting at the sophisticated electronic equipment the USSR has given to the FSLN regime.

Honduras's strategic location has also made it one of the most important routes for Cuban and Nicaraguan arms shipments to communist insurgents in El Salvador. For example, in January 1981, Honduran authorities captured six Salvadoran guerrillas unloading weapons from a truck enroute from Nicaragua. Inside the truck were forged passports, M-16 rifles, mortar rounds, ammunition, and other military equipment. By the end of 1981, the Salvadoran ERP guerrilla group had formed a joint command with Honduran subversives in Tegucigalpa. On July 4, 1982, this group sabotaged the main power station in the Honduran capital, and the next month it bombed various U.S. businesses with offices in Tegucigalpa, including IBM and Air Florida. Salvadoran guerrillas also maintain clandestine bases inside Honduras, as evidenced by the August 1982 raid on an FMLN safe house, which resulted in the capture of several high-level guerrilla leaders.[19]

According to Sandinista defector Miguel Bolanos Hunter, the Nicaraguan communists and their Cuban and Soviet mentors have a timetable for conquering Central America. El Salvador is "the test case", while Guatemala is "the next revolutionary situation," followed by Honduras. As for Costa Rica:

> [T]he situation [*there*] is not so volatile. The Sandinistas are trying to destabilize Costa Rica by advising the unions to make unreasonable demands in their negotiations with the government. They are trying to force a confrontation between the government and the unions which will lead to repression. Repression would justify the creation of armed bands.[20]

In the Soviet Union's long-term strategy for Central America, "Mexico is slated to be the last country to fall." Bolanos has stated that high-ranking Cuban intelligence officials he worked with in the DGSE "were very confident of their position in Mexico. . . . They have a large number of agents in the unions and political parties. If they just snap their fingers, the situation will explode. They have also paid off and blackmailed the Mexican security forces, which would thus be paralyzed in a crisis."[21]

Because of the Soviet Union's effective use of proxies to project its power in Central America, there is, as yet, limited information in the public domain showing a direct Soviet involvement in the countries reviewed in this chapter. However, recent actions by Moscow's military surrogates in the region, such as the invasion of Honduras by Sandinista forces on March 22, 1986, indicate growing aggressiveness on behalf of such Soviet client states. This is probably due to a strategic perception that military and revolutionary gains must be made before the tide of regional and international opinion shifts against the Sandinistas. While the FSLN remains in power, further such aggression can be expected against neighboring Latin American nations.

7

Jamaica, Guyana, and Suriname

Renewed Soviet Interest

Some recently decolonized nations of the Caribbean remain targets of Soviet power projection, even though the loss of Grenada made access to these countries more difficult. Three years after the October 1983 intervention in Grenada, there were signs that the English-speaking Caribbean was receiving renewed attention by Moscow. The burgeoning economic malaise afflicting the archipelago running from Jamaica to Trinidad, coupled with the social tensions caused by an alarming population growth, make this area a breeding ground for a new generation of revolutionaries.

In Grenada, the New Jewel Movement has been reincarnated as the Maurice Bishop Patriotic Movement (MBPM), whose chairman, Kenrick Radix, recently said: "The Grenada events were a disaster for the left but what is clear is that the right doesn't have the solutions. We are the party of the future."[1] On Dominica, the Marxist-oriented Dominica Labour Party (DLP) won three parliamentary seats in the island's 1985 elections, while turmoil engendered by two leftist independence movements engulfed the nearby French island of Guadeloupe.[2] In July 1985, more than seventy youths from Grenada, Barbados, St. Vincent and the Grenadines, St. Lucia, Dominica, Guadeloupe, Martinique, Guyana, Trinidad and Tobago, Jamaica, and the Bahamas were flown to Moscow by Cubana airlines to attend the Twelfth World Festival of Youth and Students. All expenses connected with the festival, including accom-

Facing page: Soviet naval combatants in Caribbean waters during their March–April 1984 deployment. Since 1969, the Soviet Navy has deployed task forces at times to participate in training exercises with the Cuban Navy and to establish a periodic naval presence in the Caribbean. *Department of Defense photo*

modation and traveling costs, were paid for by Komsomol, the youth arm of the CPSU.[3]

Jamaica

Soviet and Cuban influence in Jamaica expanded in a now familiar pattern of incremental stages during the late 1970s. Nearly five hundred Cubans, including DA/DGI operatives and military instructors, were based in Jamaica by 1980. Fidel Castro had made a state visit to the island in October 1977 amid much adulation by the People's National Party (PNP) government of Prime Minister Michael Manley.[4] Numerous Jamaicans were sent to Cuba for training and indoctrination, including Manley's son and twenty-five senior members of his government.[5]

As elsewhere in the Caribbean, the Soviet Union initially kept its distance from the Manley government. Michael Manley made his first visit to the USSR in April 1979—one month after the NJM coup in Grenada—during which he signed various agreements with Soviet officials. These included a contract for alumina sales to the Soviet Union and a long-term loan made to Jamaica to finance imports of Soviet goods.[6] The Manley government also signed trade agreements with Hungary and Yugoslavia, and established ties with Bulgaria, Czechoslovakia, Poland, Romania, and East Germany. The PNP's growing ties with the Soviet bloc were a major factor in the 1980 Jamaican electoral campaign that led to Michael Manley's defeat by Edward Seaga's Jamaica Labour Party (JLP).

During the summer of 1980, two defectors, a Russian and a Cuban, sought refuge in North America, bringing with them firsthand testimony of the far-reaching subversive activities of their countries' intelligence services in Jamaica and elsewhere in the Caribbean. These defectors were Alexei Leshtchouk, second secretary at the Soviet embassy in Kingston, Jamaica; and Carlos Pedro Tariche Reina, an interpreter at the Cuban embassy in Grenada. During their debriefings by U.S. intelligence officers, both men focused attention on the important role played by Cuba's former ambassador to Jamaica, Armando Ulises Estrada Fernandez.[7]

Born in 1935, Estrada participated in the Cuban Revolution and was one of the leaders of an unsuccessful guerrilla raid into the

Dominican Republic in 1959. Following this adventure, he was given responsibility for running subversive networks inside Haiti. As a DGI officer, Estrada was known to his colleagues under a series of pseudonyms, including *Pantera Negra* (Black Panther) and *El Pelado* (Baldy).

From 1961 until 1971, Estrada served as chief of the DGI's African department. He is known to have made at least six trips to Africa during this period, and to have spent several months in the Soviet Union during 1968, where he attended a specially tailored training course run by the KGB. In 1969, he was one of a team of DGI officers who accompanied a unit of the PLO on a night raid into the Sinai desert.[8]

When Manuel Piñeiro was transferred from control of the DGI to the directorship of the newly created DA in 1971, Estrada—one of the Cuban spy chief's closest associates—moved with him. Between October 1971 and June 1979 (when he was appointed ambassador to Jamaica and to the "Haitian Government-in-Exile," a Castroite front), Estrada ranked as deputy chief of the DA, responsible for supporting revolutionary groups in all parts of the Western Hemisphere. Although he is not publicly listed as a member of the Central Committee of the Cuban Communist Party, Estrada is believed to be a secret member like other senior officers of the Cuban intelligence services.[9]

The two Soviet bloc defectors confirmed the early assumptions of informed Western observers that the reason for Estrada's appointment to the Cuban embassy in Kingston was to orchestrate covert actions designed to maintain Prime Minister Michael Manley in office so that Jamaica could be converted into a secure base for further Soviet-sponsored subversive activities in the Caribbean basin.

Following the electoral victory of the pro-U.S. Jamaica Labour Party in October of 1980, Ambassador Estrada was withdrawn from his post at the personal request of newly elected Prime Minister Edward Seaga. Estrada was subsequently named as Cuba's ambassador to South Yemen, where he played a key role in the "sale" of still undelivered MiG-17 jet fighters to Nicaragua. As mentioned in the chapter on Nicaragua, Estrada had earlier been largely responsible for unifying the three FSLN guerrilla factions.[10]

Although the Jamaican government decided to maintain diplomatic relations with Cuba following Estrada's expulsion, Prime Minister Seaga issued a stern warning to Fidel Castro to stop meddling in Jamaica's affairs. In January 1981, the Jamaican government terminated the brigadista program (designed to train Jamaican revolutionaries in Cuba) and recalled Jamaican students who were ostensibly studying in Cuba under this program. Despite repeated warnings, Cuba continued to maintain some fifteen intelligence operatives at its embassy in Kingston. Finally, on October 29, 1981, the Jamaican government broke diplomatic relations with Cuba, citing Havana's failure to return three Jamaican fugitive criminals as the immediate cause for this action. However, on November 17, 1981, the government of Jamaica issued a bulletin detailing Cuba's role in providing covert military training to its citizens under the brigadista program.[11]

By the end of 1986, Jamaica's economic crisis had led to widespread dissatisfaction with the Seaga government and a corresponding increase in popularity for both Michael Manley's PNP and the island's pro-Moscow communist party, the WPJ. There can be little doubt that the PNP's return to power would be quickly exploited by the Soviet Union as a means of regaining access to the English-speaking Caribbean. Photographs of Fidel Castro and Che Guevara are still taped to office walls in the PNP's headquarters, and members of Manley's party refer to one another as "comrade."[12]

Guyana

Guyana has had a leftist-oriented political system for over thirty years. The pro-Moscow People's Popular Party (PPP), formed in 1946 by Cheddi Jagan (party leader) and Linden Forbes Sampson Burnham (chairman), won control of what was then British Guiana's colonial legislature in the elections of 1953. However, the PPP's aggressively "anti-imperialist" program caused the British colonial administration to suspend the constitution and remove the party from office. An official British white paper charged that there was evidence that the PPP was part of a "communist plot" to "turn British Guiana into a state subordinate to Moscow."[13] A 1954 report of an investigation by the British Constitutional Commission

concluded that Cheddi Jagan and other PPP members "accepted un-
reservedly the 'classical' doctrines of Marx and Lenin, were enthu-
siastic supporters of the policies and practices of modern communist movements, and were contemptuous of social democratic
parties."[14] The report placed Burnham and other party leaders in a
more moderate category, classifying them as "socialists."[15]

In 1955 the PPP split. The smaller faction, led by Burnham,
formed a new party called the People's National Congress (PNC).
Over the following two years, the PPP suffered further defections
by Marxists disillusioned by Khrushchev's 1956 "secret speech" denouncing Stalin as well as by the Soviet invasion of Hungary the
same year.[16] Until 1964, the PPP was the dominant political party.
With covert British and U.S. help, Burnham's PNC formed a coalition government with the more conservative United Front party following the 1964 elections.[17] Believing that a communist regime had
been prevented, Great Britain granted Guyana its independence in
1966.

As opposition leader, Jagan lost no time in fostering close relations with the Soviet Union. At its party congress in August 1968,
the PPP openly committed itself to Marxism-Leninism. During the
International Conference of Communist and Workers' Parties held
in Moscow in June 1969, Jagan formally aligned the PPP with the
Soviet Union. The Kremlin, in turn, recognized the PPP as a bona
fide communist party.[18] The following year, the PPP was reorganized on the pattern of the Soviet and Eastern European communist
parties.[19]

As the PNC's power grew through successive fraudulent elections, Burnham's Marxist leanings became more evident. In 1970,
Guyana was proclaimed a "cooperative republic" based on socialist
principles. Over the next six years, most major foreign economic
holdings were nationalized, bringing more than 80 percent of Guyana's goods and services under government control. Burnham also
adopted a militant stance on Third World issues, funding "freedom
fighters" in southern Africa as early as 1970 and pledging support
for other Marxist revolutionaries throughout the world.[20]

After 1970, the Burnham regime actively sought close relations
with the communist bloc. By 1979, Guyana had formal diplomatic
ties with the Soviet Union, Cuba, the People's Republic of China,

and six other communist countries. Because of the orthodox PPP's enmity toward the PNC, the Soviet Union refused to exchange ambassadors with Georgetown until 1976, after Cheddi Jagan ended a three-year boycott of the Guyanese parliament and announced a new policy of "critical support" for the Burnham government. This turn toward rapprochement with Burnham was announced several weeks after Jagan's return from the Conference of Communist Parties of Latin America and the Caribbean held in Havana in June 1975.[21]

Burnham's interest in becoming a member of the Soviet bloc is demonstrated by Guyana's application for membership in COMECON and the PNC's attempt to gain formal association with the CPSU.[22] Despite these overtures and President Burnham's visit to Moscow, Burnham never seems to have been trusted by the Kremlin, where he was viewed as an erratic opportunist who flirted with the PRC and the United States as well as the Soviet Union. Relations between Georgetown and Moscow soured in 1979 after the Guyanese government released a story linking People's Temple leader Jim Jones with the KGB in a bizarre plot to move the Jonestown residents to the Black Sea while allowing senior Soviet officials access to more than $7 million of People's Temple funds on deposit in foreign banks.[23]

With one brief hiatus, Guyana has maintained close ties with Cuba since diplomatic relations with the Castro regime were established in December 1972. Fidel Castro visited Georgetown the following year, although it was not until 1975 that Burnham began making regular trips to Havana. After Burnham's first official visit to Havana, Guyana allowed Cuban aircraft transporting troops to Angola to refuel at Georgetown's Timehri airport; the Burnham government also gave strong diplomatic support to Castro's African interventions at the United Nations and elsewhere.[24]

The PNC's relations with Cuba were encouraged by the PPP. In 1976, Cheddi Jagan called upon the Burnham government to invite Cuban soldiers to Guyana to guard against "aggression" from Venezuela.[25] During the PPP's party congress in 1979, the Central Committee issued a report stating that Guyanese communists "must defend the Cuban Revolution as a principled duty, and as a prerequisite for the attainment of our freedom and the freedom of all peoples fighting against imperialism."[26]

Following the Kremlin's policy line, the PPP has been critical of the PNC's relations with the People's Republic of China since Georgetown established relations with Peking in 1972. Burnham became the first elected chief of state from the Commonwealth Caribbean to visit the PRC in 1975, and received various forms of aid from Peking throughout his administration. In 1981, the PNC's fourth party congress was attended by Zhu Liang, a high-ranking member of the PRC's International Liaison Department.[27] The meeting was also attended by a Soviet delegate.

By 1978, as many as two hundred Cuban technicians, advisers, and medical personnel were stationed in Guyana. In March, Cuban General Senén Casas Regueiro met with Brigadier Clarence Price, chief of staff of the Guyana Defence Force, to discuss military cooperation.[28] This was followed by a visit to Georgetown in March by Cuban Foreign Minister Isidoro Malmierca for a series of unpublicized talks with President Burnham and Guyanese Foreign Minister Rashleigh Jackson. Although claiming "fraternal relations" with the socialist Burnham government during this time, DA agents operating from the Cuban embassy in Georgetown maintained contact with a variety of Guyanese opposition groups. In August 1978, five Cuban diplomats were expelled for involvement in "illegal activities"—an action reminiscent of the Soviet–Cuban quarrel over the "microfaction's" activities some ten years earlier. In the case of Guyana, the DA had been recruiting members of the radical Working People's Alliance (WPA) for guerrilla training in Cuba. The WPA, a small, multiracial communist organization formed in 1973, had received tacit support from the PPP while experiencing open suppression and harassment from the PNC. Due to its subsequent history (it became a formal Marxist-Leninist party in 1979 and subsequently became affiliated with the Socialist International), the WPA was probably being cultivated by Cuba as a hedge against both Burnham and Jagan.[29]

Following the expulsion of the DA operatives, Cuba worked to smooth its strained relations with the Burnham regime. New fishing, technical, and trade agreements were signed with Guyana in

November, and in December 1978 an official PCC delegation led by Ulises Estrada visited Georgetown for a meeting with Burnham. Reportedly, the agenda for this meeting included Guyanese assistance in the Grenada coup d'état, which took place exactly four months to the day after Estrada's return to Cuba.[30]

Cuba has attempted to unite the PNC, the PPP and, possibly, the WPA into a single party, but has met with no success.[31] This mission was reportedly the reason for DA chief Manuel Piñeiro's meeting with a delegation from the PPP in Havana in May 1979.[32] Nonetheless, Cuba has trusted agents in every Guyanese political party, union, and key government positions. Senior DA officer Pedro Silvio Gonzalez Perez—operating under the diplomatic cover of minister-counselor at the Cuban embassy in Georgetown—increased Cuban influence in the Guyana Defence Force and government ministries.[33]

Following the eighth meeting of the Guyana–Cuba Joint Commission in March 1983, the Cuban delegation was assured that "Guyana will continue on its present socialist policies."[34] The following month, the Guyana Teachers' Association pledged "unqualified support for government efforts to develop a socialist society"—a task made easier by the growing number of Cuban teachers in Guyana.[35] In November 1984, Cuba and Guyana issued a joint communiqué asserting their agreement on all major foreign policy issues, including solidarity with Nicaragua, the FDR-FMLN-guerrilla forces in El Salvador, and the South West Africa People's Organization (SWAPO).[36]

Following the People's Revolutionary Government's (PRG) accession to power in Grenada, Guyana became one of the island's closest Caribbean allies, even though the Bishop regime maintained friendly relations with the PPP and WPA as well as the PNC. President Burnham was responsible for alerting Grenada's Revolutionary Military Council to the impending invasion by U.S. and Caribbean forces in October 1983. Burnham had learned of the plans during a Caribbean Community (CARICOM) heads-of-government meeting in Trinidad, and was also probably responsible for alerting Cuba and the Soviet Union.[37] Following the intervention, Guyana provided haven to several of the island's more militant Marxists.[38]

Increasingly ostracized by the English-speaking Caribbean after the Grenada rescue mission, Guyana moved closer to the Soviet Union and its allies. Cooperation with Nicaragua and Libya grew, and various forms of military, technical, and educational assistance were provided by the USSR, East Germany, Czechoslovakia, Bulgaria, Cuba, and North Korea.[39]

The pro-Soviet nature of the ruling PNC became evident. Speaking at a rally in Georgetown in November 1983 to commemorate the Bolshevik Revolution, a "comrade" from President Burnham's office called the Russian Revolution "a significant step in the history of mankind." Guyana's minister of Manpower and Cooperatives, Comrade Kenneth Denny, told his audience—which included Soviet Ambassador Konstantin Karchev—"about the lessons to be learned from the 1917 Socialist Revolution in the USSR," and stated that "the USSR served as an inspiration to Guyana in the struggle to build socialism." Denny also noted that Marxism-Leninism was now "the ideology of the working class."[40]

Guyana's military capability, while still limited in comparison to neighboring Venezuela and Brazil, was enlarged and upgraded by the Soviet bloc over the past few years. The Guyana Defence Force, comprising ground, air and sea units, currently numbers seven thousand personnel.[41] Some four hundred Cuban military advisers provided training and technical support to all branches of the Guyanese armed forces.[42] On February 12, 1983, two ships, flying no national colors unloaded artillery pieces and small arms at the Linden Alumina Plant wharf on the Demerara River. The unloading was done at night by soldiers who cordoned off both sides of the river—a tactic similar to that employed to unload Soviet arms shipments in Grenada. One of the vessels, the *Como VI*, was identified as being of Cuban registry, and the arms had originated in North Korea.[43]

The military hardware exported to Guyana has become increasingly sophisticated. In addition to Soviet artillery pieces and mortars, Guyana has reportedly received several armed North Korean patrol boats.[44] In October 1985, three Soviet Mi-8 Hip helicopters were unloaded in Georgetown for use by the Guyana Defence Force, making Guyana the fourth country in the Western Hemisphere to receive such aircraft after Cuba, Nicaragua, and Peru.[45]

Also in 1985, Romania signed an agreement with Guyana to send Romanian aircraft personnel to Guyana to provide training for "civilian as well as Army pilots."[46] Guyana was reportedly negotiating with the USSR for MiG aircraft and with Brazil for Bandeirante patrol aircraft.[47] The state-owned Guyana Airways Corporation is currently operating a Soviet-built Tu-154B leased from Romania, and has purchased three Tu-154s from the USSR and Romania in exchange for bauxite.[48]

President Burnham died on August 6, 1985, while undergoing surgery by a team of Cuban doctors for a throat ailment.[49] Burnham's successors, President Desmond Hoyte and Prime Minister Hamilton Green, appear to differ on Guyana's future relations with Moscow. President Hoyte has expressed a desire to adopt a more nonaligned and pragmatic foreign policy based on greater integration with the CARICOM.[50] On the other hand, Prime Minister Green said that he would "continue working faithfully to maintain the fundamental policies and programmes of our late, great comrade leader," adding that he was "personally a socialist" and would "work to advance the socialist objectives of our party and government."[51] The PNC's sixth party congress, held three weeks after Burnham's death, attracted considerable attention in Moscow, as evidenced by its coverage by *Pravda* and attendance by an official CPSU delegation. PNC General Secretary Ranji Chandisingh's keynote speech stressed the need to ensure "Guyana's continued progress along the road of socialist restructuring . . . and noted the importance of strengthening party ties between the PNC, the CPSU, and the Communist Parties of Cuba and the other socialist countries."[52]

Until the middle of 1986, Guyana's progress toward adoption of a Soviet-style economic system seemed to parallel that of Nicaragua. Cuban advisers reportedly shared office space with Guyanese bureaucrats in the Ministries of Finance, Agriculture, Planning, and Manpower and Cooperatives. Cubans also helped establish a Soviet-style hard-currency shop in Georgetown that was "run in a manner somewhat similar to foreign currency shops in a number of socialist countries," and which sold goods "obtained through an arrangement with a similar business in Cuba."[53]

The PNC again won control of the Guyanese government during the December 9, 1985, general elections. The PNC won forty-two of the fifty-three seats in the National Assembly, while the PPP's previous ten seats were reduced to eight. The WPA received one of the remaining seats, with the other two going to the United Force. Following the elections, President Hoyte expressed an interest in amalgamating the PNC and PPP into a single party, but said such a move would not be possible while Cheddi Jagan remained PPP party leader.[54]

In December 1985, Guyana's Foreign Minister Rashleigh Jackson announced that it was necessary for his country to expand and consolidate its relations with the Soviet Union. Jackson also announced Soviet plans to exploit Guyana's extensive bauxite, gold, and diamond reserves.[55] However, the expansion of Soviet influence in Guyana seems to have faltered during 1986, probably due to an internal PNC power struggle between Moscow-line ideologues and nationalist–socialist pragmatists. The Kremlin is also probably wary of becoming more involved in another strategic Caribbean nation while the fate of the Sandinista government of Nicaragua hangs in the balance.

Suriname

Suriname, another former colony on the northern coast of South America, gained its independence from the Netherlands in 1975. A February 25, 1980, coup d'état overthrew the moderate parliamentary government established at the time of independence and proclaimed a "socialist republic" under the leadership of Lieutenant Colonel Desi Bouterse.

As elsewhere in the Caribbean, Cuba paved the way for Soviet influence in Suriname. A large Cuban embassy was established in Paramaribo under Ambassador Oswaldo Cardenas Junquera, a senior DA officer. Cuban technicians and military advisers arrived to fill key government and military posts.

On May 14, 1981, Suriname and the Soviet Union signed their first "cultural and scientific cooperation agreement." This allowed the USSR to provide Suriname with personnel in the fields of radio, television, public health, and "institutions of higher learning." Soviet Ambassador L. M. Ramanov "hailed it as an important step in the promotion of relations between the two countries."[56]

In December 1982, on the advice of Grenada's Prime Minister Maurice Bishop, Bouterse arrested thirty opposition leaders, including Suriname's most prominent lawyers, journalists, and union leaders. The next day, it was announced that nineteen of these men had been "shot while trying to escape," along with fifty other people who were shot to death in the streets of Paramaribo.[57]

Immediately after the executions, a spokesman for the military government said that Suriname "will study the possibility of inviting Soviet and Cuban troops in."[58] Apparently this was already a fait accompli, as Surinamese sources in The Hague said that five hundred Cuban troops were quartered in hotels in Paramaribo, apparently to provide a "palace guard" for the ruling National Military Council.[59] The Soviet Union extolled the "vigorous actions of the Armed Forces and the National Military Council," praising the "group of young, progressively-minded military [who] overthrew the corrupt colonial regime of [Prime Minister Henck] Arron and led the country onto the road of democratic transformations in the interests of the broad mass of the people."[60]

As evidence emerged of growing Soviet and Cuban activities in Suriname, neighboring South American nations became alarmed. An editorial in the Brazilian newspaper, O *Estado De São Paulo*, said:

> Under the present circumstances we cannot pretend to be ignorant of the developments in Suriname. . . . [Their] success and ideological development undoubtedly are of great interest to Castro's expansionist policy. . . . The Latin American democracies still have time to react.[61]

COPEI, the ruling Social Christian Party of Venezuela, charged that:

> Soviet and Cuban soldiers are organizing a militia in Suriname. . . . [A]nother Cuba is being established on the Latin American continent. . . . All democratic peoples should condemn the Suriname military regime's violation of elemental human rights.[62]

Despite the Brazilian government's attempts to halt the Cuban-ization of Suriname through arms sales, Cuban and Soviet influence in Paramaribo grew steadily until October 1983. In May 1983, a joint Surinamese–Cuban commission met to prepare a "programme of cooperation for 1983–84 in such areas as agriculture, public health, culture, education, planning, transport, trade, finance, public workers, telecommunications and construction."[63] On July 6, 1983, the Cuban airline, Cubana, made its inaugural flight from Havana to Paramaribo with a Soviet Tu-154 aircraft.[64]

Immediately after the U.S.–OECS intervention in Grenada, it was reported that nearly one hundred Cubans, including the ambassador, had been expelled from Suriname. This appears to have been a calculated move on Bouterse's part to establish better relations with the United States, Brazil, and the Netherlands, all of whom had expressed grave concern over Soviet and Cuban involvement with Suriname. However, the Soviet Union maintained its diplomatic and KGB presence in Paramaribo, and Libyan personnel have reportedly been trickling into Suriname over the past two years.[65] The future of Soviet involvement in Suriname will probably depend on the success of U.S. and Brazilian efforts to draw the Bouterse regime into the Western camp.

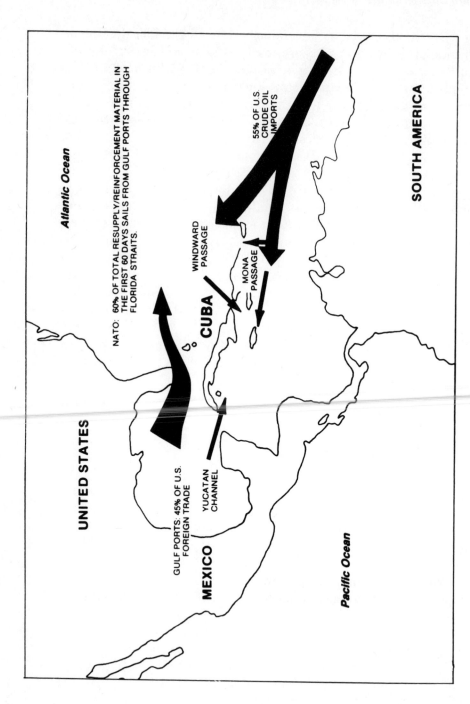

The sea lanes of the Caribbean and Gulf of Mexico are vital to the economic stability and security of the United States. The Soviet Union is attempting to create unrest in this "strategic rear" so that the United States will be less able to respond to Soviet aggression elsewhere in the world. *Department of Defense figure*

8
Summary and Conclusion

A Soviet Strategy for the Caribbean

By the mid-1980s, the Soviet Union's sixty-five-year history of relations with Latin America and the Caribbean had evolved into a sophisticated strategy based on a comprehensive analysis of the geopolitical environment and a realistic understanding of the USSR's own strengths and weaknesses in the international arena as well as those of the United States. The growth of the Soviet Union's strategic nuclear and conventional military capabilities had resulted in a concomitant increase of attempts to project its influence into areas of the world far removed from the Eurasian landmass. The Soviet Union's strategic planning for the Caribbean was therefore a facet of its global strategic objective: a world not only dominated by that brand of "socialism" developed and vigorously promulgated by the USSR, but under actual Soviet hegemony.

A new Soviet policy for the Third World developed during the Khrushchev era and was refined and expanded under Leonid Brezhnev. Recognizing the great opportunities for the projection of Soviet power in the postcolonial era, the USSR actively sought to penetrate the Third World in order to destabilize it and thus threaten and weaken the United States and its allies.

Moscow's grand strategy toward the Third World was an extrapolation of its foreign policy toward the "capitalist–imperialist" West. This policy was pursued on two levels. The first level sought penetration and influence via "peaceful" means such as diplomatic ties, trade and economic assistance, cultural links, and propaganda. The second level of policy was designed to achieve penetration and control through direct and indirect military means within the frame-work of "wars of national liberation," funding of Marxist revolu-tionaries, and KGB-sponsored "active measures" aimed at subver-sion of nonsocialist governments.[1] With the exception of the Soviet invasion of Afghanistan in 1979, the overt introduction of Soviet armed forces was avoided in order to support the fiction of indige-nous "people's revolutions."

Latin America emerged as a potential target for Soviet strate-gists after the Twentieth CPSU Congress in 1956. Recognized as the "strategic rear" of the United States, the Kremlin nonetheless as-sumed that the area was firmly under U.S. control and could not be successfully penetrated to strategic advantage until the "correlation of world forces" had shifted decisively in favor of Soviet-style "socialism."

Fidel Castro's turn toward Moscow following his 1958 coup d'état surprised the Kremlin, as did the almost inexplicable aber-ration of U.S. policy in allowing a communist state to survive and develop in the strategically vital heart of the Caribbean. The appar-ent eagerness of successive U.S. administrations to overlook Soviet activities in Cuba—culminating in President Jimmy Carter's tacit acceptance of a permanent Soviet military presence there in 1979[2]— seemed to the Kremlin's strategists and Marxist-Leninist theoreti-cians to offer proof that the "correlation of forces" had indeed shifted in Moscow's favor. In 1974, a midpoint in the era of East–West detente, Brezhnev said:

> Having assessed the overall correlation of forces in the world, we came to the conclusion several years ago that there existed a real possibility of securing a radical turnabout in the international situation.[3]

A genuine belief that the United States and its allies were in decline engendered a reappraisal of Caribbean and Latin American strategic importance. Writing in *Kommunist* soon after the Cien-fuegos incident, Boris Ponomarev said:

> Today the attention of Marxist scientists is focused more and more on the recent experience of the revolutionaries on the Latin American continent. . . . [T]his leads us to believe that the revo-

lutionary process there is continuing to develop at a faster pace than in other parts of the nonsocialist world. This is truly a 'continent in upheaval.'[4]

Out of Moscow's new perception of the United States and its geostrategic relationship to its southern neighbors grew the Soviet Union's strategic policy toward the Caribbean. In the words of Anatoly Gromyko, chief of the Africa Institute of the USSR Academy of Sciences and son of the Soviet president, the goal of such a strategy must be to "sap and undermine U.S. positions" in the region, as well as "inflict significant damage to the U.S. power position not only in the region but in the world at large."[5]

Strategic Objectives

A strategy must, by definition, have an objective, and Soviet strategy for the Caribbean incorporates five major objectives:

1. Erosion of the United States' historical predominance in the region.

2. Expansion of Soviet influence and power.

3. Establishment and maintenance of Soviet proxies.

4. Proliferation of Soviet military and C³I facilities.

5. Forced withdrawal of U.S. influence from other parts of the world due to an enhanced security threat along the U.S. southern flank, thereby leaving the "principal theaters" of Europe and Asia vulnerable to Soviet aggression.[6]

All of these objectives are closely related, although the tactical means of reaching them vary depending on the prevailing geopolitical and geostrategic circumstances. Objectives 1 through 4 should, theoretically, create the conditions for objective 5 upon reaching a certain point. Destabilization of the area lays the groundwork for the attainment of objectives 1 and 2 by playing upon the "inherent contradictions" of U.S. society through disinformation designed to mobilize popular opinion against regional policy both within the United States and in other Western democracies.

The USSR is fully aware of the United States' strategic dependence on what Boris Ponomarev has called "reliable rear lines of American imperialism."[7] An article in the Soviet theoretical journal *Kommunist* noted that "U.S. industry draws a considerable share of its raw materials" from SLOCs in this region, "including 40 to 100 percent of its imports of various strategic materials."[8] Another Soviet geostrategist has commented that the Caribbean's importance "can hardly be exaggerated. In military strategic terms, it is a sort of hinterland on whose stability freedom of United States action in other parts of the world depends."[9]

The Caribbean is more than a U.S. hinterland. The region (covering a distance of more than four thousand linear miles from Bridgetown, Barbados, to Tijuana, Mexico) is in a very real sense the United States' fourth, and longest, border. History has demonstrated that a great power's ability to maintain its global balance of power can only be achieved by ensuring the security of its borders, including its littoral zones. The natural moat of the English Channel protected the borders of Britain from invasion attempts by its Continental enemies, allowing it to govern its vast empire even while engaged in numerous international conflicts.

Since the War of 1812, the United States has come to take for granted that its security would be defended by the twin moats of the Atlantic and Pacific oceans, while nonhostile independent nations or colonies of European allies guaranteed our northern and southern borders. In the past, the United States has taken decisive action to preempt the creation of bases for hostile powers in the Western Hemisphere. This was the policy of the United States even before the enunciation of the Monroe Doctrine, was paramount throughout the nineteenth century, and persisted well into the twentieth century. For example, the Virgin Islands were purchased from Denmark to forestall their acquisition by Germany. Even before the outbreak of World War II, the chief of naval operations was authorized to devise plans for a U.S. expeditionary force to South America to prevent the establishment of a Nazi puppet regime in Brazil.[10]

Like Britain during the nineteenth and early twentieth centuries, the United States' ability to maintain its security commitments in Europe, Asia, and the Middle East rests on the security not only of its national borders but that of the entire Western Hemisphere, particularly the strategically vital Caribbean. U.S. overseas defense commitments necessitate secure SLOCs to supply U.S. and allied forces. The ability to interdict these strategic supply routes could determine the outcome of a regional or global conflict.

Although Leonid Brezhnev's threat to "take retaliatory steps that would put . . . the United States itself, its own territory, in an analogous position"[11] has been generally interpreted in the context of the deployment of intermediate-range nuclear missiles, it seems far more likely that nonnuclear means would be employed to achieve strategic objective 5. As the preceding chapters have demonstrated, the utilization of subversion, surrogate forces, and military assistance to the peripheral theatres of the Caribbean are creating a potent threat to the United States without the deployment of Soviet strategic nuclear forces within this hemisphere (the tactical nuclear weapons stored in Cuba are probably intended for wartime use to deal the United States a Pyrrhic victory).[12] A Central American isthmus dominated by Soviet client states would almost certainly lead to a Managua-style regime in Mexico, thereby confronting the United States with a populous enemy along what is presently an undefended, contiguous border some two thousand miles long.

Having been a keen observer of the United States' loss of international prestige during the 1970s due to a perceived deficiency in its national will (which the USSR was quick to exploit for its strategic benefit), the Soviet Union knows that a communist-dominated Central America would have a calamitous effect on U.S. allies and nonaligned nations in other parts of the world. Such an occurrence would be offered by Soviet propagandists as conclusive evidence that the "correlation of forces" had irrevocably shifted in favor of "socialism." This is a thesis that would probably be quickly accepted by vulnerable governments seeking to make an accommodation with the USSR. With the United States fully immersed in a region that Andrei Gromyko described as "boiling like a cauldron,"[13] Moscow would be free to impose its will on myriad countries that had heretofore felt protected not only by actual U.S. defense commitments, but by the relative balance of power that these commitments had provided.

From the vantage point of the Kremlin, it must appear that this process is already well under way. Regardless of over $200 million in military aid given to the government of El Salvador between 1984 and 1986, Salvadoran guerrilla forces—trained, supplied, and coordinated by Managua—remain undefeated and continue their economic and political destabilization efforts. The recently elected government of Costa Rican President Oscar Arias Sanchez is seeking to appease the Sandinistas diplomatically even though a five-hundred-man brigade of Costa Rican revolutionaries is currently being trained in Nicaragua for the purpose of overthrowing the Arias government.[14] Colombia, a country bordering the Caribbean that continues to support the flawed Contadora proposal for a resolution of the Sandinista threat, has seen a significant increase in Soviet-sponsored guerrilla activity since the latter part of 1985.[15]

The deployment of U.S. carrier battle groups off both the Pacific and the Caribbean coasts of Central America during military exercises over the past few years could become a permanent necessity if the regional security situation deteriorates further. For example, the U.S. Navy's large-scale Caribbean exercises in 1983 involved two aircraft carrier battle groups, the battleship *New Jersey,* and escort and auxiliary vessels totaling forty-three warships. This exercise cut so deeply into what was then the U.S. Navy's total force of 204 major surface combat vessels that it prompted the editor of *Jane's Fighting Ships* to comment that the Caribbean deployment stretched the U.S. Navy "desperately tight. . . . The U.S. Navy simply does not have enough ships; NATO does not have enough ships."[16]

The U.S. Army's Chief of Staff, General John A. Wickham, Jr., has also stated that U.S. overseas military commitments already exceed existing force capabilities. Forty-three percent of the U.S. Army is now deployed abroad; five of the thirteen U.S. aircraft carriers are currently in foreign waters with two of the remainder immobile in port for refitting. Of the roughly thirty E-3A/B airborne warning and control System (AWACS) aircraft in the inventory of the U.S. Air Force, approximately half are deployed on overseas duty. Among those AWACS deployed in the United States, one is on duty with the North American Aerospace Defense Command, eight are employed in training or narcotics interdiction missions, and another six are either undergoing depot or routine flight-line maintenance. Senator Sam Nunn, among others, has pointed to the widening gap between forces on hand and forces needed to achieve U.S. national and international security commitments as an indication that the United States' "military strategy far exceeds our present capability and projected resources."[17]

As the Soviet Union knows, any serious threat developing close to the borders of the United States—such as a major revolutionary upheaval in Mexico—would probably lead to a retraction of U.S. forces from Europe, Asia, and the Middle East. These are the areas referred to by Soviet strategist Admiral Sergei Gorshkov as the "main sectors," as opposed to the "secondary sectors," of the Caribbean and Southern Africa.[18]

One of the basic tenets of military strategy is to deploy one's own forces so as to deprive the enemy of the freedom to act effectively.[19] Admiral Gorshkov enlarged upon this theme in *Naval Power in Soviet Policy*, published in 1979, a year of seminal achievements in Soviet Caribbean strategy:

> To achieve superiority of forces over the enemy in the main sector and pin him down in the secondary sectors . . . means to achieve sea control in a theater or a sector of a theater. . . . [T]he enemy will be paralyzed or constrained in his operations . . . and thereby hampered from interfering with our operations.[20]

The geopolitical value of the Caribbean, in general, and Cuba, in particular, has been recognized for centuries. As early as 1562, King Philip II of Spain said "He who owns the island of Cuba has the key to the new world."[21] In the late nineteenth century, the U.S. naval strategist Alfred Thayer Mahan noted Cuba's command of the major Caribbean chokepoints of the Yucatán Channel and the Straits of Florida, through which all sea traffic from the Gulf of Mexico had to pass.[22] Gorshkov, who based much of his own strategic thinking on Mahan's theories,[23] stated that the United States was able to gain a dominant position in the Caribbean by taking over Cuba in 1898, thereby securing the Caribbean approaches to the Panama Canal, which was subsequently completed by the United States.[24] The acquisition of Cuba by the Soviet Union gave Moscow the strategic capability of pinning the United States down "in the secondary sectors" through a combination of subversion,

offensive ground operations of proxy forces, and air and sea interdiction of SLOCs.

The proliferation of Soviet-controlled bases in the United States'
"strategic rear" would definitely imperil United States and allied
SLOCs. Logistics planning for the U.S. military currently estimates
that almost half of the shipping tonnage that would be needed to
reinforce NATO, and about 40 percent of that required by a major
East Asian conflict, would have to pass from the Gulf of Mexico
through the Caribbean–Central American zone. These same routes
also carry roughly 50 percent of all other foreign cargo, including
crude oil, imported to the United States. As the 1984 Report of the
President's National Bipartisan Commission on Central America
pointed out:

> The Soviets have already achieved a greater capability to interdict
> shipping than the Nazis had during World War II. . . . German U-
> boats then sank 260 merchant ships in just six months, despite the
> fact that Allied forces enjoyed many advantages, including a two-
> to-one edge in submarines and the use of Cuba for resupply and
> basing operations. Today this is reversed. The Soviets now have a
> two-to-one edge overall in submarines and can operate and re-
> ceive air cover from Cuba, a point from which all 13 Caribbean
> sea lanes passing through four chokepoints are vulnerable for
> interdiction.[25]

The weakening of the United States' historical political and economic predominance in the region, with or without a concomitant
increase in Soviet influence, serves to create the type of regional
instability that fosters the growth of leftist insurgent movements.
The economic crises besetting nearly all Caribbean and Latin American countries have led to anti-U.S. feeling and growing economic
nationalism that the Cubans are actively exploiting to create even
greater divisiveness between the United States and its southern
neighbors.[26] For example, the governments of Costa Rica, Guatemala, Colombia, and Venezuela have stated their opposition to the
Reagan administration's policy of providing military assistance to
the anti-Sandinista insurgent forces—positions that have received
highly favorable publicity from Cuba, Nicaragua, and leftist opposition parties throughout the regions.[27] To date, the U.S. govern-

ment's much-vaunted Caribbean Basin Initiative (CBI) has largely failed to fulfill its promises of economic revitalization for the region, and will probably not have any significant impact on the area's problems even if fully implemented.[28] As a result, Caribbean Marxists are regaining some of the political ground lost after the 1983 intervention in Grenada, where remnants of the New Jewel Movement have regrouped to enter the political arena again under the guise of the Maurice Bishop Patriotic Movement (MBPM). Recent polls taken in Jamaica indicate that the apparent failure of the Seaga government's economic policies has engendered a surge in popularity for Michael Manley's PNP, which some analysts feel is now dominated by the party's pro-Cuban left wing.[29]

Elements of the Strategy

The Soviet Union's Caribbean strategy is distinguished by nine identifiable elements, based on an analysis of the USSR's relations with Latin America in general since 1920 and with the Caribbean region in particular since 1959. These elements are:

1. Opportunism
2. Subversion
3. Use of proxies
4. Deception
5. Tactical probes
6. Incremental power projection
7. Confrontational avoidance
8. Military assistance
9. Unification of factions

Opportunism
Fidel Castro's turn to the Soviet bloc was probably not anticipated by Moscow: Castro's agents began courting the USSR seven months after the Cuban Revolution. The U.S. government had few doubts during this time that Cuba was still firmly within its sphere of influence, while neither the existing Cuban social structure nor even

many members of the revolutionary government can be said to have been receptive to Soviet influence.[30] The USSR saw the opportunities offered by Castro's overtures and exploited them. The growth of Soviet influence in Cuba would not have been possible, however, without the strategic elements of *subversion, use of proxies, and deception*. All were provided by the Cuban Communist Party, which functioned as a Soviet proxy by forging an early alliance with Castro's Twenty-sixth of July Movement and infiltrating key positions in the revolutionary regime. Similar opportunities were exploited in a more sophisticated form in the cases of Grenada and Nicaragua, where political discontent united the populace and essentially transcended ideology.

Opportunism has also been a feature of the USSR's transformation of Cuba into both a Soviet military bastion in the Western Hemisphere and a reliable international proxy. Cuba's proximity to the United States was seized upon by Nikita Khrushchev as an opportunity for a relatively rapid and low-cost improvement in the Soviet Union's strategic nuclear capability to provide the USSR with a diplomatic bargaining chip.[31] Although this tactic failed, Moscow was able to exploit the Kennedy administration's pledge not to invade Cuba to achieve a long-term strategic gain that may prove to profoundly affect the global balance of power. The U.S. government's subsequent reluctance to jeopardize SALT and other East–West events of the détente period offered further opportunities to expand Soviet influence and military power in the Caribbean.

Moscow's successful employment of Cuba as an international military, political, and technical surrogate was also achieved due to the USSR's tactical flexibility and ability to exploit opportunities for strategic gain. For example, although limited numbers of Cuban advisers had been present in Africa and elsewhere prior to 1975, they do not appear to have been used as a direct proxy of Moscow until Fidel Castro approached the Kremlin with an offer to intervene in the Angolan civil war with a large professional Cuban combat force.[32] The Soviet Union was able to take advantage of Castro's egotism and domestic political need for an overseas adventure to achieve a series of strategically important victories in Africa with minimal risk to its other interests.[33]

At the theoretical level, the successful and generally unimpeded consolidation of what were initially genuinely popular revolutionary regimes in Cuba, Grenada, and Nicaragua served to support the contention of Soviet geostrategists that certain "objective and subjective conditions" must exist in a country to render it "ripe for a revolution of deep social character."[34] The failure of Marxist-oriented governments in Guatemala and Chile as well as the abortive Dominican Republic coup of 1965 appeared to Soviet Latin Americanists such as Mikhail Kudachkin to confirm this theory.[35] Since 1978, the element of opportunism has been heavily tempered by greater cautiousness and closer attention to the laying of "revolutionary foundations" through subversion and the work of proxies.

Subversion

The subversive element of Soviet Caribbean strategy takes many forms. In the early days of the USSR's relationship with Latin America, clumsy attempts were made to create civil unrest via strikes and riots, or through what were often equally counterproductive efforts to infiltrate governments with Comintern–Cominform agents. An attempt by Soviet agents to subvert even the declaredly Marxist-Leninist regime of Fidel Castro backfired badly in the late 1960s and could have resulted in Cuba's loss to the USSR had the United States been as skillfully opportunistic as its Soviet antagonist.[36]

Since Cuba's acceptance as the Soviet Union's most important proxy, subversive operations in Latin America and the Caribbean have generally been the responsibility of the DA and DGI (notable exceptions include the work of Soviet agents among plantation workers in Costa Rica and unions in the Dominican Republic). The identification, cultivation, and training of potential revolutionaries, as in the cases of the New Jewel Movement and the Sandinistas, appear to be the favored form of initiating subversion in the region during the 1980s. This is usually accomplished by inviting young Caribbean leftists to conferences such as the First Consultative Meeting of Anti-Imperialist Organizations of the Caribbean and Central America, held in Havana in June 1984, which was attended by twenty-eight parties, fronts, and other organizations from twenty-one Caribbean regional countries.[37] The attendance by several hundred young people from Central America and the Caribbean at the July–August 1985 Moscow Youth Festival may indicate a more overt trend on behalf of the Soviet Union to influence the next political generation throughout the Caribbean. Transportation and other expenses were paid for by the USSR, and festival participants included a significant number of representatives from moderate, traditionally anticommunist political parties.[38]

Cuba's intelligence arms, as well as the Nicaraguan DGSE, are so closely connected with the KGB and GRU that they effectively function as Latin American branches of the Soviet espionage services.[39] The subversive activities of these proxies can and do draw on the resources of a comprehensive international subversive network, including terrorist advisers and operatives from the Soviet bloc, Vietnam, Libya, Ethiopia, the PLO, the Basque ETA, and various Latin American organizations.[40]

The collaboration and joint action of these groups represent a powerful means of projecting a subtle Soviet influence over every nation in the Western Hemisphere, including the United States.[41] Because of the Caribbean region's geostrategic importance and vulnerability, subversion has proven particularly effective in political coercion, economic destabilization through workers' strikes, assassinations, and clandestine support for coups d'état. For example, ETA "internationalists" based in Managua were responsible for the 1984 assassination attempt on anti-Sandinista military commander Edén Pastora—a former FSLN hero who threatened the Managua regime by his enduring popularity throughout Nicaragua.[42] Several Soviet client states, including Cuba, Nicaragua, Libya and Vietnam, have also been implicated in the Marxist M-19 guerrilla movement's continuing efforts to destabilize Colombia.[43]

A new form of subversion directed against the United States through the Caribbean is now evident from the extensive involvement of the Soviet Union's surrogate regional actors in narcotics trafficking, possibly under Soviet direction and with Soviet technical and logistics support.[44] Cuba, Nicaragua, and Marxist guerrilla movements such as the Colombian M-19 now obtain a percentage of their operational funds for subversive activities from collaboration with international narcotics dealers.[45] Facilitating the flow of drugs to the United States is also seen as a means of destabilizing U.S. society; Fidel Castro is quoted as having said, "We are going to make the people up there [the United States] white, white with cocaine."[46] Nicaraguan Interior Ministry defector Alvaro Baldizon has documented Sandinista Comandante Tomás Borge's involvement in cocaine trafficking for the purpose of obtaining U.S. currency to help finance the FSLN's revolutionary and subversive operations.[47] Augmentation of the operating budgets of the DGI, DA, and DGSE with narcotics proceeds also benefits Moscow by reducing financial obligations to its Caribbean proxies.

The evolution of subversion as an important tactic of Soviet strategy toward the Caribbean is therefore demonstrated by two recent developments: the utilization of the Sandinista regime in Nicaragua as a staging base for terrorism in both the Central American and Caribbean theaters; and the development of a significant narcotics trafficking and arms smuggling operation based in Cuba as an adjunct to Cuban-supported terrorist activities in Latin America and the Caribbean. These developments are evidence of the dynamic nature of Moscow's Caribbean strategy as well as the flexibility of its tactics.

Use of Proxies

The Soviet Union has achieved remarkable success in its utilization of Caribbean proxy forces to advance its strategic objectives not only in the Western Hemisphere but throughout the world. Today more than fifty-thousand uniformed Cuban military personnel are serving in sixteen known countries on four continents, and are engaged in combat against pro-Western forces in Nicaragua, Angola, and other countries.[48] The permanent presence of Soviet surrogate naval, air, and ground forces in the Caribbean already represents a significant projection of Soviet power into this important geostrategic region; dealing with these forces in time of war would cause a serious diversion of U.S. military assets from other parts of the world.

The Soviet Union has enjoyed a high degree of success with its Caribbean surrogates because of their belief that they are *not* proxy forces controlled by an extrahemispheric superpower but *partners* with the USSR in a global crusade to replace "imperialism" with "socialism." Although some members of the Cuban, Grenadian, and Nicaraguan governments had undoubtedly given their primary allegiance to Moscow, the nationalistic leaders of these countries willingly accepted Soviet support and resources in pursuit of their personal revolutionary goals. The fact that the objectives of Fidel Castro, Maurice Bishop, and Daniel Ortega coincided with those of the Soviet Union was seen as completely natural within their shared ideological context. Although Fidel Castro has complained, probably correctly, that the Soviet Union has usurped many of his revolutionary initiatives, he nonetheless sees this as a form of self-vindication.[49] As demonstrated by the Grenada documents, the Kremlin has grown adept at manipulating the egos and aspirations of those countries' leaders who are almost certainly regarded, albeit with great secrecy, as the USSR's proxies.

A factor of even greater value to the attainment of Soviet strategic objectives in the Caribbean is the existence of a proxy *system*—again stemming from shared ideological sentiments and political goals—by which a wide variety of leftist groups, some of which are unfriendly to the USSR, coordinate their activities. These organizations, ranging from the powerful Cuban armed forces to the tiny WPJ, are able to carry out actions that serve Soviet interests, yet in which the USSR could not openly engage without jeopardizing its international standing or risking a confrontation with the United States. The most striking example of this is the deployment of tens of thousands of Cuban troops whose presence in nations as diverse as Nicaragua and Angola arouses only mild Western reaction, whereas the presence of large numbers of Soviet soldiers in their place would undoubtedly serve, albeit briefly, to unite the West in ways similar to those provoked by the 1979 invasion of Afghanistan. This proxy system is sustained and coordinated by conferences such as the 1984 Consultative Meeting of Anti-Imperialist Organizations in Havana, and the First Latin American Congress on Anti-Imperialist Thought, held in Managua in February 1985.[50] These meetings, all of which are attended by Soviet delegates, function as strategy sessions, allowing Caribbean revolutionaries to develop "close unity, diverse means of rapid communication, mutual support, encouragement and shared criticism in order to survive, struggle and win."[51]

In the Caribbean, Moscow's successful use of Cuba as a proxy had been extrapolated since 1979 by Havana's employment of its own surrogates—in effect, proxies of a proxy. Numerous examples of this primary and secondary system have been documented, especially in the areas of political subversion.

Grenada proved to be a valuable secondary proxy due to its black, English-speaking population and its ties with democratic leftist governments and parties throughout the world. After the electoral defeat of the PNP in Jamaica, Grenada was designated to play a role in Moscow's Caribbean strategy as "a bridge between the CPSU and the Left Parties in the English-speaking Caribbean."[52] Both Grenada and Nicaragua have sought to influence the SI by the attempted tactical use of the SI in promoting "progressive and revolutionary forces" in the region while criticizing the United States.[53] The Soviet Union and Cuba, barred from membership in the SI, used Grenada's NJM, Nicaragua's FSLN, Jamaica's PNP, and Guyana's WPA "to thwart the maneuvers of the [SI's] center right, strongly stimulated by the Panamanians, and avoid a setback of S.I. positions on Latin America and the Caribbean."[54]

A Grenadian delegate to a conference of international radicals held in Libya admitted that "Cuba was using Grenada to influence the other Caribbean parties and organizations."[55] Regardless of Cuba's command and control role and close cultural, racial, and geographic ties with its secondary Caribbean proxies, most regional Marxists maintained an ideological allegiance to Moscow. Grenada's NJM viewed its revolution as "a world-wide process with its original roots in the Great October Revolution," and were eager to enhance Grenada's "importance in the Soviet scheme of things."[56] During a visit to Moscow in March 1980, Sandinista Defense Minister Humberto Ortega told his Soviet hosts that the FSLN was "willing to sacrifice the revolution in Nicaragua" in the interests of Soviet global strategy.[57] In January 1977, Guyanese PPP leader Cheddi Jagan stated in Parliament that he was "not ashamed of being a Moscow puppet, if you want to put it that way, because Moscow stands for socialism, for democracy, for proletarian internationalism. It helps liberation movements. . . ."[58]

Deception
As evidenced by the Grenada documents and Bayardo Arce's remarks to the PSN, deception features as prominently in Soviet Caribbean strategy as it does in the USSR's other strategies. Penetration

of the United States' traditional sphere of influence requires the most sophisticated deception techniques, again often utilizing proxies as diverse as the Spanish niños in Cuba to black Cuban commandos in Grenada. Once pro-Soviet regimes have been installed, continuing forms of deception are used to prevent U.S. intervention during the months or years necessary to achieve consolidation. The cases of Cuba, Grenada and, increasingly, Nicaragua, demonstrate that Soviet strategists seem to feel that the United States will come to accept a Marxist-Leninist regime as part of the status quo after it has survived beyond a certain point, thus allowing the "democratic socialist" facade to crumble and the Soviet presence to become more overt.

The similarity between the tactics of the Grenadian and Nicaraguan "revolutions" is evidence that the strategy meetings of regional and international leftists have resulted in a coordinated attempt to deceive the United States and its Western allies. In his "Line of March for the Party" speech spelling out the NJM's tactics for consolidating a Marxist-Leninist regime, Maurice Bishop said that to deceive the West into thinking that the PRG was moderate, the party had formed an alliance with members of the middle class. This was ". . . done deliberately so that imperialism won't get too excited . . . and as a result wouldn't think about sending in troops." Bishop emphasized that this tactic was also necessary to ensure a steady flow of capital from the West so that the NJM could "consolidate and build the revolution."[59]

Comandante Bayardo Arce's speech to the political committee of the PSN (a small, Moscow-line communist party closely allied with the Sandinistas) has close parallels to the deceptive tactics spelled out by his Grenadian counterpart. Arce explained that Nicaragua's November 1984 elections were to be used as a tactical device to influence world opinion and "remove one of the United States' policy justifications for aggression against Nicaragua." Arce also said that the FSLN's "strategic allies"—Cuba and the Soviet Union—had warned the Sandinistas "not to declare themselves Marxist-Leninists, not to declare socialism," so they could achieve their goal of "building socialism with the dollars of capitalism."[60]

Deception is a vital part of military as well as political strategy. Though the most graphic example of this is the 1962 Cuban missile crisis, the USSR has also attempted to deceive the United States by constructing military installations in Cuba, Grenada, and Nicaragua that were ostensibly under the sovereign control of these client states. The introduction of both tactical and strategic assets into the region is accomplished in much the same way, as illustrated by the reported basing of Tu-95 Bear D aircraft in Cuba under the guise of Cuban Air Force markings, as well as by the apparent plan to provide the tiny island of Grenada with its own air force as a means of legitimizing a military presence at the island's Cuban-built "international airport."

Tactical Probes

Demonstrably, Soviet strategy for the Caribbean is a synthesis of Marxist-Leninist doctrine, superpower rivalry, and unbridled imperialism. The continuing influence of V. I. Lenin on Soviet strategic policy cannot be underrated, particularly in its application to the Caribbean. One of Lenin's most basic tenets, "If you strike steel, pull back; if you strike mush, keep going"[61] constitutes the most enduring theoretical factor in the USSR's Caribbean strategy: *tactical probes,* which, in turn, form the basis for *incremental power projection.*

Tactical probing in the Caribbean is a recognizable feature of the USSR's grand strategy, as illustrated by Richard Pipes:

> Soviet global strategy is implemented by means of a series of pressures exerted at various points of the globe in a bewildering succession of shifts and causes. . . . [T]he Soviet Union may be said to be laying siege in the same manner in which medieval castles were blockaded.[62]

The most recent case of a major Soviet tactical probe in the Caribbean was the planned visit of a naval task force to the Mexican port of Veracruz. The Soviet flotilla consisted of a Kashin-class guided missile destroyer, a Krivak-I-class guided missile frigate, a refueling ship, and a Tango-class attack submarine. Moscow tested U.S. reaction to such a visit (which would have marked the first port call ever made by Soviet warships to a Mexican port) by leaking the story via Cuba's Prensa Latina offices in Mexico City. The probe resulted in a statement from the U.S. State Department that the United States was "concerned about naval activities in the region, but Mexico is a sovereign nation that can make its own decisions on such matters." Diplomatic sources indicate that Mexico cancelled the visit under pressure from Washington.[63]

Both the planned Soviet Navy visit to Veracruz and the Soviet airline Aeroflot's attempt to gain landing rights in Costa Rica in October 1985[64] served a dual purpose in the Kremlin's Caribbean strategy. These activities probed U.S. and Latin American reaction to an expanded Soviet presence in the region. They were also a deliberate challenge to the United States in its traditional sphere of influence as a reminder that Moscow remains committed to Khrushchev's statement "that the Monroe Doctrine has outlived its time, has outlived itself—has died, so to speak, a natural death. Now the remains of this doctrine should best be buried. . . . That would be the correct thing to do, and this is what will happen. . . ."[65]

The attempted introduction of Soviet intermediate-range (IRBM) and medium-range (MRBM) ballistic missiles into Cuba in 1962 was based on the strategic element of opportunism rather than the more sophisticated policy of tactical probing, which appeared in 1969. The appearance of Soviet naval and naval air units in the Caribbean during 1969 and 1970 was designed to test the United States' reaction during a watershed period in U.S.–Soviet relations brought about by the historical coincidence of SALT, Vietnam, a new U.S. administration, and the USSR's strategic nuclear parity with the United States. When such probes encounter Leninist "mush," the strategic thrust is maintained via the cautious projection of power.

Incremental Power Projection

The use of tactical probes has continued unabated to the present day, and has exhibited growing sophistication vis-à-vis the utilization of disinformation and deliberate leaks of genuine material to the Western media to test the U.S. government's reaction. The cases of alleged MiG and L39 aircraft shipments from Bulgaria to Nicaragua in late 1984 and early 1985 may well have been part of this strategy, which has the more subtle purpose of allowing the U.S.

government to establish its own criteria for the introduction of offensive weapons systems into the Caribbean, thereby facilitating the tactic of *incremental power projection*. The public outcry over the possible introduction of fixed-wing Soviet aircraft allowed Mi-24 helicopter gunships—the most lethal counterinsurgency weapon in the Soviet arsenal—to be landed in Nicaragua with negligible comment by either the U.S. State Department or the media. The same tactic has been successfully used in Cuba for over twenty years; combat aircraft such as the MiG-23BN have a far more potent offensive capability than the Il-28s ordered removed by President Kennedy in 1962, yet these nuclear-capable warplanes have been based in Cuba for nearly ten years. Incremental power projection is also accomplished by introducing into the Caribbean successively more powerful Soviet warships such as the *Leningrad* helicopter carrier and Golf- and Echo-class submarines, as well as by the development of seaport projects in Grenada and Nicaragua for "peaceful" purposes.

Confused U.S. responses to direct and indirect Soviet aggression in Africa, Asia, and Latin America during the 1970s served to encourage the USSR's expansionist tendencies, as Soviet theoreticians pointed to the seeming powerlessness of the Carter administration as evidence of the inevitable decline of the West. With the "correlation of forces" now perceived as visibly shifting in their favor, Soviet strategists appear increasingly determined to pursue Moscow's "mission" of hastening the spread of global communism.

Periodic testing of Washington's reaction to Moscow's tactical probing in the Caribbean (very similar to Soviet tactical probing of U.S. continental defenses such as NORAD[66]) made U.S. responses so predictable that it has been theorized that the Kremlin's strategists may have developed a model for U.S. behavior.[67] Washington's consistent ambiguity about what constituted a Soviet strategic threat in the Caribbean left broad loopholes for a gradual and purposeful military buildup with nominal risk. Highly provocative coups de main (such as Khrushchev's deployment of MRBMs in Cuba) were to be avoided, although it was found that other strategic assets (such as variants of the Tu-95 Bear bomber and Golf-II SSBNs) could be introduced if the U.S. political climate was correctly gauged. The strategy therefore sought success in the long run instead of large and dramatic achievements in the short run. The essence of Soviet incremental power projection in the Caribbean is the setting of an initial precedent, followed by a desensitizing of that action's strategic significance. Once this has taken place, a new precedent is set and the process begins again.

Confrontational Avoidance

Tactical probes and subsequent incremental power projection are actually facets of a strict, universal Soviet policy of avoiding, until a propitious time, a direct military confrontation with the West. Again, this strategic element has its basis in Lenin's admonition not to "deprive ourselves in advance of any freedom of action" by openly informing "an enemy who is at present better armed than we are, whether we shall fight him and when."[68] This suggests that, as the military balance and "correlation of forces" are perceived as shifting decisively in Moscow's favor, the Soviet Union may lose much of the cautiousness with which it pursues its global expansionism.

Although the Soviet Union has sought to reassure the Castro government of its "fraternal" support by ambiguous warnings such as "Washington . . . should be clearly aware of the consequences with which aggressive actions against the island of freedom are frought,"[69] Fidel Castro is too experienced a geopolitician to believe that the USSR would engage in a war with the United States solely for the defense of Cuba. The best compromise the Kremlin can make on the defense of Cuba is to build up the island's own defensive capability to a point where any U.S. military action against the Castro regime short of an attack with nuclear weapons would result in a Pyrrhic victory, at best, for the United States.

In the Caribbean region and other parts of the Third World, the tactic of *confrontational avoidance* is served by the sophisticated use of indirect means to achieve strategic objectives. These include the various forms of military assistance, employment of surrogates, covert action, and other means of spreading Soviet power and influence at low risk. However, the Soviet Union's level of strategic cautiousness may be dropping in direct proportion to its increasing international power, as demonstrated by the 1979 invasion of Afghanistan as well as by a presence in the Caribbean today that would have been virtually unthinkable to U.S. policymakers less than thirty years ago. The new generation of Soviet leadership represented by Mikhail Gorbachev has also been shaped by its limited or complete lack of experience of Stalinist purges, World War II, and the era of strategic inferiority to the United States, and may therefore be more willing to demonstrate the USSR's powers in areas more distant from Moscow.

Any perception among the Kremlin's strategists—based on the remarkable record of Soviet politico-military gains in the Western Hemisphere since 1960—that their objectives are steadily being achieved makes it even more unlikely that a direct military confrontation with the United States would be allowed to take place. Thus, a great emphasis is placed on building up the military capabilities of Soviet proxy forces such as Cuba and Nicaragua. Regardless of the Soviet Union's policy of avoiding a direct confrontation with the United States, it has sought to cover all possible strategic contingencies by establishing its own military facilities in Cuba and planning for similar bases elsewhere in the Caribbean. The use of Cuba for intelligence collection, servicing of Soviet submarines, reconnaissance, and ASW support has a more universal strategic application than Cuba's regional role as a base for the export of revolution. For the equivalent of the annual cost of supporting one U.S. aircraft carrier battle group, the Soviet Union, in Cuba, maintains an invaluable strategic asset that has yet to reach its full potential.[70]

Military Assistance

Even though the tactical device of *military assistance* to "peripheral theatres" of the Third World seems to have been formally incorporated into Soviet strategic doctrine in the mid-1970s, it had been employed, albeit haphazardly, for some years before its enunciation by General I. Ye. Shavrov. Raúl Castro publicly stated that Soviet military assistance was the "decisive factor" in the 1961 Bay of Pigs invasion attempt,[71] and Czech arms were sent to the Arbenz regime in Guatemala as early as 1954. However, it was not until the Brezhnev regime that military assistance appears to have become an official part of military and foreign policy. On the fiftieth anniversary of the Bolshevik Revolution in 1967, Leonid Brezhnev said:

We must never forget that the mission that falls to the Communists is the grandiose and complex mission of the revolutionary transformation of the entire society. . . . Experience shows that it is possible to defeat such a strong and perfidious opponent as imperialism. . . . The Communists are confronting this opponent with a strategy that is supported by a scientific analysis of the correlation of forces, both within countries and in the international arena.[72]

The progression of Brezhnev's "strategy" is significant. The following year, a new sentence appeared in the third edition of Marshal Sokolovskiy's *Soviet Military Strategy:*

The USSR will render, when it is necessary, military support, as well, to people subject to imperialist aggression.[73]

One year later, in 1969, Brezhnev reiterated Moscow's doctrine of support for global Marxist-Leninist revolution:

We have always been guided by the well-known Leninist definition that to be an internationalist is to do "the utmost possible in one country for the development, support and awakening of the revolution in all countries." The CPSU has always striven . . . to support and develop the revolutionary struggle throughout the world. Such is our idea of internationalist duty to the world communist and working-class movement.[74]

By the spring of 1970, within days of the opening round of the Vienna SALT negotiations and during Raúl Castro's visit to the USSR, Brezhnev asserted the Soviet Union's growing aggressiveness in global affairs:

Today no question of any importance in the world can be decided without our participation and without consideration of our economic and military might.[75]

Only weeks after the signing of SALT I in 1972, in the midst of Western self-congratulation over the achievement of détente with the Soviet Union, Premier Aleksei Kosygin clearly stated Moscow's support for revolutionary armed struggle:

> The policy of peaceful coexistence . . . in no case means the rejection of the right of peoples, arms in hand, to oppose aggression or to strive for liberation from foreign oppression. This right is holy and inalienable and the Soviet Union unfailingly assists peoples which have risen in struggle against the colonialists or have become victims of aggression.[76]

The chronological context of the above statements must be noted to provide an understanding of this tactic's evolution, as well as the evolution of overall Soviet strategy toward the Caribbean. Brezhnev's 1967 quote originated the year after the Soviet Union preempted Fidel Castro's plan to be the leader of the Third World revolutionary movements by expressing Moscow's support for "people's liberation wars, the armed struggle of oppressed peoples"[77] during the Tricontinental Conference in Havana. The Soviet delegate apparently felt compelled to take a decisive action in support of armed struggle to maintain Moscow's status as the key player in global revolution. However, this position was almost certainly taken with the approval of the Kremlin, indicating that the enormous strategic potential of low-intensity conflicts in the Third World had already made an impact on Soviet strategists, probably due to the escalating Vietnam war. The expanding Soviet strategic nuclear, air, and sea capabilities also made military assistance to "peripheral theatres" a viable tactic due to Moscow's acquisition of the material means to project power internationally.

Military assistance involves far more than providing arms, ammunition, and other materiel to pro-Soviet forces. Essentially, military assistance must lead to the creation of a de facto Soviet proxy faithful to the dictates of Moscow. Soviet military assistance (now undertaken largely by its primary Caribbean surrogate, Cuba) therefore includes political and ideological elements to build an effective means of command and control. This includes unification of factions, as in the cases of Nicaragua and El Salvador, indoctrination and training of cadres in Soviet and Soviet satellite institutions, and the purging of unreliable or noncommunist members of insurgent movements.

Military assistance was vital to the Sandinista victory in 1979, while the flow of arms and equipment to Marxist insurgents in El Salvador and other Central American nations continues to fuel a large and well-organized guerrilla network. Although conventional Soviet military assistance to established Caribbean client states such as Cuba and Nicaragua is now largely overt, material assistance to Marxist guerrillas such as the Colombian M-19 and the Salvadoran FMLN is usually "laundered" by channeling weapons and equipment through Soviet-allied intermediaries such as Libya and Vietnam.[78] Ironically, the large stockpile of U.S. military equipment abandoned in Vietnam serves as a major source of supply for pro-Soviet insurgents in Central America and the Caribbean.[79]

Unification of Factions
The Soviet Union's Caribbean proxy forces were forged by successfully unifying various leftist factions into coalitions then developing them into willing surrogates by purging them of ideologically unreliable members. Although it is debatable whether the Cuban Communist Party's (PSP) early alliance with Fidel Castro's Twenty-Sixth of July guerrilla movement was carried out on Moscow's orders, there is no doubt that the unification of the two factions proved to be of eventual strategic benefit to the Soviet Union.[80] Well-positioned pro-Soviet communists in the early revolutionary government were responsible both for influencing Fidel Castro's turn to the Soviet bloc and for opening Cuba to Marxist-Leninist "internationalists" even before the establishment of a Soviet–Cuban pact.[81] However, the notorious "microfaction trial" of 1968 and Moscow's subsequent "taming" of Fidel Castro taught Soviet strategists that creation of a reliable client regime must take place at a much earlier stage in the revolutionary process to ensure the emergence of a stable proxy.[82]

The creation of Grenada's New Jewel Movement (NJM) via an amalgamation of the radical Marxist Movement for the Assemblies of the People (MAP) with the moderately socialist Joint Endeavor for Welfare, Education, and Liberation (JEWEL) marked a more sophisticated stage in the development of the *unification of factions* tactic, that is, alliances with social democratic or even rightist opposition elements to give Marxist-Leninist revolutionary movements a moderate facade.

Such a tactic was also employed by Fidel Castro during the final stages of the Nicaraguan revolution against the Somoza regime. Cuban military assistance to the Sandinista forces was made contingent upon the three Sandinista factions achieving effective unity. Not only did such an alliance present to the world an image of a broad-based, united front against the Somoza government, it also allowed the pro-Soviet Marxist-Leninist minority among the insurgents to gain political control of the movement.[83]

Unification of factions has also been practiced by Castro among the guerrilla factions of El Salvador, although in this case the result has been greater Soviet–Cuban–Nicaraguan command and control rather than the creation of a broad revolutionary front with a moderate facade.[84] In Guyana, where both the ruling People's National Congress party and the opposition People's Popular Party were Marxist-oriented organizations, Cuban and Soviet efforts were made to unify the two factions into a single party. People's Popular Party leader Cheddi Jagan reportedly resists unification more for reasons of personal egotism than for ideological differences.[85]

Conclusion

The USSR's strategic ventures in the Caribbean are part of one great strategic objective that has preoccupied Soviet strategists since the end of World War II: the destabilization and subordination of the Soviet Union's "main adversary," the United States. While the United States remains an international power, the Soviet Union will feel compelled to approach its goal of global hegemony cautiously. To gain the requisite freedom of action to defeat "imperialism," the USSR has decided to take the struggle to the United States' often overlooked, and therefore most vulnerable, southern flank.

The decisive U.S. and allied action to remove Grenada's pro-Soviet regime did not halt the proliferation of Soviet influence in the Caribbean. The incremental expansion of Moscow's power in "the traditional zone of U.S. dominance"[86] continues to erode the security of the entire Western Hemisphere. Regardless of occasional, and perhaps expected, tactical setbacks, the Soviet Union's strategy toward the Caribbean continues to prove its effectiveness.

Soviet strategists have learned to exploit the United States' weaknesses—the "inherent contradictions" of a democratic society. Each display of weakness by the U.S. government has been met with an incremental expansion of Soviet power in the Caribbean region. Thus, it can be demonstrated that political decisions made in Washington may be as important to the Soviet Union's Caribbean, and other, strategies as military assistance to a communist guerilla movement in Central America or the construction of a new Soviet military base in Grenada.

The final chapter suggests that the best means available to the United States to counter Soviet expansionism in the Caribbean is the usurpation of Moscow's own tactics: the use of proxies, military assistance, and unification of factions. However, any successful U.S. counterstrategy must be based on a strong bipartisan policy toward the Caribbean that is free of domestic political encumbrances that ignore the future national security interests of the United States.

9
A U.S. Counterstrategy

The final outcome of the USSR's strategic thrust into the Caribbean region has yet to be determined. The people of the United States and their government still have it within their power not only to contain Soviet aggression in the Caribbean and Central America but to turn it back and cast it permanently from the Western Hemisphere. To do so will not only strengthen the security of the United States, but will also assist in bringing economic growth and political stability to our southern neighbors and fellow Americans—goals that will be unattainable as long as Soviet-sponsored destabilization in this region continues.

The Soviet strategy for the Caribbean is vulnerable in many of its features.[1] Among these are the region's great distance from the USSR, making Soviet SLOCs to Caribbean client states such as Cuba and Nicaragua highly vulnerable to U.S.–NATO interdiction. The United States also remains the dominant military power in the region, notwithstanding the growing military potential of the Cuban and Nicaraguan armed forces. Perhaps Moscow's greatest vulnerability in the Caribbean basin is local resistance to the type of alien totalitarian political system accompanying Soviet expansionism. Such a political system, now largely followed by Cuba, Nicaragua, and Guyana, is so unsound economically that Soviet imperial outposts must depend on steady infusions of financial assistance, thus placing a greater burden on the USSR's own shaky economy.

These vulnerabilities are skillfully concealed by "active measures" orchestrated by the International Department of the CPSU Central Committee in concert with the Central Committee's International Information Department and Service A of the KGB's First

Main Directorate.[2] Creating the impression of growing Soviet power on an international scale represents a vital strategic asset in itself, insofar as it reinforces the sometimes vacillating political orientation of leaders of de facto and aspiring Soviet client states in the Caribbean. Using propaganda to convince these states that they are on the winning side of history is an important feature in winning and keeping a reliable proxy. Admiral Sergei Gorshkov endorsed "showing the flag" for the purpose of demonstrating

> the achievements of Soviet science, technology and industry. Soviet mariners, from rating to admiral, bring the peoples of other countries the truth about our socialist country, our Soviet ideology and culture and our Soviet way of life.[3]

Although the leaders of Cuba, Grenada (until October 1983), Nicaragua, and various other groups and parties may consider themselves Marxist-Leninists, they are as realistic as their benefactors in Moscow, and are well aware, especially in the case of Cuba, that the severance of Soviet assistance would leave them only the choice of political demise or some form of accommodation with the United States. Despite their rhetorical assertions that the Monroe Doctrine is dead, Caribbean Marxists know as well as their Soviet supporters do that they are still very much within the United States' sphere of influence. To continue its strategic momentum in the region, the Soviet Union must always maintain the psychological fiction that the "correlation of forces" is visibly shifting in its favor; no weakness or lack of resolution can ever be exhibited, particularly in the military sphere, for the heavily militarized regimes of the USSR's Caribbean client states respect the tangible symbols of power above the abstruseness of Marxist-Leninist doctrine. This is why lavish displays of military hardware and martial parades were as commonplace in Cuba, Grenada, and Nicaragua as in the Soviet Union and other totalitarian regimes, past and present.

Regular appearances in the Caribbean of sophisticated, well-maintained Soviet warships (in contrast to unkempt vessels observed in the Baltic and elsewhere) serve the time-honored purpose of "showing the flag" as well as testing the United States. Although a Soviet naval task force has not yet called at a Nicaraguan port (a visit to El Bluff was apparently planned for the *Leningrad* in March 1984 but canceled after a Soviet tanker was damaged by a mine off Corinto[4], taped footage of joint Soviet–Cuban naval exercises is given air time on Managua's *Sistema Sandinista Televisión* network; Prensa Latina ensures that the task force's maneuvers are covered by the media in other Caribbean and Latin American countries. Striking pictorial images of powerful Soviet fleets cruising at will in "America's Lake" have an important psychological impact on democratic nations in the region as well as totalitarian ones; the USSR hopes that the former will be receptive to Soviet diplomatic and trade overtures if their governments think that the Monroe Doctrine's validity is truly questionable. The unprecedented visit of a Soviet flotilla to the Mexican port of Veracruz apparently planned for the fall of 1985 would have marked a significant incremental increase in Soviet influence in the Caribbean while bolstering the Mexican government's growing relationship with the Soviet bloc.[5]

This is the vital point of vulnerability in the Soviet Union's Caribbean strategy: its dependence on regional proxies to project its power and influence. Without the existence of a reliable, surrogate regime in Cuba, the USSR would have found the logistical obstacle of providing military assistance to Latin America's small, disorganized, and generally unpopular communist insurgent movements to be almost insurmountable. Maurice Bishop's acknowledgment that "if there had been no Cuban revolution in 1959 there could have been no Grenadian revolution nor Nicaraguan revolution in 1979,"[6] is a testimonial of Cuba's key role in Soviet Caribbean strategy. However, Cuba's geographic insularity made the establishment of other regional proxies a strategic necessity. The consolidation of the Sandinista regime in Nicaragua is the prerequisite for a Marxist Central America, as Grenada was the bridgehead for the subversion of the English-speaking Caribbean.

The lessons of Grenada demonstrate the vulnerability factor. The *internally* motivated disintegration of the NJM—a developing proxy on which Soviet strategists evidently pinned great expectations—caused a major reversal in plans to subvert Suriname and the English-speaking Caribbean.[7] Although it is possible that Soviet KGB personnel in Grenada knew about and even instigated the Coard faction's coup against Maurice Bishop, they could not have

anticipated the volatility of the Grenadian people—the catalyst that
touched off the tragic events of October 19, 1983, and engendered
the U.S.–OECS military action, which preempted the reestablish-
ment of an even more ardently pro-Soviet regime, à la Afghanistan.
The most significant, yet often overlooked, strategic result of the
Grenada intervention was *not* the removal of a Soviet proxy and
forward base but the psychological impact this had on the entire
region; an impact that demonstrated that countering Soviet aggression by the demonstration of force of *will* may be of equal importance to actual use of arms.

The military government of Suriname—a country specifically
targeted as an entrepôt for Soviet influence in South America[8]—
responded to the Grenada action by expelling nearly a hundred Cuban diplomats and military advisers. There is evidence that Surinamese leader Desi Bouterse had been considering this action for
some time, but had not acted until the United States demonstrated
by its Grenada action that Soviet and Cuban influence in the Caribbean was not inviolate.[9] Russel Stendal, a U.S. missionary taken
captive by the Cuban-supported Revolutionary Armed Forces of
Colombia (FARC) for five months in 1983, reported that news of
the Marxist defeat on Grenada had a profound impact on the Colombian insurgents:

> There was a general mood of depression among the guerrilla lead-
> ership after the Cuban defeat on Grenada. Some of them started
> asking worried questions about whether or not America would
> intervene militarily in Colombia if the guerrillas seemed in danger
> of taking over the country. . . . Another factor contributing to the
> guerrillas' mood of depression was the rumor circulating around
> camp that a large weapons shipment, destined for them, had been
> captured on Grenada by the Americans.[10]

The evident unreliability of the Bishop and Bouterse regimes
must have inspired a thorough strategic reexamination in Moscow
as Soviet policymakers waited to see if the United States would follow up its Grenada actions by effectively "calling their bluff"
throughout the Caribbean—a move the Nicaraguans and Cubans
obviously considered feasible. The Kremlin must have therefore

been immensely relieved when the U.S. government not only failed to take any decisive actions—military or otherwise—elsewhere in the Caribbean, but actually cut off aid to the anti-Sandinista Nicaraguan democratic resistance fighters the following year.

This history of the Soviet Union's policy demonstrates that it invests its resources and risks its international prestige only when a substantial strategic gain is expected. The enormous economic burden of Cuba is borne by Moscow not for an altruistic desire to build socialism but because the island has been able to justify the expenditure by fulfilling its important surrogate military and subversive role in the Caribbean region and Africa. Were this not the case, it is highly unlikely that the economically troubled USSR would continue subsidizing the Castro regime. If Cuban initiatives in Angola, Ethiopia, Nicaragua, El Salvador, and other places had been as decisively foiled as the Grenadian venture was, Fidel Castro probably would have been cast adrift in the Caribbean to await the inevitable economic and political collapse of his regime.

The same holds true for Nicaragua. The most reliable reports of Daniel Ortega's visit to the Soviet bloc in April and May 1985 indicate that the USSR and its Eastern European satellites were unresponsive to the Nicaraguan president's request for some $200 million in emergency hard-currency economic assistance to purchase food and other essential products.[11] In addition to its massive military aid program to the Sandinistas, now totaling more than $750 million, the Soviet Union supplies more than half of all Nicaragua's oil needs and may be forced to take on the entire burden if Mexico follows Venezuela's lead in suspending oil deliveries because of Nicaragua's inability to pay for the shipments.[12] Nicaragua, like Cuba, is nothing more than a strategic asset to the USSR. If the asset becomes a liability, it may well be quickly jettisoned so that Soviet fortunes can be recouped elsewhere.

The Sandinista regime has grown increasingly vulnerable to both internal and external forces—a fact now openly acknowledged by the FSLN comandantes. In January 1986, Víctor Tirado Lopez, a Mexican-born member of the FSLN National Directorate, said that he foresaw a difficult year ahead for the Sandinistas. Tirado admitted that "there has been a great change in the balance of military forces" in Nicaragua as a result of the loss of two Soviet-supplied combat helicopters to a SAM-7 missile used by anti-Sandinista forces. Comandante Tirado stated that the Sandinistas were disturbed that other Latin American nations had not condemned either the incident or the acquisition of SAM-7s by the anticommunist insurgents, and acknowledged that the "unity between Latin America and the Sandinist revolution" had been strained "because the political interests in the region have changed."[13] Another demoralizing factor for the Sandinistas is the realization that U.S. military and economic assistance to the once beleaguered government of El Salvador has crippled the communist guerrilla movement in that country and reversed its momentum. The democratically elected Salvadoran government has also been accepted as a legitimate member of the Latin American family of nations, while Nicaragua is increasingly being ostracized by former friends and supporters throughout the world.[14]

All the principal parties now involved in supporting the FSLN regime—including the USSR, Cuba, and leftists in the United States and Western Europe—are cognizant of the Sandinistas' vulnerability, and can only hope that a combination of diplomatic maneuvering, military aid, and (most importantly) domestic U.S. politics will allow the time necessary to consolidate the regime and expand the revolution. The FSLN's three principal leaders, Daniel and Humberto Ortega and Tomás Borge, have said that despite rebel attacks, a disintegrating economy and rising complaints from the Nicaraguan public they will persevere "in the expectation that opposition to the rebels from Honduras, Costa Rica and possibly the U.S. public ultimately will combine to force President Reagan to abandon his anti-Sandinista campaign."[15]

In a very real sense, Marxist-Leninist revolution must keep its dynamism and permeate all of Central America if the Sandinista government itself is to survive. Soviet strategists know that, ipso facto, their multifaceted strategy toward the Caribbean region is largely dependent on the survival and consolidation of Moscow's Nicaraguan proxy. The subversion of Nicaragua's neighbors, as well as South American countries such as Colombia and Ecuador, has therefore been given priority by the FSLN and its Soviet bloc supporters. DGSE defector Miguel Bolanos Hunter, an authority on revolutionary strategy for Central America, has said, "El Salvador is the test case. Subversion is a double-edged sword. If they are successful, the Sandinistas will remove some of the pressure on themselves by surrounding Nicaragua with allies."[16]

Paralleling the Soviet doctrine that the USSR's ultimate national security will be guaranteed through global revolution,[17] Nicaraguan communists believe that a Marxist-Leninist Central America will provide them with collective security and eradicate their regime's most critical threat: the Nicaraguan democratic resistance forces operating across Nicaragua's contiguous borders with Honduras and Costa Rica.

The anti-Sandinista insurgent movement prevents the consolidation of the FSLN's control because it serves to remind the Nicaraguan people that an alternative exists to the type of alien political system Daniel Ortega and his comandantes seek to impose upon them. The growing insurgency encourages the erosion of active support for the Sandinistas by creating uncertainties about the FSLN's future not only among the Nicaraguan people but also in the minds of Cuban tacticians and Soviet geostrategists.

The U.S. Congress' vote in the summer of 1986 to provide $100 million in military and "non-lethal" aid to the Nicaraguan Freedom Fighters immeasurably strengthened their morale and bolstered pro-U.S. governments in other Central American countries. As a result, the Nicaraguan democratic resistance (which by late 1986 claimed some eighteen thousand armed troops with another three thousand in training) increased its operations and succeeded in placing the EPS on the defensive along the Honduran border and in the Atlantic coastal region.[18] Bipartisan U.S. congressional support for military aid to the "contras" also prompted leaders of Nicaragua's neighboring countries to voice their opposition to the Sandinistas. For example, Honduran President José Azcona Hoyo asserted that "the Nicaraguan Government must be overthrown by the Nicaraguan people," adding that the $100 million aid package "could resolve the problem."[19]

Adopting the tactic used by Fidel Castro in unifying the FSLN, by late 1986 most of the various anti-Sandinista exile groups had united under an umbrella organization called the United Nicaraguan Opposition (UNO). Even the UNO's enemies admit that it is rapidly becoming a viable national liberation force; it is believed that the organization will demand observer status at the United Nations and the Organization of American States following the precedent set by the PLO and SWAPO. The UNO is also in the process of setting up offices in several world capitals. Given sufficient support, UNO leaders believe their armed forces could double within twelve months—a possibility acknowledged even by Sandinistas such as Víctor Tirado Lopez, who predicted that UNO's military arm, the Nicaraguan Democratic Force (FDN) would "perhaps reach a total of some 35,000 men."[20]

However, continued U.S. military and economic assistance beyond the $100 million approved by the U.S. Congress in 1986 must not fall victim to political vagaries or budget cuts. Confronting a Soviet-equipped enemy that outnumbers it by six to one, the FDN must be guaranteed a consistent supply of shoulder-fired antiaircraft weapons, artillery to use in besieging towns and defending territory, large stockpiles of ammunition, and adequate logistical support. Without strong and unwavering U.S. assistance, the Nicaraguan resistance will neither restore democracy to their country nor deter the Soviet strategic objective of destabilizing Central America. Halfway measures taken to counter an implacable and highly sophisticated enemy strategy are actually counterproductive. A stalemated situation in Nicaragua would benefit only the USSR and its proxies, who can afford the luxury of waiting until attrition among the UNO forces and shifting political currents in Washington clear their path of this last major obstacle.

As Cuba is the key to Soviet strategy in the Caribbean, then Nicaragua must be the key to a U.S. counterstrategy. Mere containment of the unabashedly Marxist-Leninist Sandinistas will have no greater success in stemming the spread of Soviet influence in the Western Hemisphere than did the feeble polemics of Public Law 87–733. Dissolution of the FSLN regime would provide the single greatest setback possible to Soviet ambitions in Central America and the Caribbean. This would be a far more serious blow than even the loss of Cuba would be at this time in history, for without Nicaragua the leftist insurgent forces of Central America would have no secure base on the American mainland.

U.S. policymakers are fortunate to have an existing military force, well-trained and highly motivated, that is determined to truly liberate Nicaragua and remove what is also a grave threat to U.S. national security. The anti-Sandinista forces ask for no U.S. commitment beyond an adequate supply of weapons and other equipment, as well as the confirmation that the U.S. government's support for their struggle will not fall victim to domestic political expediency. The credibility of the United States is weakened when drastic measures are taken to promote a free society in such places as South Africa and El Salvador, but a blind eye is turned to the equally legitimate aspirations of the Nicaraguan people.

Accordingly to high-ranking FSLN defectors,[21] the Sandinistas believe that their regime will fall if Nicaraguan democratic resistance forces gain the type of offensive momentum generated by a string of victories. If simultaneous offensives are launched on several fronts, as they were in 1979, large numbers of peasants would join the anticommunist insurgency, swelling the ranks of the anti-Sandinista forces. This action would be accompanied by widespread mutiny and defections among the Nicaraguan Army (EPS), a force that is already so demoralized by poor living conditions and antipathy toward Marxism that its troops are not trusted with loaded weapons during visits by Sandinista comandantes such as Humberto Ortega.[22]

At this point, a coup d'état by officers of the EPS—not yet purged of non-Marxist elements—is considered possible, followed by an alliance with UNO in a government of national reconstruction.[23] If events reach this stage, the United States should impose a blockade of Nicaragua to prevent Soviet and Cuban resupply operations, and should use force, if necessary, to interdict any reinforcements or supplies, as allowed under the provisions of Public Law 87–733.[24]

The author believes, from the evidence available to him, that the Sandinista regime can be removed by the force of arms of the Nicaraguan people if given U.S. military assistance. However, if the U.S. Congress is unwilling to commit itself to an unequivocal policy of rendering military and economic assistance to the Nicaraguan democratic resistance forces, direct U.S. military intervention in Central America will become inevitable.

If the USSR's Caribbean strategy fails in Central America as it did in Grenada and the English-speaking Caribbean, will the Kremlin consider its massive investment in Cuba to be worth maintaining? The continuing utilization of Cuban proxy forces in Africa will probably become unnecessary if Jonas Savimbi's UNITA forces are victorious in Angola and if Ethiopia develops its own capacity for both national defense and service as a Soviet military proxy. There are already signs that the Soviet Union is losing patience with Cuba's abysmal economic performance: Soviet demands that Cuba fulfill its commitments to supply sugar to Soviet bloc countries in 1985 forced Havana to spend $100 million buying sugar on the world market.[25]

The United States should pursue a graduated offensive strategy to exploit Cuba's weaknesses and place greater burdens on Moscow. The greatest priority should be given to continued military assistance to both UNO in Nicaragua and UNITA in Angola to raise the casualty and financial burdens of Castro's foreign adventures. Greater cooperation between the U.S. and Latin American governments is also needed to eradicate the narcotics trade. Halting the flow of funds from drug sales would serve a strategic as well as a moral purpose, placing a greater strain on Castro's limited economic resources and thereby making it more difficult for him to finance subversion and guerrilla warfare without an infusion of fresh Soviet support. The United States should also take measures to interdict Cuban arms shipments to Latin American insurgents—again, under the legal provisions of Public Law 87–722—and should adopt a tougher stance on the large number of Soviet military personnel in Cuba. In addition, the United States must resist initiatives to "normalize" relations with Cuba while it remains a Soviet proxy. Such an action would prove a major strategic benefit to Moscow by allowing it to substitute Western economic support for its own while still retaining Cuba as an important military asset.

The U.S. counterstrategy for the Caribbean must extend beyond the regional level. The proposed annual summit meetings between the president of the United States and the general secretary of the Communist Party of the Soviet Union represent the most direct means of indicating U.S. resolve toward Soviet expansion in the Caribbean region. The demonstration of consistency in U.S. policy toward the Caribbean, using Grenada and U.S. support for Nicaraguan anti-Sandinista forces as examples, must be clearly emphasized to the Kremlin.

The domino theory in reverse may prove to be valid in the Caribbean. The United States still has time to counter the USSR's Caribbean strategy without the loss of a single U.S. life in battle. However, this time is limited. Once the proliferation of Soviet influence reaches a certain point in the Western Hemisphere, no amount of economic or military aid will reverse it, and the United States will inevitably be forced, at great cost, to remove an intolerable threat to its national security.

Although the U.S. intervention in Grenada was a major strategic victory for the West, operations at the tactical level during the invasion of the island have been criticized by a variety of defense analysts.[26] Although some of this criticism is unjustified,[27] Operation Urgent Fury nonetheless demonstrated that overwhelming force was required by U.S. and allied forces to defeat a mixed force of Cuban and Grenadian troops and Cuban militia-trained construction workers numbering less than two thousand combatants. Nineteen, or 20 percent, of the U.S. helicopters deployed in Operation Urgent Fury were lost, nearly double the rate of daylight bomber losses during World War II.[28] Seven full-strength U.S. combat battalions plus elements of two others took part in the invasion, supported by a fifteen-ship U.S. naval task force including an aircraft carrier and two amphibious assault ships. The engagement of such a small Soviet proxy force with a U.S. force nearly seven times larger was carefully observed in Moscow via the Cosmos 1504 surveillance satellite, which was deliberately maneuvered into a lower orbit to allow it to pass near Grenada at an altitude of 125 miles from October 26 to November 1, 1983.[29]

Without the use of tactical nuclear weapons, a U.S. invasion of Nicaragua or Cuba would almost certainly preclude a significant reinforcement and resupply operation to U.S. NATO or South Korean forces, especially if two such major Caribbean operations took place simultaneously. In *Kingdoms of the Blind,* Harold Rood hypothesizes that a conventional invasion of Cuba would require one Marine Amphibious Force (consisting of a marine division plus a marine aircraft wing), one or two airborne divisions, an armored division, perhaps half of the fifty-four tactical air squadrons deployed in the continental United States, plus at least one carrier battle group, and between forty-five and seventy-five other ships, not including mine clearance vessels.[30]

In a 1982 Rand Corporation study prepared for the U.S. Department of State and the U.S. Air Force, the military cost of a U.S. operation against Cuba was extrapolated. The study concluded that Washington would have to take into account the possibility of unexpected resistance or a protracted conflict in Cuba, necessitating a major sea blockade of the island plus ample air cover to minimize the risk of Cuban attacks against U.S. surface vessels. Additionally, the United States would have to be prepared to defend itself from Cuban air attacks against Miami and the Gulf Coast, as well as Cuban DOE raids and sabotage by DGI "sleeper" agents.[31] Although a simultaneous operation against Nicaragua would probably not require such a large allocation of U.S. military assets, it would nonetheless require a carrier battle group, five tactical air squadrons, at least one armored division, and elements of Ranger regiments and airborne divisions.[32] It is worth noting that the Rand Corporation study concludes that:

> [I]f left unchecked, the latent security threat now posed by Cuban and Soviet activities in the Basin could become so grave in the years ahead that Washington would have no recourse but to resort to a military solution for the "Cuba problem" as occurred in 1962.[33]

It is incumbent upon the current generation of U.S. policymakers to take measures that will ensure the security and economic well-being of generations yet unborn, not only in the United States, but elsewhere in the hemisphere as well. Unless decisive actions are taken, the Soviet Union's Caribbean strategy may well succeed in its objective of crippling the United States as a global power.

Notes

Introduction

1. The Monroe Doctrine, a policy statement enunciated by U.S. President James Monroe on December 2, 1823, was designed to counter the imperial ambitions of the Holy Alliance founded in 1815 by Tsar Alexander I of Russia. Russian expansionism on the Pacific coast of North America became of particular concern to the United States in 1821, after the tsarist government issues a ukase forbidding foreign vessels from coming within one hundred miles of the shore of territories claimed by Russia on the North American continent. Monroe's declaration was an extrapolation of a statement made by U.S. Secretary of State John Quincy Adams to the Russian minister in Washington that the United States "would contest the right of Russia to *any* territorial establishment on this continent" (Samuel Flagg Bemis, *The Latin American Policy of the United States* [New York: Harcourt Brace & Company, 1943], p. 54).
2. Mario Lazo, *American Policy Failures in Cuba* (New York: Twin Circle Publishing Co., 1968), p. 52.

Chapter 1. Historical Soviet Interest in Latin America and the Caribbean

1. Lenin had adopted Marx's belief that "final victory of socialism in a single country is impossible." He therefore decreed that Soviet Russia was the base for world revolution and enjoined all other communists to recognize this. Regardless of Stalin's dispute with Trotsky over "socialism in one country," he also believed that the Soviet Union would degenerate into a "bourgeois republic" if it did not consistently pursue "a revolutionary policy uniting around the working class of the USSR the proletarians and oppressed of all countries." Jan Librach, *The Rise of the Soviet Empire* (New York: Praeger, 1964), p. 14.
2. Adam B. Ulam, *Expansion and Coexistence* (New York: Praeger, 1975), p. 776.

3. Elias Lafertte, *Vida de un Comunista* (Santiago: 1961), p. 210. In *Marxism in Latin America* Luis E. Aguilar, ed. (Philadelphia: Temple University Press, 1978).

4. Víctor R. Haya de la Torre, *Nuestra America y el mundo* (Lima: 1961), pp. 158–159. In Aguilar, *Marxism in Latin America*.

5. V. I. Lenin, *Imperialism: The Highest Stage of Capitalism* (Moscow: 1934), p. 78.

6. Jane Degras, *The Communist International 1919–1943: Documents*, vol. 1, 1919–22 (London: Oxford University Press, 1956), pp. 179–93.

7. Stephen Clissold, "Soviet Relations with Latin America between the Wars," in *The Soviet Union and Latin America* J. Gregory Oswald and Anthony J. Strover, eds., (New York: Praeger, 1970), p. 16.

8. Ibid, p. 17.

9. Donald Herman, ed., *The Communist Tide in Latin America* (Austin: University of Texas Press, 1973), p. 22.

10. Clissold, "Soviet Relations," p. 17n.

11. *International Press Correspondence*, no. 78, Berlin, November 8, 1928, p. 1465. In Aguilar, *Marxism in Latin America*.

12. Clissold, "Soviet Relations," p. 17n.

13. *International Press Correspondence*, no. 39, July 25, 1928, p. 706. In Aguilar, *Marxism in Latin America*.

14. Clisshold, "Soviet Relations," p. 19.

15. *El Trabajador Latino Americano*, September 15, 1928, p. 1. In Aguilar, *Marxism in Latin America*.

16. Rodrigo Garcia Trevino, *La ingerencia rusa en Mexico* (Mexico City: Editorial America, 1959), pp. 79–83.17. *El Movimiento revolucionario latinoamerican: resena de la primera conferencia latinoamericano de partidos comunista* (Buenos Aires: Editorial La Correspondencia Sudamericana, 1929), pp. 89–90.

17. Louis E. Aguilar, ed., *Marxism in Latin America*, rev. ed. (Philadelphia: Temple University Press, 1978), p. 21.

18. *International Press Correspondence*, September 1, 1928. In Aguilar, *Marxism in Latin America*.

19. Mark Falcoff, "Somoza, Sandino, and the United States: What the past Teaches—and Doesn't," *This World* 6 (Fall 1983): 56.

20. "Struggles of the Communist Parties of South and Caribbean America," *The Communist International* 12, no. 10 (May 20, 1935): 564–76. In Aguilar, *Marxism in Latin America*.

21. Robert J. Alexander, *Communism in Latin America* (New Brunswick, N.J.: Rutgers University Press, 1957), pp. 368–69.

22. *Foreign Relations of the United States, 1932* (Washington: U.S. GPO, 1948), vol. 5, p. 615.

23. *A Insurreicao de 17 Novembro—relatorio do Delegado E. Bellens Porto* (Rio de Janiero, 1936). In Aguilar, *Marxism in Latin America*.

24. *International Press Correspondence*, vol. 60, July 19, 1921, p. 732. In Aguilar, *Marxism in Latin America*.

25. *Dokumenty vneshney politiki SSSR* 12, no. 329 (Moscow: 1957): 572–74. In *Soviet Relations with Latin America 1918–1968: A Documentary Survey* Stephen Clissold, ed.,(London: Oxford University Press, 1970).

26. Emilio Portes Gil, *Quince Años de Politica Mexicana* (Mexico City: 1941), pp. 373–81. In Aguilar, *Marxism in Latin America.*

27. J. Valtin, *San Patrie ni Frontieres* (New York: 1941), pp. 254–57. In Aguilar, *Marxism in Latin America.*

28. *League of Nations Official Journal,* annex 1586 (Geneva: February 1936), pp. 233–35.

29. Ibid, pp. 91–92.

30. *Seventh Congress of the Communist International* (Moscow: Foreign Languages Publishing House, 1939), pp. 182–83. In Aguilar, *Marxism in Latin America.*

31. *Communist* 18, no. 7 (July 1939): 576–89. In Aguilar, *Marxism in Latin America.*

32. Alvin J. Rubinstein, ed., *The Foreign Policy of the Soviet Union* (New York: Random House, 1966), p. 172.

33. Joseph L. Nogee and Robert H. Donaldson, *Soviet Foreign Policy since World War II (Elmsford N.Y.: Pergamon Press, 1981), p. 67.*

34. F. G. Zuev, I. V. Ivashin, and V. P. Nikhamin, eds., *International Relations and Foreign Policy of the USSR, 1917–1960* (Moscow: State Publishing House of the Higher Party School of the CPSU Central Committee, 1961), pp. 506–18. In Rubinstein, *Foreign Policy of the Soviet Union.*

35. Enrique E. Rivarola, "Some Aspects of Soviet–Latin American Relations," in *The Soviet Union and Latin America* J. Gregory Oswald and Anthony J. Strover, eds., (New York: Praeger, 1970), pp. 59–66.

36. A. I. Sizonenko, *Ocherki istorii Sovetsko-Latinoamerikanskikh otnoshenii* (Moscow: 1971), p. 89. In Clissold, *Soviet Relations with Latin America.*

37. F. Parkinson, *Latin America, the Cold War and the World Powers, 1945–1973* (Beverly Hills: Sage Publications, 1974), p. 53.

38. U.S. Congress, Senate Subcommittee of the Committee on the Judiciary to Investigate Internal Security, part 5, testimony of William Wieland, Jan. 9, Feb. 8, 1961; Feb. 2, 1962, pp. 638–39.

39. Ibid.

40. *Actas Novena Conferencia, Bogotá, 1948,* Dictamen Sobre "Defensa y Preservacion de la Democracia en America Frente a la Eventual Instalacion de Regimenes Antidemocraticos en el Continente" (Washington, D.C., 1948), pp. 441–49.

41. Although the Inter-American Treaty of Reciprocal Assistance, the Rio Treaty, established the political framework for an inter-American collective security system, it did not provide for the establishment of armed forces under collective command, as in the case of NATO, nor did it establish a structure for military cooperation.

42. *En defensa del pueblo* (Havana: Ediciones del Partido Socialista Popular, 1945).

43. Rodney Arismendi, "El Fin de la guerra y el nuevo imperialismo norteamer-

icano," in *Para un prontuario del dolar* (Montevideo: Ediciones Pueblos Unidos, 1947), pp. 16, 198, 205, 245. In Aguilar, *Marxism in Latin America.*

44. The Soviet government's opportunistic accord with Germany did not prevent it from actively conspiring with German communists and left-wing socialists to provoke a communist revolution in the Reich via strikes and armed insurrection. See Ulam, *Expansion and Coexistence*, p. 155.

45. *World Marxist Review* (Prague; March 1966): 37.

46. J. Gregory Oswald, "Studies on Latin America by Soviet Political Economists," in *The Soviet Union and Latin America* J. Gregory Oswald and Anthony J. Strover, eds. (New York: Praeger, 1970), pp. 72–80.

47. Parkinson, *Latin America*, p. 40.

48. Ibid.

49. U.S. Congress, House *Select Committee on Communist Aggression, Ninth Interim Report of Hearings before the Subcommittee on Latin America* (Washington, D.C., 1954), p. 120.

50. Thomas P. Anderson, *Politics in Central America* (New York: Praeger, 1982), p. 23.

51. Parkinson, *Latin America*, p. 55. See also J. Slater, *The OAS and United States Foreign Policy* (Columbus: Ohio University State Press, 1967), p. 131.

52. Nikita S. Khrushchev, *The Disintegration of the Imperialist Colonial System—Report of the Central Committee of the CPSU to the Twentieth Party Congress, Feb. 4, 1956* (Moscow: Foreign Languages Publishing House, 1956). In Rubinstein, *Foreign Policy of the Soviet Union.*

53. Parkinson, *Latin America*, p. 40.

54. Robert Wesson, ed., *Communism in Central America and the Caribbean* (Stanford: Hoover Institution Press, 1982), p. 148.

55. Richard H. Shultz and Roy Godson, *Dezinformatsia* (McLean, Va.: Pergamon-Brasseys, 1984), p. 22.

56. A. I. Sizonenko, Ed., *SSSR–Argentina 30 let* (Moscow, 1976), p. 16. In Parkinson, *Latin America.*

57. Parkinson, *Latin America*, p. 56.

58. Ibid.

59. Cole Blasier, *The Giant's Rival: The USSR and Latin America* (Pittsburgh: University of Pittsburgh Press, 1983), p. 34.

Chapter 2. Cuba's Role in Soviet Strategy

1. Joseph L. Nogee and Robert H. Donaldson, *Soviet Foreign Policy since World War II* (Elmsford, N.Y.: Pergamon Press, 1981), p. 174.

2. Robert J. Alexander, *Communism in Latin America* (New Brunswick: Rutgers University Press, 1957), p. 278.

3. Donald Herman, ed., *The Communist Tide in Latin America* (Austin: University of Texas Press, 1973), p. 19.

4. *Bohemia,* November 9, 1962, p. 62. Washington, D.C., Joint Publications Research Service (JPRS), November 22, 1962.

5. Andres Suarez, *Cuba, Castroism and Communism, 1957–1966* (Cambridge, Mass.: MIT Press, 1967), p. 26.

6. Mario Lazo, *American Policy Failures in Cuba* (New York: Twin Circle Publishing Co., 1970), p. 118. See also Fulgencio Batista, *Cuba Betrayed* (New York: Vantage Press, 1962), p. 118.

7. Maurice Halperin, *The Rise and Decline of Fidel Castro* (Berkeley and Los Angeles: University of California Press, 1972), pp. 50, 153.

8. Carlos Franqui, *Diario de la revolucion cubana* (Barcelona: Ediciones R. Torres, 1976), pp. 94, 96.

9. U.S. Congress, Senate Committee on the Judiciary, *Hearings on the Communist Threat to the United States through the Caribbean*, 86th Cong., 1st sess., p. 1, July 14, 1959, pp. 7, 13.

10. *New York Times*, February 24 and February 25, 1957, p. 1. Information on this period also provided by Dr. Emilio Adolfo Rivero, Twenty-sixth of July veteran.

11. Earl E. T. Smith, *The Fourth Floor* (New York: Random House, 1962), p. 100.

12. *Partiinaia zhizn'*, no. 20 (1958): 51–53. As quoted by Cole Blasier, *The Giant's Rival: The USSR and Latin America* (Pittsburgh: University of Pittsburgh Press, 1983), p. 102.

13. Fidel Castro and Janette Habel, *Proceso al sectarismo* (Buenos Aires: 1965), p. 49.

14. Konstantin M. Obyden, *Kuba v bor'be za svobodu i nezavismost* (Moscow: 1959), in JPRS 3563, July 18, 1960, p. 6.

15. Robert Murphy, *Diplomat among Warriors* (New York: Doubleday, 1964), p. 442.

16. Daniel James, *Cuba: The First Soviet Satellite in the Americas* (New York: Avon, 1961), pp. 234–41. Supported by author's interviews with Dr. Emilio Adolfo Rivero, Dr. Claudio Benidez, and Ambassador Nicholas Arroyo.

17. Paul D. Bethel, *The Losers* (New Rochelle, N.Y.: Arlington House, 1969, p. 162). See also Hugh Thomas, *The Cuban Revolution* (New York: Harper and Row, 1977), pp. 503–504.

18. Senate Committee on the Judiciary, *Communist Threat*, part 3, testimony of C. P. Cabell, November 5, 1959, p. 171.

19. James, *Cuba*, p. 248. See also Thomas, *Cuban Revolution*, p. 474.

20. Bethel, *Losers*, pp. 221, 252, 418.

21. Ibid, pp. 205–206. See also Thomas, *Cuban Revolution*, p. 486.

22. Interview with Dr. Herminio Portell-Vila, Boston, Virginia, August 27, 1983.

23. Brian Crozier, "Soviet Pressures in the Caribbean," *Conflict Studies* (London), no. 35 (May 1973): 87.

24. Robert E. Tucker, *The Soviet Political Mind, Stalinism and Post-Stalin Change* (New York: Norton, 1971), p. 596.

25. Robert S. Walters, "Soviet Economic Aid to Cuba: 1959–1964" *International Affairs* 42, no. 1 (January 1966): 76–81.

26. Bethel, *Losers*, p. 250. See also J. Slater, *The OAS and United States Foreign Policy* (Columbus: Ohio State University Press, 1967), p. 112.

27. *Pravda,* February 11, 1960. Quoted in *Mikoyan in Cuba* (New York: Cross-currents Press, 1960), p. 83.
28. U.S. Foreign Broadcast Information Service (FBIS), Radio Moscow, May 8, 1970.
29. Strobe Talbott, trans. and ed., *Khrushchev Remembers: The Last Testament* (Boston: Little, Brown & Co., 1974), p. 461. See also Roy and Zhores Medvedev, *Khrushchev: The Years in Power* (New York: Columbia University Press, 1976), pp. 165–75.
30. Bethel, *Losers,* p. 223. See also *Report of the Royal Commission on Espionage of the Dominion of Canada,* June 1946.
31. *Pravda,* July 10, 1960. Quoted in *Soviet Relations with Latin American 1918–1968 A Documentary Survey,* Stephen Clissold, ed., (London: Oxford University Press, 1970), p. 212.
32. Richard M. Nixon, "Cuba, Castro and John F. Kennedy," *Readers' Digest,* November 5, 1964, p. 288.
33. Quoted in James, *Cuba,* p. 258.
34. Bethel, *Losers,* p. 224. See also Blas Roca, *The Fundamental Principles of Socialism in Cuba* (JPRS, August 20, 1962), p. 303.
35. This vague warning, issued by the OAS at U.S. prompting, was directed to "the Sino–Soviet powers" even though the Chinese influence in Cuba was neglible.
36. Alexander L. George, "The Operational Code: A Neglected Approach to the Study of Political Leaders and Decisionmaking," in *The Conduct of Soviet Foreign Policy,* Erik P. Hoffman and Frederick J. Fleron, eds. (Chicago: Aldine-Atherton, 1971), p. 179 n. 33.
37. F. G. Zuev, I. V. Ivashin, and V. P. Nikhamin, eds., *International Relations and Foreign Policy of the USSR, 1917–1960* (Moscow: State Publishing House of the Higher Party School of the CPSU Central Committee, 1961), pp. 506–18. In Rubinstein, *Foreign Policy of the Soviet Union.*
38. Ibid.
39. Lazo, *American Policy Failures,* p. 230. See also Ernesto Guevara, *Guerrilla Warfare* (Washington, D.C.: Department of the Army, Assistant Chief of Staff for Intelligence, 1960), p. 23.
40. Franqui, *Diario,* p. 362.
41. James, *Cuba,* p. 262.
42. Wynfred Joshua and Stephen P. Gilbert, *Soviet Military Aid as a Reflection of Soviet Objectives* (Washington, D.C.: Georgetown University Research Project, 1968). See also *New York Times,* November 19, 1960, p. 1.
43. Pierre Salinger, *With Kennedy* (New York: Doubleday, 1966), p. 146. See also Ania Francos, *La Fête Cubaine* (Paris: Rene Juilliard, 1962), for corroboration from the Cuban side.
44. *Pravda,* April 19, 1961, p. 1.
45. James Reston, *New York Times Magazine,* November 15, 1964. See also *Khrushchev: The Last Testament,* pp. 487–501.

46. Arnold L. Horelick, *The Cuban Missile Crisis: An Analysis of Soviet Calculations and Behavior* (Santa Monica: Rand Corporation, 1963), p. 53.
47. Ibid.
48. Strobe Talbott, trans. and ed., *Khrushchev Remembers* (Boston: Little, Brown and Co., 1970), pp. 493–94.
49. Michael Tatu, *Power in the Kremlin: From Khrushchev to Kosygin* (New York: Viking, 1967), pp. 236–37. See also Franqui, *Diario*, p. 362.
50. U.S. Congress, Senate Committee on Government Operations, Subcommittee on Natural Security Staffing and Operations, *Staffing Procedures and Problems in the Soviet Union,* Washington, D.C.: 88th Cong. 1st sess., 1963, p. 24. See also Horelick, *Cuban Missile Crisis,* p. 47. Ponomarev, a senior Comintern official prior to taking over the CPSU Central Committee's International Department in 1957, was also responsible for liaison with non-Soviet bloc communist parties; Andropov, in charge of liaison with Soviet bloc parties, was in 1962 a secretary in the International Department of the CPSU Central Committee. He was appointed KGB chief in 1967.
51. U. S. Congress, House Committee on Appropriations, Subcommittee on Department of Defense Appropriations, *Hearings,* 88th Cong., 1st sess., 1963, pp. 15–19.
52. *New York Times,* September 23, 1962.
53. U.S. Department of Defense, Special Cuba Briefing, February 6, 1963. See also U.S. Congress, Senate Committee on Armed Services, Preparedness Investigating Subcommittee, *Interim Report on Cuban Military Buildup,* 88th Cong., 1st sess., 1963, pp. 2–4.
54. See Horelick, *Cuban Missile Crisis;* Thomas, *Cuban Revolution;* and Harold W. Rood, *Kingdoms of the Blind* (Durham, N.C.: Carolina Academic Press, 1980), for geopolitical and strategic analyses of this event.
55. Henry A. Kissinger, *The White House Years (Boston: Little, Brown and Co., 1979), p. 633.*
56. Adam B. Ulam, *Expansion and Coexistence* (New York: Praeger, 1971), pp. 667–77.
57. Rood, *Kingdoms of the Blind,* p. 109.
58. Herbert S. Dinerstein, "Soviet Policy in Latin America," *The American Political Science Review* 61 (March 1967): 87.
59. *Congressional Record—Senate,* "Testimony of Senator Steve Symms," April 25, 1983, vol. 129, no. 53, pp. S5233–37.
60. Theodore C. Sorenson, *Kennedy* (New York: Harper and Row, 1965), p. 673. See also Elie Abel, *The Missile Crisis* (New York: Lippincott, 1966), pp. 211–12.
61. Carlos Franqui, "Castro's Worst Week," *Penthouse,* February 1983, p. 150. See also Franqui, *Diario,* p. 97.
62. *Bohemia,* November 9, 1962, pp. 64–65. Quoted in Bethel, *Losers,* p. 357. See also Thomas, *Cuban Revolution, p. 489.*
63. *Hoy,* November 3, 1962, p. 1. In Bethel, *Losers,* p. 357.

64. *Bohemia,* November 9, 1962, p. 65. In Bethel, *Losers,* p. 490.

65. Ibid, pp. 39–40.

66. Edward Weintal and Charles Bartlett, *Facing the Brink: An Intimate Study of Crisis Diplomacy* (New York: Scribner, 1967), p. 67.

67. Maurice Halperin, *The Taming of Fidel Castro* (Berkeley and Los Angeles: University of California Press, 1981), pp. 9–10. See also Thomas, *Cuban Revolution,* p. 702.

68. M. V. Danilevich, M. F. Kudachkin, M. A. Okuneva, eds., *Latinskaia Amerika: Kratkii politiko-ekonomicheskii sprovochnik* (Moskva: Gosudarstvennone izdatel'stvo politicheskoi literatura, 1962), pp. 121–24. In Clissold, *Soviet Relations with Latin America,* pp. 303–305.

69. Blasier, *Giant's Rival,* pp. 277–90.

70. Ernesto Guevara, "Cuba, Historical Exception or Vanguard in the Anti-Colonial Struggle? in *Marxism in Latin America,* Luis E. Aguilar, ed., (Philadelphia: Temple University Press, 1978), pp. 206–13.

71. Georges Fauriol, ed., *Latin American Insurgencies* (Washington, D.C.: National Defense University, 1985), pp. 11–16.

72. A. F. Shul'govskii, "Rasstanovka klassovikh sil v bor'be za osvobozhdenie," in *Ekonomicheskie problemy stran Latinskoi Ameriki,* V. Ia. Avarina and M. V. Danilevich, eds. (Moskva: Izdatel'stvo Akademii nauk SSSR, 1963), pp. 482–84.

73. Ibid.

74. N. Mostovets and M. Kudachkin, "Osvoboditel'noe dvizhenie v Latinskoi Amerike," *Kommunist,* no. 11 (July 1964): 121–30. Quoted in Dinerstein, "Soviet Policy", p. 86.

75. Ibid.

76. A. Sivolobov, "Krestianskoe dvizhenie v Latinskoi Amerike," *Kommunist,* no. 12 (August 1964): 100–107. Quoted in Dinerstein, "Soviet Policy," p. 87.

77. "Pamiatnaia zapiska Palmiro Togliatti," *Pravda,* September 10, 1964. Quoted in Dinerstein, "Soviet Policy," p. 87.

78. Dinerstein, "Soviet Policy," p. 87.

79. "Communicado: Conferencia de los Partidos Communistas de America Latina," *Revolución,* Havana, January 19, 1965. From collection of Dr. Emilio Adolfo Rivero.

80. *Politica Internacional,* no. 9 (1st trimester, 1965): 116–20.

81. Marcel Niedergange, *Le Monde,* January 8, 1966.

82. Carlos Nunez, "Y ahora, en que camp esta Cuba?" *Marcha* (Montevideo; February 18, 1966): Information from Dr. Daniel James, Georgetown University Center for Strategic and International Studies.

83. Andres Suarez, "Soviet Influence on the Internal Politics of Cuba," in *Soviet and Chinese Influence in the Third World,* Alvin J. Rubinstein, ed. (New York: Praeger, 1976), pp. 184–85.

84. "Speech by Armed Forces Minister Raúl Castro to the Graduating Class of the Maximo Gomez Superior School of Military Training," Radio Progreso, July 24, 1967. In Bethel, *Losers,* p. 276.

85. *Granma,* January 28, 1968, p. 1. See Thomas, *Cuban Revolution, pp. 692–993.*

86. Ibid.

87. *Granma,* January 30, 1960. Quoted in Bethel, *Losers,* p. 547.

88. Bethel, *Losers,* p. 551. See also Thomas, *Cuban Revolution,* pp. 602–603.

89. Suarez, "Soviet Influence," p. 183.

90. *Diario las Americas,* Miami, October 25, 1967, p. 3.

91. Bethel, *Losers,* p. 547. Corroborated by Dr. Daniel James, editor of *The Complete Bolivian Diaries of Che Guevara and Other Captured Documents* (Briarcliff Manor, New York: Stein and Day, 1969).

92. Cecil Johnson, *Communist China and Latin America, 1959–1967* (New York: Columbia University Press, 1970), pp. 128, 172–73, 228–29.

93. *Granma,* (Havana), January 28, 1968. Quoted in Bethel, *Losers,* p. 559.

94. *El Mundo,* January 17, 1968. Quoted in Bethel, *Losers,* p. 551.

95. *Le Monde,* March 21, 1968.

96. *Cuba Socialista* 17, no. 65 (January 1967): 33.

97. *Politica Internacional* 22–24 (2nd, 3rd, and 4th trimesters, 1968), 88, pp. 278–83 (private collection). See also eyewitness reports from Dr. Emilio Adolfo Rivero, Dr. Jorge Mas, and Ms. Barbara Gordon.

98. *Bohemia* January 19, 1968, p. 79.

99. *Granma Weekly Review,* June 30, 1968, p. 2.

100. Suarez, "Soviet Influence," p. 194.

101. U.S. Congress, Senate Committee on the Judiciary, Subcommittee to Investigate the Administration of the Internal Security Act, testimony of Orlando Castro Hidalgo, October 16, 1969, pp. 1423–29.

102. Ibid. See also Edward Gonzalez and David Ronfeldt, "Post-Revolutionary Cuba in a Changing World," a report prepared for the assistant secretary of defense for International security affairs (Santa Monica: Rand Corporation, December 1975), p. 55.

103. *New York Times,* August 23, 1968, p. 1.

104. *Granma Weekly Review,* August 25, 1968, p. 1.

105. Ibid.

106. *Ogonek* (Moscow), no. 21 (June 1970): 3. Quoted in Suarez, "Soviet Influence," p. 195.

107. Leon Goure and Julian Weinkle, "Cuba's New Dependency," *Problems of Communism* (March-April 1972): 74.

108. *New York Times,* March 24, 1971. See also Gonzalez and Ronfeldt, "Post-Revolutionary Cuba," p. 45.

109. Radio Havana, January 4, 1973. Quoted in Suarez, "Soviet Influence," p. 195.

110. Carmelo Mesa-Lago, *Cuba in the 1970s: Pragmatism and Institutionalization* (Albuquerque: University of New Mexico Press, 1978), pp. 17–53.

111. U.S. Central Intelligence Agency, National Foreign Assessment Center, *The Cuban Economy: A Statistical Review* (Washington, D.C.: 1981), p. 39. See also U.S. Department of State, *Dealing with the Reality of Cuba* (Washington, D.C.: December 14, 1982), p. 4.

112. Lester A. Sobel, ed., *Castro's Cuba in the 1970s* New York: Facts on File, 1978), pp. 167ff.
113. Suarez, "Soviet Influence," p. 191.
114. Ibid., p. 192.

Chapter 3. Cuba: A Base for Soviet Power Projection

1. Jeffrey T. Richelson, *Sword and Shield: Soviet Intelligence and Security Apparatus* (Cambridge, Mass.: Ballinger Publishing Co., 1986), pp. 210–24.
2. John Barron, *KGB: The Secret Work of Soviet Secret Agents* (New York: Readers' Digest Press, 1974), p. 148.
3. U.S. Congress, Senate Committee on the Judiciary, Subcommittee to Investigate the Administration of the Internal Security Act, testimony of Orlando Castro Hidalgo, October 16, 1969, pp. 1423–29. See also U.S. Congress, Senate Committee on the Judiciary, *The Role of Cuba in International Terrorism and Subversion* (Washington, D.C., 1982), p. 11.
4. Ibid.
5. U.S. Congress, Senate Committee on the Judiciary, *Role of Cuba,* p. 24.
6. Brian Crozier, "The Soviet Involvement in Violence," *Soviet Analyst* 1, no. 11 (July 20, 1972): 5–9.
7. Richelson, *Sword and Shield,* p. 212.
8. Interview with Dr. Emilio Adolfo Rivero, exiled Twenty-sixth of July Movement veteran, Washington, D.C., October 7, 1985. See also Crozier, "Soviet Involvement," p. 6.
9. Havana Radio Progreso Network, December 3, 1985; FBIS Latin America, December 3, 1985, p. Q1.
10. U.S. Air Force Office of Special Investigations, *Special Report: The Cuban Intelligence Service* (Washington, D.C.: AFOSI, 1976), p. 1.
11. U.S. Congress, House Committee on Foreign Affairs, Subcommittee on Inter-American Affairs, *Impact of Cuban–Soviet Ties in the Western Hemisphere, Spring 1979* (Washington, D.C., April 25 and 26, 1979), pp. 25, 26. See also Richelson *Sword and Shield,* p. 211.
12. Richelson, *Sword and Shield,* p. 211.
13. See the testimony of DGI defector Gerardo Jesus Peraza Amechazuara in *London Evening News,* March 26, 1973. See also U.S. Congress Senate, Committee on the Judiciary, *Role of Cuba,* pp. 5–22.
14. *Washington Post,* April 20, 1983, p. A17.
15. U.S. Congress, Senate Committee on the Judiciary, Subcommittee on Western Hemisphere Affairs, *The Cuban Government's Involvement in Facilitating International Drug Traffic* (Washington, D.C., April 30, 1983), p. 658.
16. U.S. Congress, Senate Committee on the Judiciary, Subcommittee on Security and Terrorism, *The Role of the Soviet Union, Cuba and East Germany in*

Fomenting Terrorism in Southern Africa (Washington, D.C., March 1982), pp. 340–41.

17. Ibid.

18. Viktor Suvorov, *Inside Soviet Military Intelligence* (New York: Macmillan, 1984), pp. 158, 160, 164.

19. Richelson, *Sword and Shield*, p. 212. See also Jay Mallin, "Cuban Intelligence Elite Pushes Subversion in Americas," *Washington Times*, August 25, 1983, p. 7A.

20. U.S. Congress, Senate Committee on the Judiciary, *Role of Cuba*, p. 16. See also Mallin, "Cuban Intelligence Elite."

21. U.S. Congress, Senate Committee on the Judiciary, testimony of Orlando Castro Hidalgo, p. 11.

22. Barron, *KGB*, p. 147.

23. *Strategic Situation in Central America and the Caribbean*, current policy no. 352 (Washington, D.C.: U.S. Department of State, December 14, 1981), p. 5.

24. Moscow Radio Magallanes (in Spanish to Chile), November 14, 1985; FBIS Soviet Union, November 20, 1985, p. K1.

25. *Pravda*, September 3, 1985, p. 5; FBIS Soviet Union, September 16, 1985, p. K3.

26. James D. Theberge, ed., *Russia in the Caribbean: A Special Report*, pt. 2 (Washington, D.C.: Georgetown University Center for Strategic and International Studies, 1973), pp. 54–55.

27. U.S. Department of State, "Cuba's Renewed Support for Violence in Latin America," *Special Report No. 90* (Washington, D.C.: U.S. Department of State, December 14, 1981) pp. 212–13.

28. *Strategic Situation in Central America*, p. 4.

29. Ibid.

30. Radio Havana, July 10, 1981.

31. Interview with Mark Isaac, minister-counselor, Embassy of Grenada (Washington, D.C.), December 20, 1985. See also *Indies Times*, July 20, 1985, p. 1.

32. As early as 1963, Marshal V. D. Sokolovskiy had written that "The CPSU and all the Soviet people . . . consider it our duty to support the sacred struggle of oppressed peoples and their just wars of liberation against imperialism. This duty the Soviet Union discharges . . . by helping the peoples . . . not only ideologically and politically but materially as well." (*Soviet Military Strategy*, 1st and 2nd eds.). In the 3rd edition of *Soviet Military Strategy*, published in 1968, Sokolovskiy added the sentence: "The USSR will render, when it is necessary, military support, as well, to people subject to imperialist aggression." See V. D. Sokolovskiy, *Soviet Military Strategy*, ed. Harriet Fast Scott (New York: Crane, Russak and Co., 1975), pp. 168, 183–84.

33. I. Shavrov, "Local Wars and Their Place in the Global Strategy of Imperialism," in *The Soviet Union and the Arms Race*, David Holloway, ed. (New Haven: Yale University Press, 1983), p. 87.

34. Ibid.

35. N. I. Gavtilov and G. V. Statushenko, eds., *Africa: Problems of Socialist Orientation* (Moscow: Nauka, 1976), p. 10.

36. Karen N. Brutents, *National Liberation Revolutions Today: I* (Moscow: Progress Publishers, 1977). In Robert S. Leiken, *Soviet Strategy in Latin America* (New York: Praeger, 1982).

37. Adam B. Ulam, *Expansion and Coexistence (New York: Praeger, 1971), pp. 135–36, 448. See also Anton Antonov-Oveseyenko, The Time of Stalin* (New York: Harper and Row), 1980), p. 214.

38. U.S. Department of the Navy, *Understanding Soviet Naval Developments* (Washington, D.C.: Office of the Chief of Naval Operations, 1981), p. 26. See also Theberge, *Russia in the Caribbean*, p. 97.

39. *Krasnaia zvezda*, December 2, 1969, in Mose L. Harvey, *Soviet Combat Troops in Cuba* (Miami: Advanced International Studies Institute, 1979), p. 27.

40. Henry A. Kissinger, *The White House Years* (Boston: Little, Brown and Co., 1979), p. 636.

41. *Pravda*, July 13, 1960. Quoted in Mose L. Harvey, *Soviet Combat Troops in Cuba* (Miami: Advanced International studies Institute, 1979), p. 13.

42. Public Law 87–733, "A Joint Resolution Expressing the Determination of the United States with Respect to the Situation in Cuba," approved October 3, 1962.

43. U.S. Congress, House Committee on Armed Services, Subcommittee on Air Defense of the Southeastern United States, *Air Defense of Southeastern United States* (HASC No. 91–39), pp.11–32.

44. Ibid.

45. U.S. Congress, House Committee on Foreign Affairs, Subcommittee on Inter-American Affairs, *Cuba and the Caribbean*. Statement of G. Warren Nutter, assistant secretary of defense for international security affairs, July 13, 1970, p. 104.

46. "L. I. Brezhnev meets with R. Castro," *Pravda*, May 13, 1970, p. 1.

47. Theberge, *Russia in the Caribbean*, p. 107. See also U.S. Congress, House Committee on Foreign Affairs, *Cuba and the Caribbean*, p. 105.

48. Leon Goure and Morris Rothenberg, *Soviet Penetration of Latin America* (Washington, D.C.: Advanced International Studies Institute, 1975), p. 31. See also U.S. Congress, House Committee on Foreign Affairs, *Cuba and the Caribbean*, p. 104.

49. Kissinger, *White House Years*, p. 637.

50. Ibid.

51. James D. Theberge, ed., *Soviet Seapower in the Caribbean: Political and Strategic Implications* (New York: Praeger, 1972), p. 53. See also U.S. Congress, House Committee on Foreign Relations, Subcommittee on Inter-American Affairs, *Soviet Naval Activities in Cuba* (Washington, D.C.: September 30, October 13, November 19 and 24, 1970).

52. Richard M. Nixon, *The Memoirs of Richard Nixon* (New York: Grosset and

Dunlop, 1978), pp. 486–89. See also George Quester, "Missiles in Cuba—1970," *Foreign Affairs* (April 1971).

53. Christopher A. Abel, "A Breach in the Ramparts," *Naval Institute Proceedings* (July 1980): 49.

54. Quoted in *Russia in the Caribbean* Theberge, p. 151.

55. *International Herald Tribune* (Paris), January 9–10, 1971. See also Barry M. Blechman and Stephanie E. Levinson, "Soviet Submarine Visits to Cuba," *Naval Institute Proceedings* (September 1975): 31–35.

56. Kissinger, *White House Years,* p. 651.

57. Ibid, p. 637.

58. Ibid, p. 651.

59. Leslie J. Fenlon, Jr., "The Umpteenth Cuban Confrontation," *Naval Institute Proceedings* (July 1980): 44.

60. The Pentagon responded to this incident by stating: "this looks like steady escalation. All that's left now is for them to bring in a nuclear sub with ballistic missiles and they'll be crowding the so-called 'understanding' between us. . . ." Quoted in *New York Times,* May 5, 1972, p. 4.

61. For an excellent analysis of this incident see Harold W. Rood, *Kingdoms of the Blind* (Durham, N.C.: Carolina Academic Press, 1980), pp. 109–22.

62. Rowland Evans, Jr., and Robert D. Novak, *Nixon in the White House* (New York: Random House, 1971), pp. 406–7.

63. Abel, "A Breach in the Ramparts," p. 50.

64. Ibid. See also U.S. Congress, House Committee on Foreign Affairs, Subcommittee on Inter-american Affairs, *Impact of Cuban–Soviet Ties in the Western Hemisphere* (March 26, 27; and May 14, 1980), p. 7.

65. Abel, "A Breach in the Ramparts," p. 50.

66. *New York Times,* March 28, 1978, p. 9. See also *Congressional Record–Senate,* "Testimony of Senator Steve Symms," April 25, 1983, Vol. 129, no. 53, pp. S5233–37.

67. Quoted in *New York Times,* February 11, 1979, p. 11.

68. U.S. Congress, House Committee on Foreign Affairs, *Impact of Cuban–Soviet Ties,* p. 6.

69. Quoted in *Economist,* September 15, 1979, p. 38.

70. *Congressional Record–Senate,* September 17 to September 27, 1979, vol. 125, nos. 119 to 129, S13213, S13440, S13533.

71. "Testimony of Senator Steve Symms," pp. S5233–37. See also Christopher Whalen, "The Soviet Military Buildup in Cuba," Heritage Foundation *Backgrounder* (June 11, 1982): 6–7.

72. U.S. Congress, House Committee on Foreign Affairs, *Impact of Cuban–Soviet Ties,* p. 7.

73. Quoted in *Economist,* September 15, 1979, p. 38.

74. *New York Times,* February 15, 1983.

75. *Soviet Military Power 1985* (Washington, D.C.: U.S. Department of Defense), p. 120.

76. "Testimony of Senator Steve Symms," pp. S5233–37.

77. _The Soviet-Cuban Connection in Central America and the Caribbean_ (Washington, D.C.: U.S. Departments of State and Defense, March 1985), p. 4.
78. _Baltimore Sun,_ June 27, 1982, p. 9.
79. "Testimony of Senator Steve Symms," pp. S5233–37.
80. _Defense and Foreign Affairs Handbook, 1985_ (Washington, D.C.: Perth Corporation, 1985), p. 158.
81. Joseph A. Douglass and Amoretta H. Hoeber, _Soviet Strategy for Nuclear War_ (Stanford: Hoover Institution Press, 1979), p. 6.
82. _The Soviet–Cuban Connection in Central America and the Caribbean_ (Washington, D.C.: U.S. Departments of state and Defense, March 1985), pp. 3–4. See also Richelson, _Sword and Shield,_ pp. 100–101.
83. Ibid.
84. _Soviet Military Power 1984,_ p. 126. See also William J. Broad, "Evading the Soviet Ear at Glen Cove," _Science_ (September 1982): 910–11.
85. U.S. Congress, Senate Committee on Commerce, Science, and Technology, _Soviet Space Programs 1976–1980, Part I,_ (Washington, D.C.: 1976), p. 124.
86. "Testimony of Senator Steve Symms," pp. S5233–37. See also Whalen, "The Soviet Military Buildup in Cuba," p. 7.
87. _Congressional Record–House,_ "Presence of Soviet Combat Troops in Cuba," September 17 to September 26, 1979, H7956, H8411, H8576, H8746, E4811. See also "Testimony of Senator Steve Symms," pp. S5233–37.
88. "Soviet–Cuban Buildup Told," _San Francisco Chronicle,_ June 10, 1983, p. 22. See also _Soviet–Cuban Connection,_ p. 6.
89. "Testimony of Senator Steve Symms," pp. S5233–37. Additional information from tape-recorded interrogation of Cuban DGI defector provided by Brigadier General Albion W. Knight, U.S. Army (ret'd.), September 21, 1983.
90. Ibid.
91. _Krasnaia zvezda,_ January 1, 1969, p. 2.
92. _Soviet–Cuban Connection,_ p. 9.
93. Ibid, p. 6.
94. "Cuban Armed Forces and the Soviet Military Presence," _Special Report No. 103_ (Washington, D.C.: U.S. Department of State, August 1982), p. 3.
95. _Soviet–Cuban Connection,_ p. 3.
96. Edward Gonzalez, _A Strategy for Dealing with Cuba in the 1980s_ (Santa Monica: Rand Corporation R-2954-DOS/AF, September 1982), p. 6.
97. Robert S. Leiken and M. Vego, "The Cuban Navy 1959–1982," _Navy International_ (May 1983): 1064.
98. Ibid.
99. _Understanding Soviet Naval Developments,_ pp. 42–43.
100. Thomas D. Anderson, _Geopolitics of the Caribbean_ (Stanford: Hoover Institution Press, 1984), p. 121.
101. _The Military Balance, 1983–1984_ (London: International Institute for Strategic Studies, 1983), p. 119.

102. U.S. Congress, House Committee on Foreign Affairs, *Impact of Cuban–Soviet Ties*, p. 21. See also R Bruce McColm, "Central America and the Caribbean: The larger Scenario," *Strategic Review* (Summer 1983): 34.

103. *Soviet–Cuban Connection*, pp. 8–9.

104. Ibid.

105. Arkady N. Shevchenko, *Breaking with Moscow* (New York: Alfred A. Knopf, 1985), pp. 271–72.

106. See testimony of Assistant Secretary of State Elliott Abrams, Jr., before the Subcommittee on Western Hemisphere Affairs of the House Foreign Affairs Committee, December 5, 1985.

107. Boris Ponomarev, "Topical Problems of the Theory of the Revolutionary Process," *Kommunist* (October 1971): 75. Ponomarev, a candidate Politburo member and chief of the CPSU Central Committee's International Department, was also secretary for liaison with all nonruling communist parties.

Chapter 4. Grenada

1. Interview with Donald Street, St. George's, Grenada, April 18, 1980.

2. Interview with General Wallace H. Nutting in *Attack on the Americas* (documentary), (American Security Council Foundation, 1982).

3. *BP Statistical Review of the World's Oil Industry* (London, 1980).

4. Gregory Sandford and Richard Vigilante, *Grenada: The Untold Story* (Lanham, Md. Madison Books, 1984), p. 28.

5. Ibid.

6. "Guidelines for Caribbean Conference in Martinique, February 11–15, 1972 in *Grenada Documents* (Washington, D.C.: National Archives, (G.D., unnumbered).

7. "Minutes of JEWEL Meeting, Jan. 7, 1973; 'A Review of the Organizational Structure of the NJM. Paper to be presented to the 1st International Conference of Grenadians to be held in Grenada from 23rd–26th August 1974'," (G.D., unnumbered).

8. *Grenada Documents: An Overview and Selection* (Washington, D.C.: U.S. Departments of State and Defense, September 8, 1984): "Line of March for the Party, 13th September 1982."

9. *Grenada: A Preliminary Report* (Washington, D.C.: U.S. Departments of State and Defense, December 16, 1983), p. 7.

10. Sandford and Vigilante, *Grenada*, p. 54.

11. Based on author's conversations with numerous Grenadians, including Ambassador Albert Xavier, Alva James, Leslie Pierre, Sir Eric Gairy, and others, including members of the PRA.

12. Albert Xavier, "Plotting That Had the Eastern Caribbean on Edge," *Wall Street Journal*, November 1, 1983, p. 30.

13. U.S. Department of State, *U.S.–Grenada Relations since the Coup: A Background Paper,* by Lawrence G. Rossin (case control no. 8402598, Amembassy, Bridgetown, Barbados, January 17, 1983), p. 18.
14. *Forward Ever!: Three Years of the Grenadian Revolution* (Sidney: Pathfinder Press, 1982), p. 12.
15. *Congressional Record–House,* vol. 123, pt. 17, p. 20620, June 23, 1977.
16. "Line of March for the Party," p. 49.
17. "General Political Factors to be Considered" (G.D., undated, unnumbered).
18. *U.S.–Grenada Relations,* p. 16.
19. Ibid, p. 7.
20. "Report of Mission to Moscow 3rd to 10th December, 1981," (G.D. no. 103068), p. 4.
21. *Grenada Documents,* "Meeting between Chiefs of Staff of Soviet Armed Forces and the People's Revolutionary Armed Forces of Grenada, 10 March 1983" (doc. no. 24).
22. "Record of Meeting between Prime Minister Maurice Bishop and First Deputy Prime Minister and Minister of Foreign Affairs Andrei Gromyko at the Kremlin April 15th, 1983" (G.D. no. 104261), pp. 3–4.
23. *Grenada Documents,* "Top Secret Agreement between Grenada and the USSR" (doc. no. 13).
24. Ibid., "Letter to Maurice Bishop from Gail Reed" (doc. no. 31).
25. Ibid., "Minutes of the Political Bureau Meeting, Wednesday, 7th April, 1982" (doc. no. 77).
26. "Minutes of the Political Bureau Meeting Wednesday, 15th December 1982" (G.D., unnumbered).
27. *Grenada Documents,* "Comrades to Complete Five (5) Years by March 13th '84" (doc. no. 10).
28. *Grenada: A Preliminary Report,* p. 9.
29. *Torchlight,* St. George's, Grenada, March 18, 1979.
30. *U.S.–Grenada Relations,* p. 18.
31. "Material Means Received from Foreign Countries, within the Period 1979–81," September 9, 1981 (G.D. no. 102170).
32. The author visited the La Sagesse training school in January 1980 with a dissident relative of Maurice Bishop. The facility had only recently been abandoned by Cuban instructors and still contained revolutionary posters, torn pages from guerrilla warfare manuals, and copies of *Granma.*
33. *Advocate-News,* May 18, 1979, p. 1.
34. *Trinidad Guardian,* January 9, 1980, p. 1.; FBIS Latin America, January 14, 1980.
35. *Newsweek,* March 31, 1980, p. 22.
36. *Daily Gleaner,* November 21, 1979, p. 9; FBIS Latin America, November 28, 1979.
37. *Grenada Documents,* "Report from Moscow Embassy, June 1982" (doc. no. 29), p. 3.
38. Ibid., "Summary of Prime Minister's Meeting with Soviet Ambassador, 24th May, 1983" (doc. no. 21).

39. *Grenada: A Preliminary Report,* p. 8.
40. *Free West Indian,* April 19, 1980.
41. *Grenada Documents,* "Grenada's Relations with the USSR, July 11, 1983,"by W. Richard Jacobs (doc. no. 26).
42. *Advocate–News,* January 25, 1980; FBIS Latin America, January 30, 1980.
43. *Pravda,* May 31, 1980; FBIS Soviet Union, June 5, 1980.
44. Havana International Service, June 25, 1980; FBIS Latin America, June 25, 1980.
45. *Newsweek,* March 31, 1980, p. 22.
46. *Miami Herald,* March 14, 1980.
47. *Free West Indian,* March 28, 1981.
48. *Grenadian,* July 1981, p. 2.
49. "Material Means" (G.D. no. 102170).
50. *News Briefing on Intelligence Information on External Support of the Guerrillas in El Salvador* (Washington, D.C.: U.S. Departments of State Defense, August 8, 1984), pp. 16–17.
51. Letter to Raúl Castro Ruz, November 14, 1981 (G.D. no. 102647).
52. Tass, July 28, 1982; FBIS Soviet Union, July 29, 1982.
53. Ibid.
54. *Cana* (Barbados), July 28, 1982; FBIS Soviet Union, July 29, 1982.
55. Radio Free Grenada, August 5, 1982; FBIS Latin America, August 2, 1982.
56. *Miami Herald,* March 17, 1983, p. 1A.
57. *Grenada: A Preliminary Report,* p. 10.
58. *Grenada Documents,* "Top Secret Agreement between Grenada and the USSR, July 27, 1982" (doc. no. 14).
59. Ibid., "Report from Grenada Embassy in Moscow on Grenada's Relations with the USSR, July 11, 1983" (doc. no. 26).
60. Ibid., "Letter to Commander Andropov from General of the Army Hudson Austin, February 17, 1982" (doc. no. 27).
61. Ibid., "Report to Bishop from Moscow Embassy, June 30, 1982," (doc. no. 29).
62. Ibid., "Grenada's Relations with the USSR, July 11, 1983" (doc. no. 26), p. 2.
63. Ibid., "Report to Bishop from Moscow Embassy, June 30, 1982" (doc. no. 29), p. 2.
64. Ibid.
65. Ibid.
66. Ibid., "Grenada's Relations with the USSR, July 11, 1983" (doc. no. 26), p. 5.
67. Ibid., "Report to Bishop from Moscow Embassy, June 30, 1982" (doc. no. 29), p. 2.
68. Richard F. Staar, *USSR Foreign Policies after Detente* (Stanford: Hoover Institution Press, 1985), p. 30.
69. *Grenada Documents,* "Report to Bishop from Moscow Embassy, June 30, 1982" (doc. no. 29), p. 3.
70. This information is based on complaints made in Grenada during early 1983

by Gail Reed to several Grenadian residents not wishing to be identified. Ms. Reed blamed this action on Bernard Coard.

71. *Cana,* March 14, 1983; FBIS Latin America, March 15, 1983.
72. "Minutes of the NJM Central Committee," undated (G.D. no. 100278), p. 5.
73. "Minutes of Meeting of Committee of Economic Ministers Held on 9th May, 1983" (G.D. no. 100719), p. 5.
74. "On the Possible Establishment of a State Trading Corporation for Effecting Grenada's Trade with the Socialist Countries," undated (G.D. no. 100013), p. 10.
75. *Cana,* May 14, 1983; FBIS Latin America, May 17, 1983.
76. *Free West Indian,* May 21, 1983, p. 3.
77. *Cana,* March 14, 1983; FBIS Latin America, March 15, 1983.
78. Radio Free Grenada, June 15, 1983; FBIS Latin America, June 17, 1983.
79. *Cana,* March 14, 1983; FBIS Latin America, March 15, 1983.
80. *Grenada Documents,* "Grenada's Relations with the USSR" (doc. no. 26), p. 4.
81. Sandford and Vigilante, *Grenada: The Untold Story,* p. 175.
82. Ibid.
83. *Washington Post,* June 19, 1984.
84. *Grenada: A Preliminary Report,* p. 30.
85. Grenada Documents, "Page from Liam James' Notebook" (doc. no. 23).
86. *Grenada: A Preliminary Report,* p. 30.
87. "Minutes of the Political Bureau Dated 22nd June 1983" (G.D. no. 100291).
88. *Grenada Documents,* "Summary of Prime Minister's Meeting with Soviet Ambassador—24th May, 1983" (doc. no. 21), p. 3.
89. "Minutes of Organising Committee, 18-4-83" (G.C. no. 100718).
90. *Grenada Documents,* "Meeting between Chiefs of General Staff, March 10, 1983," (doc. no. 24), p. 4.
91. *Grenada: A Preliminary Report,* p. 20.
92. *Grenada Documents,* "Note from Grenadian Ambassador in Cuba, 18, 2, 82" (doc. no. 18).

Chapter 5. The Role of Nicaragua in Soviet Strategy for the Caribbean

1. Interview with Humberto Belli, Washington, D.C., January 15, 1986. See also David Nolan, *The Ideology of the Sandinistas and the Nicaraguan Revolution* (Coral Gables, Florida: Institute of Interamerican Studies, University of Miami, 1984), pp. 17–20.
2. Ibid.
3. Information from Dr. Antonio Ybarra-Rojas, Humberto Belli, and Arturo Cruz.
4. Nolan, *Ideology of the Sandinistas,* p. 20.

5. Humberto Belli, *Breaking Faith* (Garden City, Mich.: The Puebla Institute, 1985), p. 8.
6. Douglas W. Payne, "The 'Mantos' of Sandinista Deception," *Strategic Review* (Spring 1985): 12.
7. Nolan, *Ideology of the Sandinistas,* p. 20.
8. Information from Dr. Antonio Ybarra-Rojas.
9. Information from Humberto Belli.
10. Interview with Tomás Borge in *Playboy,* September 1983, p. 60.
11. Interview with Humberto Belli, Washington, D.C., March 5, 1986.
12. FSLN National Directorate, *Nicaragua: On the General Political–Military Platform of Struggle of the Sandinista Front for National Liberation for the Triumph of the Sandinista Revolution,* 1977.
13. "What the Sandinistas Say about Sandinismo," *White House Digest,* June 20, 1984, p. 2.
14. "Line of March For the Party," *Grenada Documents: An Overview and Selection* (Washington, D.C.: U.S. Departments of State and Defense, September 1984) (doc. no. 1).
15. U.S. Department of State *Airgram,* December 26, 1979, from: Amembassy Managua; Subject: "The 72-hour Document: An FSLN Blueprint"; reference no. Managua 6189, pp. 1–4.
16. Ibid., p. 4.
17. Ibid.
18. Ibid.
19. "What the Sandinistas Say," p. 3.
20. U.S. Department of State, *Comandante Bayardo Arce's Secret Speech before the Nicaraguan Socialist Party (PSN)* (Washington, D.C.: March 1985), pp. 5–6.
21. Ibid.
22. Ibid.
23. *Barricada,* April 25, 1983, p. 2.
24. Speech to the Sandinista military, quoted by Branko Lazitch in *Est Et Ouest* (Paris), August 25, 1981.
25. Stephen de Mowbray, "Soviet Deception and the Onset of the Cold War," *Encounter* (July–August 1984): 57–58.
26. Interviews with Humberto Belli and Ambassador Albert Xavier.
27. Payne, "The 'Mantos' of Sandinista Deception," p. 11.
28. U.S. Department of State, *The Sandinistas and Middle Eastern Radicals* (Washington, D.C.: August 1985), p. 1.
29. Interview with Comandante Adolfo Chamorro, Washington, D.C., January 28, 1986.
30. Interviews with Humberto Belli, Antonio Ybarra-Rojas and Adolfo Chamorro.
31. I. Shavrov, "Local Wars and Their Place in the Global Strategy of Imperialism" in *The Soviet Union and the Arms Race,* David Holloway, ed. (New Haven: Yale University Press, 1983), pp. 83–94.

32. Payne, "The 'Mantos' of Sandinista Deception," p. 15. Information also from Humberto Belli.

33. Nolan, *Ideology of the Sandinistas,* p. 72. Information also from Humberto Belli, Alfonso Robelo, Arturo Cruz, and Leonel Teller.

34. Interview with Arturo Cruz and Adolfo Calero, Washington, D.C., March 5, 1986.

35. Information from Edén Pastora, Comandante Adolfo Chamorro, and Antonio Ybarra-Rojas.

36. Bernard Diederich, *Somoza: And the Legacy of U.S. Involvement in Central America* (New York: E. P. Dutton, 1981), p. 221. Information also from Humberto Belli.

37. U.S. Congress, House Committee on Foreign Affairs, Subcommittee on Inter-American Affairs, *Impact of Cuban–Soviet Ties in the Western Hemisphere, Spring 1979* (Washington, D.C., April 25 and 26, 1979), p. 6.

38. Ambassador Thomas R. Pickering and General Paul F. Gorman, *News Briefing on Intelligence Information on External Support of the Guerrillas in El Salvador* (Washington, D.C.: U.S. Departments of State and Defense, August 8, 1984), p. 15.

39. Uri Ra'anan, Robert L. Pfaltzgraff, Jr., Richard Shultz, Ernst Halperin, and Igor Lukes, eds., *Hydra of Carnage* (Lexington, Mass.: Lexington Books, 1986). Testimony of Edén Pastora Gómez, p. 324.

40. *Strategic Situation in Central America and the Caribbean,* current policy no. 352 (Washington, D.C.: U.S. Department of State, December 14, 1981), p. 6.

41. *Background Paper: Central America* (Washington, D.C.: U.S. Departments of State and Defense, May 27, 1983), p. 3.

42. Interview with former DGSE Special Investigator Alvaro José Baldizon Aviles, U.S. Department of State, October 11, 1985.

43. Ra'anan et al., *Hydra of Carnage,* testimony of Miguel Bolanos Hunter, pp. 311–12.

44. Ibid.

45. Speech by CIA Director William Casey to the San Antonio, Texas, World Business Council, *Washington Times,* May 17, 1985, p. 8A.

46. Ra'anan et al., *Hydra of Carnage,* pp. 313–14.

47. Ibid., p. 319. Information also from Comandante Adolfo Chamorro and Arturo Cruz.

48. FBIS Latin America, November 16, 1979, pp. P1–2.

49. Ibid.

50. FBIS Latin America, January 29, 1980, p. P7.

51. Cleto Di Giovanni, Jr., and Mose L. Harvey, *Crisis in Central America* (Coral Gables, Fla.: Advanced International Studies Institute, University of Miami, 1982), pp. 85–86. See also *Grenada Documents,* "Agreement in Cooperation between the New Jewel Movement and the Communist Party of the Soviet Union, Moscow, July 27, 1982" (G.D. no. 103902).

52. Quoted in Di Giovanni and Harvey, *Crisis in Central America*, p. 86.
53. Ibid.
54. Ibid. See also *Grenada Documents*, "Agreement between the Government of Grenada and the Government of the Soviet Socialist Republics on deliveries from the Union of SSR to Grenada of special and other equipment" (doc. no. 14–2).
55. CANA, December 19, 1985; FBIS Latin America, December 23, 1985, p. T1.
56. Ra'anan et al., *Hydra of Carnage*, p. 327. Information also from Comandante Adolfo Chamorro and Humberto Belli,
57. ibid.
58. *Background Paper: Nicaragua's Military Buildup and Support for Central American Subversion* (Washington, D.C.: U.S. Departments of State and Defense, July 18, 1984).
59. FBIS Latin America, April 16, 1980, p. P7.
60. Quoted in Di Giovanni and Harvey, *Crisis in Central America*, pp. 87–88.
61. FBIS Latin America, October 31, 1980, p. P9.
62. FBIS Latin America, August 1, 1980, p. P15.
63. Ibid.
64. FBIS Latin America, June 10, 1981, p. P6.
65. FBIS Latin America, June 19, 1981, p. P6.
66. FBIS Latin America, June 30, 1981, p. P11.
67. *Background Paper: Central America*, p. 15.
68. Ibid.
69. *Background Paper: Nicaragua's Military Buildup*, pp. 8–9.
70. *Background Paper: Central America*, p. 15.
71. *National Review*, April 29, 1983, p. 500. Information confirmed by Arturo Cruz and Jorge Salaverry.
72. Associated Press, March 17, 1983 and April 14, 1983. See also *New York Times*, April 26, 1983.
73. *San Francisco Chronicle*, June 8, 1983, p. C2. See also remarks by Dr. Fred C. Ikle, under secretary of defense for policy, at American Security Council White House Briefing, August 26, 1983.
74. *Times-Picayune*, May 27, 1984, p. 14.
75. *Barricada*, February 20, 1983, p. 5.
76. *El Nuevo Diario* (Managua), December 3, 1983, p. 2.
77. FBIS Latin America, July 12, 1983, p. P.25.
78. *La Prensa Libre* (San José, Costa Rica), March 25, 1983. See also *Washington Times*, April 29, 1983.
79. FBIS Latin America, July 15, 1983, p. P17.
80. *Barricada*, June 14, 1983, p. 6.
81. *Sotsialisticheskaya industriya*, June 19, 1983; FBIS Soviet Union, June 23, 1983, p. K1.
82. *Background Paper: Nicaragua's Military Buildup*, p. 11.

83. *Bohemia,* February 7, 1983, pp. 72–75.
84. Remarks of Nestor D. Sanchez, ASC Seminar, Washington, D.C., August 26, 1983, p. 7.
85. U.S. Congress, Senate Foreign Relations Committee, Subcommittee on Western Hemisphere Affairs, *Review of the President's Report on Assistance to the Nicaraguan Opposition,* 99th Cong., 1st sess., hearing, December 5, 1985, pp. 25, 32.
86. Ibid.
87. Tass, July 29, 1983; FBIS Soviet Union, August 1, 1983, p. K1.
88. Havana Domestic Service, August 3, 1983; FBIS Latin America, August 4, 1983, p. P10.
89. Managua Domestic Service, March 11, 1985; FBIS Latin America, March 12, 1985.
90. Information from William Pascoe III, Washington, D.C., August 4, 1986.
91. *Miami Herald,* June 21, 1983. See also *New York Times,* June 19, 1983.
92. *New York times,* July 27, 1983.
93. *Daily Telegraph,* July 30, 1983, pp. 1, 24.
94. FBIS Latin America, July 20, 1983, pp. A4, A5.
95. *Barricada,* September 25, 1983, p. 1.
96. *The Soviet–Cuban Connection in Central America and the Caribbean* (Washington, D.C.: U.S. Departments of State and Defense, March 1985), p. 23.
97. San José Radio Impacto, July 11, 1985; FBIS Latin America, July 12, 1985.
98. *Jane's All the World's Aircraft, 1984–1985* (London, 1984), pp. 233–34.
99. *Washington Post,* August 17, 1983, p. A4.
100. *Soviet–Cuban Connection* p. 27.
101. Ibid., p. 28.
102. Remarks of Nestor D. Sanchez, deputy assistant secretary of defense for inter-American affairs, American Security Council Speakers Bureau, Washington, D.C., August 26, 1983. See also testimony by Dr. Fred C. Ikle, under secretary of defense for policy, Senate Foreign Relations Committee, Subcommittee on Western Hemisphere Affairs, December 15, 1981, p. 7.
103. Ibid.
104. FBIS Latin America, January 29, 1980, p. P7.
105. *Nation,* November 24, 1984, p. 540.
106. "What the Sandinistas Say," p. 3.
107. "Nicaragua and the World," *Christianity and Crisis* (May 12, 1980): 141.
108. *New York* magazine, September 12, 1983, quoted in *White House Digest,* June 20, 1984, p. 4.
109. ANN (Managua), May 23, 1985; FBIS Latin America, May 29, 1985.
110. *Playboy,* September 1983, p. 192.
111. "What the Sandinistas Say," p. 4.
112. *El Tiempo* (Bogotá), December 20, 1985, p. 8a; FBIS Latin America, December 26, 1985, p. F1.
113. *Diario las Americas,* December 22, 1985, pp. 1, 15A.

114. *El Tiempo,* December 20, 1985, p. 8a.
115. *El Espectador* (Bogotá), December 20, 1985 pp. 1A, 13A; FBIs Latin America, December 30, 1985, p. F2.
116. Emisoras Caracol Network (Bogotá), January 4, 1985; FBIS Latin America, January 6, 1985, p. F1.
117. Interview with Alvaro Baldizon, U.S. Department of State, October 11, 1985.
118. Michael S. Radu, *The Origins and Evolution of the Nicaraguan Insurgencies, 1979–1985* (Philadelphia: Foreign Policy Research Institute, March 1986).

Chapter 6. The Cases of El Salvador and Honduras

1. *Background Paper: Central America* (Washington, D.C.: U.S. Department of State and Defense, May 27, 1983), p. 5.
2. Ibid.
3. Ibid, p. 6.
4. Ibid.
5. Ibid.
6. Ibid., p. 7.
7. See *The Challenge to Democracy in Central America* (Washington, D.C.: U.S. Departments of State and Defense, June 1986).
8. *Background Paper: Central America.*
9. *Washington Post,* June 8, 1985, p. A12.
10. *Washington Post,* December 20, 1985, p. A49.
11. Transcript of press briefing by Elliott Abrams, assistant secretary of state for inter-American Affairs, on evidence of Nicaraguan subversion in Central America, December 19, 1985.
12. *Miami Herald,* July 14, 1985, p. A21.
13. Transcript of Republican Study Committee briefing with Alejandro Montenegro, Washington, D.C., July 12, 1984.
14. Ibid.
15. *Background Paper: Nicaragua's Military Buildup and Support for Central American Subversion* (Washington, D.C.: U.S. Departments of State and Defense, July 18, 1984), p. 27.
16. Ibid.
17. Ibid., p. 9.
18. *Background Paper: Central America,* p. 9.
19. Ibid.
20. Uri Ra'anan, Rober L. Pfaltzgraff, Jr., Richard Shultz, Ernst Halperin, and Igor Lukes, eds., *Hydra of Carnage* (Lexington, Mass.: Lexington Books, 1986), p. 318.
21. Ibid.

Chapter 7. Jamaica, Guyana, and Suriname

1. *Albuquerque Journal,* July 21, 1985, p. B5.
2. Paris International Service, July 25, 1985; FBIS Latin America, July 26, 1985.
3. CANA, July 13, 1985; FBIS Latin America, July 17, 1985.
4. Robert Wesson, ed., *Communism in Central America and the Caribbean* (Stanford: Hoover Institution Press, 1982), p. 124.
5. *Daily Gleaner,* November 2, 1983, p. 11.
6. *Keesing's Contemporary Archives,* July 27, 1979, p. 297478.
7. Agence France-Presse (AFP), May 16, 1981; FBIS Latin America, May 16, 1981.
8. Robert Moss, "The Intelligence War," *Daily Telegraph* (London), November 7, 1980, p. 2.
9. Martin Weinstein, ed., *Revolutionary Cuba in the World Arena* (Philadelphia: Institute for the Study of Human Issues, 1979).
10. *Strategic Situation in Central America and the Caribbean,* current policy no. 352 (Washington, D.C.: U.S. Department of State, December 14, 1981), p. 9.
11. *Daily Gleaner,* November 17, 1971, p. 1.
12. *New York Times,* August 15, 1984, p. A2.
13. Leo A. Despres, *Cultural Pluralism and National Politics in British Guiana* (Chicago: Rand-McNally, 1967), p. 209.
14. Kenneth M. Glazier, "Guyana," in *World Communism: A Handbook, 1918–1965,* Wilton S. Sworakowski, ed. (Stanford: Hoover Institution Press, 1973), p. 180.
15. Robert H. Manley, *Guyana Emergent* (Cambridge, Mass.: Schenkman Publishing Co., 1979), p. 6.
16. Despres, *Cultural Pluralism,* pp., 217–20.
17. Geoffrey Wagner, "Guyana: The Basket Case Economy," *Grenadian Voice,* November 30, 1985, p. 13.
18. Richard F. Staar, ed., *Yearbook on International Communist Affairs, 1971* (Stanford: Hoover Institution Press, 1971), pp. 446–47.
19. Ibid.
20. William E. Ratliff, "Guyana," in Wesson, *Communism in Central America,* p. 153.
21. Richard F. Staar, ed., *Yearbook on International Communist Affairs, 1976* (Stanford: Hoover Institution Press, 1976), p. 489.
22. Cole Blasier, *The Giant's Rival: The USSR and Latin America* (Pittsburgh: University of Pittsburgh Press, 1983), p. 48.
23. James Reston, Jr., *Our Father Who Art in Hell* (New York: Times Books, 1981), pp. 168–204. See also *Washington Post,* February 1, 1979.
24. Ronald E. Jones, "Cuba and the English-speaking Caribbean," in *Cuba in the World,* Cole Blasier and Carmelo Mesa-Lago, eds. (Pittsburgh: University of Pittsburgh Press, 1979), p. 140.
25. *Washington Post,* March 13, 1976.

26. Cheddi Jagan, "Report of the Central Committee," in Wesson, *Communism in Central America,* p. 155.
27. Richard F. Staar, ed., *Yearbook on International Communist Affairs, 1982* (Stanford: Hoover Institution Press, 1982), p. 115.
28. U.S. Central Intelligence Agency, *Cuban Chronology 1978–80* (Washington, D.C.: National Foreign Assessment Center, 1981), p. 109.
29. *Strategic Situation,* p. 10.
30. *Cuban Chronology,* p. 109. See also Gregory Sandford and Richard Vigilante, *Grenada: The Untold Story* (Lanham, Md.: Madison Books, 1984), pp. 54–55.
31. Richard F. Staar, ed., *Yearbook on International Communist Affairs, 1985* (Stanford: Hoover Institution Press, 1985), p. 97.
32. *Cuban Chronology,* p. 109.
33. Jay Mallin, "Cuban Intelligence Elite Pushes Subversion in Americas," *Washington Times,* August 25, 1983, p. 7A. Further information from Sridatt Lakhan and Motarak Ali of the Conservative Liberal Party of Guyana.
34. *Guyana Chronicle* (Georgetown), March 22, 1983, p. 3.
35. *Guyana Chronicle,* April 7, 1983, p. 1.
36. *Bohemia* (November 1984, pp. 76–77.
37. Based on interviews with Prime Minister Eugenia Charles, Ambassador Albert Xavier, and Grenada Advisory Council Chairman Nicholas Braithwaite.
38. Wagner, "Guyana: Basket Case Economy," p. 13.
39. *New York Times,* July 6, 1984, p. A5.
40. *Sunday Chronicle,* (Georgetown), November 13, 1983, pp. 1, 6.
41. *The Military Balance, 1985–1986* (London: International Institute for Strategic Studies, 1985), p. 150.
42. *Spotlight* (Georgetown), November 15, 1981.
43. *Mirror* (Georgetown), February 27, 1983, p. 1.
44. Gregory R. Copley, ed., *Defense and Foreign Affairs Handbook, 1985* (Washington, D.C.: Copley and Associates, 1985), p. 274.
45. CANA, Oct. 19, 1985; FBIS Latin America, October 22, 1985, p. T1.
46. CANA, July 20, 1985; FBIS Latin America, July 23, 1985, p. VI.
47. *Defense and Foreign Affairs Handbook, 1985,* p. 274.
48. *Catholic Standard* (Georgetown), November 11, 1984, p. 1.
49. AFP August 6, 1985; FBIS Latin America, August 7, 1985, p. T1.
50. CANA, August 12, 1985; FBIS Latin America, August 13, 1985, p. T1.
51. CANA, July 12, 1986, FBIS Latin America, July 15, 1986, p. T1.
52. *Pravda,* August 27, 1985, p. 4; FBIS Soviet Union, August 29, 1985, p. K1.
53. *Guyana Chronicle,* December 5, 1984, pp. 1.8.
54. Bonaire Trans World Radio, December 17, 1985; FBIS Latin America, December 18, 1985, p. T1.
55. CANA, December 19, 1985; FBIS Latin America, December 23, 1985, p. T1.
56. CANA, May 14, 1981; FBIS Latin America, May 21, 1981.
57. *Le Monde,* January 7, 1983; FBIS Latin America, January 7, 1983.
58. AFP, December 12, 1982; FBIS Latin America, December 14, 1982.

59. AFP, December 13, 1982; FBIS Latin America, December 14, 1982.
60. Tass, December 14, 1982; FBIS Soviet Union, December 15, 1982.
61. *O Estado de São Paulo,* February 4, 1983, p. 3; FBIS Latin America, February 10, 1983.
62. AFP, February 9, 1983; FBIS Latin America, February 10, 1983.
63. CANA, May 17, 1983; FBIS Latin America, May 19, 1983.
64. AFP, July 11, 1983; FBIS Latin America, July 12, 1983.
65. *Prela* (Havana), February 26, 1985; FBIS Latin America, March 4, 1985, p. 2.

Chapter 8. Summary and Conclusion

1. U.S. Congress, Senate Committee on the Judiciary, Subcommittee on Security and Terrorism, *Historical Antecedents of Soviet Terrorism* (Washington, D.C.: June 11 and 12, 1981), pp. 62–65.
2. *Economist,* September 15, 1979, p. 38.
3. *Pravda,* June 15, 1974. Quoted in Cleto Di Giovanni, Jr., and Mose L. Harvey, *Crisis in Central America* (Miami: Advanced International Studies Institute, 1982), p. 38.
4. Boris N. Ponomarev, "Topical Problems in the Theory of the Revolutionary Process," *Kommunist,* no. 15 (October 1971): 59 (translated with the assistance of Dr. Mikhail Tsypkin).
5. Anatoly A. Gromyko and A. Kokoshin, "U.S. Foreign Strategy for the 1970s," *International Affairs,* no. 10 (October 1973): 71.
6. Sergei Gorshkov, *The Sea Power of the State* (Elmsford, N.Y.: Pergamon Press, 1979), p. 252.
7. Ponomarev, "Topical Problems," p. 75.
8. *Kommunist,* no. 10 (July 1970): 93. Quoted by R. Bruce McColm in "Central America and the Caribbean: The Larger Scenario," *Strategic Review* (Summer 1983): 34.
9. John Bartlow Martin, *U.S. Policy in the Caribbean* (Boulder, Colo.: Westview Press, 1978), p. 138.
10. Harold W. Rood, *Kingdoms of the Blind* (Durham, N.C.: Carolina Academic Press, 1980), p. 127.
11. *Pravda,* March 17, 1982. Quoted in McColm, "Central America and the Caribbean," p. 34.
12. *Congressional Record—Senate,* "Testimony of Senator Steve Symms," April 25, 1983, vol. 129, no. 53, pp. S5233–37.
13. "Record of Meeting between Prime Minister Bishop and First Deputy Prime Minister and Minister of Foreign Affairs Andrei Gromyko at the Kremlin, April 15, 1983," (G.D. no. 104261).
14. Remarks of Assistant Secretary of State Elliott Abrams, The White House, March 14, 1986.

15. *El Tiempo,* (Bogotá), December 20, 1985, p. 8a.
16. Quoted in the *Chicago Tribune,* August 24, 1983, p. 5.
17. Richard Halloran, "Military Forces Stretched Thin, Army Chief Says," *New York Times,* August 10, 1983, pp. 1 and 3A.
18. Sergei Gorshkov, *Naval Power in Soviet Policy* (Moscow: Voenizdat, 1979), pp. 11–12. Quoted in Robert S. Leiken, *Soviet Strategy in Latin America* (New York: Praeger, 1982), p. 64.
19. Rood, *Kingdoms of the Blind,* p. 3.
20. Gorshkov, *Naval Power in Soviet Policy,* pp. 11–12.
21. Quoted in Mario Lazo, *American Policy Failures in Cuba* (New York: Twin Circle Publishing Co., 1968), p. 52.
22. Admiral A. T. Mahan, *The Interests of America in Sea Power Present and Future* (Boston: Little, Brown and Co., 1898), p. 289.
23. Rood, *Kingdoms of the Blind,* p. 109.
24. Admiral of the Fleet S. G. Gorshkov, *Navies in War and in Peace,* excerpted in the U.S. Naval Institute *Proceedings* (March 1974): 52–62.
25. *Report of the President's National Bipartisan Commission on Central America* (Washington, D.C., January 1984), p. 92.
26. *Wall Street Journal,* July 30, 1985, p. 34.
27. Managua Domestic Service, February 21, 1986; FBIS Latin America, February 24, 1986, p. P23.
28. "Contrasting Views on CBI Potential," *Caribbean Today* 2, no. 2 (1985): 32–41.
29. *Albuquerque Journal,* July 21, 1985, p. B5.
30. Irving Louis Horowitz, ed., *Cuban Communism* (New Brunswick, N.J.: Transaction Books, 1985), pp. 213–43.
31. Michael Tatu, *Power in the Kremlin: From Khrushchev to Kosygin* (New York: Viking, 1967), pp. 63–67.
32. Arkady N. Shevchenko, *Breaking with Moscow* (New York: Alfred A. Knopf, 1985), pp. 271–72.
33. Ibid.
34. A. F. Shul'govskii, "Rasstanovka klassovikh sil v vor'be za osvobozhdenie," in *Ekonomicheskie problemy stran Latinskoi Ameriki,* V. Ia. Avarina and M. V. Danilevich, eds. (Moskva: Izdatel'stvo Akademii nauk SSSR, 1963), pp. 482–84. Quoted in Herbert S. Dinerstein, "Soviet Policy in Latin American," *The American Political Science Review* 61 (March 1967): 80–91.
35. M. F. Kudachkin, ed., *Velikii oktiabr' i Kommunisticheskii partii Latinskoi Ameriki* (Moscow: 1978), p. 175 (translated by Dr. Mikhail Tsypkin).
36. Horowitz, *Cuban Communism,* p. 553.
37. Richard F. Staar, ed., *Yearbook on International Communist Affairs, 1985,* (Stanford,: Hoover Institution Press, 1985), pp. 76–77.
38. *La Nacion* (San José), July 17, 1985, p. 6A; FBIS Latin America, July 25, 1985.

39. Jeffrey T. Richelson, *Sword and Shield: Soviet Intelligence and Security Apparatus* (Cambridge, Mass.: Ballinger Publishing Co., 1986), pp. 210–24.

40. U.S. Departments of State and Defense, *Background Paper: Nicaragua's Military Buildup and Support for Central American Subversion* (Washington, D.C.: July 18, 1984), p. 34.

41. U.S. Congress, Senate Committee on the Judiciary, Subcommittee on Western Hemisphere Affairs, *The Cuban Government's Involvement in Facilitating International Drug Traffic* (Washington, D.C., April 30, 1983), pp. 96–99.

42. *Background Paper: Nicaragua's Military Buildup,* pp. 31–32.

43. *El Tiempo* (Bogotá), December 20, 1985, p. 8A; FBIS Latin America, December 26, 1985, p. F1.

44. U.S. Congress, Senate Committee on the Judiciary, *The Cuban Government's Involvement in Facilitating International Drug Traffic,* p. 96.

45. Uri Ra'anan, Robert Pfaltzgraff, Jr., Richard Shultz, Ernst Halperin, and Igor Lukes, eds., *Hydra of Carnage* (Lexington, Mass.: Lexington Books, 1986), p. 431.

46. Ibid., p. 330.

47. Interview with Alvaro Jose Baldizon Aviles at U.S. Department of State, October 14, 1985.

48. U.S. Departments of State and Defense, *The Soviet–Cuban Connection in Central America and the Caribbean* (Washington, D.C., March 1985), p. 8.

49. Carlos Nunez, "Y ahora, en que camp esta Cuba?" *Marcha* (Montevideo, February 18, 1966).

50. Managua Radio Sandino Network, February 19, 1985; FBIS Latin America, February 21, 1985.

51. Staar, *Yearbook on International Communist Affairs,* 1985, p. 76.

52. *Grenada Documents,* "Report to Bishop from Moscow Embassy, June 30, 1982" (doc. no. 29), p. 2.

53. *Grenada Documents,* "Cuban document on Socialist International written by Manuel Piñeiro" (doc. no. 33), p. 4.

54. *Grenada Documents,* "Analysis of the 1980 Socialist International Conference in Madrid" (doc. no. 35), p. 2.

n55. *Grenada Documents,* "Report by an NJM delegate to a Congress in Libya, June 1982" (doc. no. 34), p. 2.

56. *Grenada Documents,* "Report to Bishop from Moscow Embassy."

57. Uri Ra'anan et al., *Hydra of Carnage,* p. 328.

58. *Daily Chronicle,* (Georgetown), January 9, 1979.

59. *Grenada Documents,* "Line of March of the Party" (doc. no. 1), p. 18.

60. U.S. Department of State, *Comandante Bayardo Arce's Secret Speech before the Nicaraguan Socialist Party (PSN),* (Washington, D.C.: March 1985).

61. Alexander L. George, "The Operational Code: A Neglected Approach to the Study of Political Leaders and Decisionmaking," in *The Conduct of Soviet Foreign Policy,* Erik P. Hoffman and Frederick J. Fleron, eds. (Chicago: Aldine–Atherton, 1971), p. 179 n. 33.

62. Richard Pipes, "Soviet Global Strategy," *Commentary* 67, no. 4 (April 1980): 31–39.

63. Bill Gertz, "Soviet Ships Skip Mexican Port," *Washington Times,* October 23, 1985, p. 2. See also Prensa Latina, September 19, 1985; FBIS Latin America Annex p. 2.

64. *Costa Rican Newsletter,* no. 3, (December 1985): 1.

65. *Pravda,* July 13, 1960. Quoted in Mose L. Harvey, *Soviet Combat Troops in Cuba* (Miami: Advanced International Studies Institute, 1979), p. 13.

66. U.S. Department of Defense, *Soviet Military Power 1985* (Washington, D.C., April 1985), p. 108.

67. Jiri Valenta and William Potter, eds., *Soviet Decisionmaking for National Security* (London: George Allen and Unwin, 1984).

68. Robert C. Tucker, *The Soviet Political Mind,* rev. ed. (New York: W. W. Norton, 1971), p. 596.

69. *Pravda,* November 24, 1981: FBIS Soviet Union, November 25, 1981, p. K1.

70. *Soviet–Cuban Connection,* p. 4.

71. *Red Star,* December 2, 1970. Quoted in Horowitz, *Cuban Communism,* p. 634.

72. *Pravda,* November 4, 1967. Quoted in Di Giovanni and Harvey, *Crisis in Central America,* p. 36.

73. V. D. Sokolovskiy, *Soviet Military Strategy,* ed. Harriet Fast Scott (New York: Crane, Russak and Co., 1975), p. 168.

74. L. I. Brezhnev, "The Communist Movement Has Entered a New Phase of Growth," in *The Leninist Course* (Moscow: Political Literature Publishers, 1970), pp. 427–47. Quoted in Di Giovanni and Harvey, *Crisis in Central America,* p. 36.

75. Ministry of Defense of the USSR, *CPSU on the Armed Forces of the Soviet Union* (Moscow: Voenizdat, 1981), p. 497.

76. *Pravda,* July 4, 1972. Quoted in Di Giovanni and Harvey, *Crisis in Central America,* p. 38.

77. Marcel Niedergang, *Le Monde,* January 8, 1966.

78. *El Tiempo* (Bogotá), December 20, 1985, p. 8A; FBIS Latin America, December 26, 1985, p. F1.

79. U.S. Department of State, *Revolution beyond Our Borders: Sandinista Intervention in Central America,* special report no. 132 (Washington, D.C., September 1985), p. 6.

80. William E. Ratliff, *Castroism and Communism in Latin American, 1959–1976* (Washington, D.C.: AEI–Hoover, 1976), pp. 28–33.

81. Cole Blasier, *The Giant's Rival: The USSR and Latin America* (Pittsburgh: University of Pittsburgh Press, 1983), p. 101.

82. Ibid.

83. Interview with Edén Pastora, Washington, D.C., February 28, 1986.

84. *Revolution beyond Our Borders,* p. 5.

85. Richard F. Staar, ed., *Yearbook on International Communist Affairs, 1971* (Stanford: Hoover Institution Press, 1971), p. 97.

86. *Novoe Vremia,* March 19, 1982. Quoted in Di Giovanni and Harvey, *Crisis in Central America,* p. 110.

Chapter 9. A U.S. Counterstrategy

1. For other U.S. policy options in dealing with the Soviet threat to the Caribbean region, see R. Daniel McMichael and John D. Paulus, eds., *Western Hemisphere Stability: The Latin American Connection* (World Affairs Council of Pittsburgh, April 1983), pp. 77–93. See also *The Report of the President's National Bipartisan Commission on Central America* (Washington, D.C., 1984), pp. 119–22.

2. Richard A. Shultz and Roy Godson, *Dezinformatsia* (McLean, Va.: Pergamon-Brasseys, 1984), pp. 17–21.

3. Sergei Gorshkov, *The Sea Power of the State* (Elmsford, N.Y.: Pergamon Press, 1979), p. 252.

4. *Washington Post*, March 24, 1985, pp. A1 and A33.

5. *Washington Times*, October 23, 1985, p. 2.

6. *Forward Ever! Three Years of the Grenadian Revolution* (Sydney: Pathfinder Press, 1982), p. 133.

7. *Grenada Documents*, "Report to Bishop from Moscow Embassy, June 30, 1982" (doc. no. 29), p. 2.

8. Ibid.

9. *NRC Handelsblad* (Rotterdam), December 6, 1983, p. 4.

10. Russel Stendal, *Rescue the Captors* (Burnsville, Minn.: Ransom Press International, 1984), p. 161.

11. Information from Alvaro Baldizon, Edén Pastora, and Bishop Pablo Vega.

12. ANN (Managua), February 24, 1985; FBIS Latin America, February 26, 1985.

13. *El Siglo* (Bogotá; *Nicaragua Hoy* supplement), January 8, 1986, p. 1; FBIS Latin America, January 15, 1986, p. P18.

14. William W. Pascoe III, "In Central America: A Dismal Record for the Contadora Process," (Heritage Foundation *Backgrounder*, March 5, 1986).

15. *Washington Post*, September 30, 1985, p. A20.

16. Uri Ra'anan, Robert Pfaltzgraff, Jr., Richard Shultz, Ernst Halperin, and Igor Lukes, eds., *Hydra of Carnage* (Lexington Books, 1986), p. 318.

17. Jan Librach, *The Rise of the Soviet Empire* (New York: Praeger, 1964), p. 776.

18. Interview with Adolfo Calero, Washington, D.C., July 16, 1986.

19. *Tiempo*, (San Pedro Sula), July 2, 1986, p. 2; FBIS Latin America, July 7, 1986, P5.

20. *El Siglo* (Bogotá), January 8, 1986, p. 2.

21. The FSLN defectors interviewed were former junta member Arturo Cruz, Deputy Defense Minister Edén Pastora, and Interior Ministry official Alvaro Baldizon.

22. *La Prensa* (censored article dated February 6, 1986); JPRS, March 11, 1986.

23. This scenario is considered a possibility by several Nicaraguan defectors and members of the democratic resistance, who report that they are in contact with sympathetic elements within the EPS.

24. Public Law 87–733, "A Joint Resolution Expressing the Determination of the United States with Respect to the Situation in Cuba," approved October 3, 1962.
25. *New York Times*, August 13, 1985, pp. A1 and a10.
26. Richard A. Gabriel, *Military Incompetence* (New York: Hill and Wang, 1985), pp. 149–86. See also the report on "Urgent Fury" by William S. Lind of the Congressional Military Reform Caucus.
27. See "JCS Replies to Criticism of Grenada Operation," in *Army* (August 1984): 28–37.
28. Richard A. Gabriel, *Military Incompetence*, p. 183.
29. Nicholas L. Johnson, "Soviet Satellites Eye Grenada and the Persian Gulf," *Defense Systems Review* (January 1984): 42.
30. Harold W. Rood, *Kingdoms of the Blind* (Durham, N.C.: Carolina Academic Press, 1980), pp. 134–48.
31. Edward Gonzalez, *A Strategy for Dealing with Cuba in the 1980s* (Santa Monica, Ca.: Rand Corporation R-2954-DOS/AF, September 1982), p. 105.
32. Based on author's interviews with anonymous officers of the U.S. Joint Special Operations Command (JSOC).
33. Gonzalez, *A Strategy for Dealing with Cuba*, p. 100.

Acronyms

ANL	National Liberation Alliance (Brazil) *(Aliança Nacional Libertadora)*
APRA	Aprista Party (Peru) *(Alianza Popular Revolucionaria Americana)*
ASW	Antisubmarine warfare
AWACS	Airborne Warning and Control System
CBI	Caribbean Basin Initiative
CCP	Chinese Communist Party
CDR	Committees for the Defense of the Revolution (Cuba) *(Comités de Defensa de la Revolución)*
CMEA	Council for Mutual Economic Assistance
COMECON	Council for Mutual Economic Assistance
COPEI	Social Christian Party (Venezuela) *(Comité de Organización Politica Electoral Independiente—Partido Social-Cristiano)*
CPSU	Communist Party of the Soviet Union
CST	Sandinista Workers' Federation (Nicaragua) *(Central Sandinista de Trabajadores)*
CTC	Cuban Confederation of Workers *(Central de Trabajadores de Cuba)*
C³I	Command, control, communications, and intelligence

DA   Departamento América (Cuba)

DGI   General Directorate of Intelligence (Cuba)
(Dirección General de Inteligencia)

DGRE   General Department of Foreign Relations (Cuba)
(Departamento General de Relaciones Exteriores)

DGSE   General Directorate of State Security (Nicaragua)
(Dirección General de Seguridad Estado)

DLN   Directorate for National Liberation (Cuba)
(Dirección de Liberación Nacional)

DLP   Dominica Labour Party

DNU–MRH   National Unity Directorate of the Revolutionary Movement of Honduras
(Directorio Nacional Unido–Movimiento Revolucionario Hondureño)

DOE   Directorate of Special Operations (Cuba)
(Dirección de Operaciones Especiales)

DRU   United Revolutionary Directorate (El Salvador)
(Dirección Revolucionaria Unida)

DSE   Department of State Security (Cuba)
(Departamento de Seguridad de Estado)

EFE   Spanish News Agency

ELN   Army of National Liberation (Bolivia)
(Ejército de Liberación Nacional)

EPS   Sandinista People's Army (Nicaragua)
(Ejército Popular Sandinista)

ERP   People's Revolutionary Army (El Salvador)
(Ejército Revolucionario Popular)

ETA   Basque Nation and Liberty (Spain)
(Euzkadi ta Azkatasuna)

FAL   Armed Forces of Liberation (El Salvador)
(Fuerzas Armadas de Liberación)

FARC   Revolutionary Armed Forces of Colombia
(Fuerzas Armada Revolucionarias de Colombia)

FDN	Nicaraguan Democratic Forces *(Fuerzas Democráticas Nicaragüenses)*
FDR	Revolutionary Democratic Front (El Salvador) *(Frente Democrático Revolucionario)*
FLN	Nicaraguan Liberation Front (Nicaragua) *(Frente de Liberacion Nicaragüenses)*
FMLH	Morazan Front for the Liberation of Honduras *(Frente Morazanista para la Liberación de Honduras)*
FMLN	Farabundo Martí National Liberation Front (El Salvador) *(Farabundo Martí de Liberación Nacional)*
FPMR	Manuel Rodríguez Patriotic Front (Chile) *(Frente Patriótica Manuel Rodríguez)*
FSLN	Sandinista National Liberation Front (Nicaragua) *(Frente Sandinista de Liberación Nacional)*
GRU	Chief Administration for Intelligence (Soviet Military Intelligence) *(Glavnoe Razvedivatelnoe Upravlenie)*
ICAP	Institute for Friendship With the Peoples (Cuba) *(Instituto Con Amistad Popular)*
IMF	International Monetary Fund
INF	Intermediate-range nuclear forces
IRBM	Intermediate-range ballistic missile
JEWEL	Joint Endeavour for Welfare, Education, and Liberation (Grenada)
JLP	Jamaica Labour Party
KGB	Committee of State Security (Soviet Union) *(Komitet Gossudarstvennoi Bezopasnosti)*
MAP	Movement for the Assemblies of the People (Grenada)
MBPM	Maurice Bishop Patriotic Movement (Grenada)
MNR	National Revolutionary Movement (El Salvador) *(Movimiento Nacional Revolucionario)*

M-19	Movement of April 19 (Colombia) *(Movimiento de Abril 19)*
MPL	Movement for Popular Liberation (Honduras) *(Movimiento Popular de Liberación ("Cincheneros")*
MRBM	Medium-range ballistic missile
NJM	New Jewel Movement (Grenada)
NORAD	North American Air Defense
OAS	Organization of American States
OECS	Organisation of Eastern Caribbean States
OLAS	Organization of Latin American Solidarity
OPEC	Organization of Petroleum Exporting Countries
OREL	Organization for Revolutionary Education and Liberation (Grenada)
ORI	Integrated Revolutionary Organization (Cuba) *(Organizaciones Revolucionarias Integradas)*
PCC	Cuban Communist Party *(Partido Comunista Cubano)*
PCH	Communist Party of Honduras *(Partido Comunista de Honduras)*
PCS	Communist Party of El Salvador *(Partido Comunista Salvadoreño)*
PDS	Social Democratic Party (Brazil) *(Partido Democrático Social)*
PLO	Palestine Liberation Organization
PNC	People's National Congress (Guyana)
PNP	People's National Party (Jamaica)
PPP	People's Popular Party (Guyana)
PRA	People's Revolutionary Army (Grenada)
PRC	People's Republic of China
PRG	People's Revolutionary Government (Grenada)

PRTCH	Central American Workers' Revolutionary Party of Honduras *(Partido Revolucionario de los Trabajadores Centroamericanos de Honduras)*
PSN	Nicaraguan Socialist Party *(Partido Socialista Nicaragüense)*
PSP	Popular Socialist Party (Cuba) *(Partido Socialista Popular)*
PUR	Revolutionary Union Party (Cuba) *(Partido Unión Revolucionario)*
PURS	United Party of the Socialist Revolution (Cuba) *(Partido Unido de la Revolución Socialista)*
RMC	Revolutionary Military Council (Grenada)
SALT	Strategic Arms Limitation Talks
SAM	Surface-to-air missile
SI	Socialist International
SLOC	Sea Lines of Communication
SSBN	Ballistic missile submarine (nuclear)
SSG	Guided missile submarine
SSGN	Guided missile submarine (nuclear)
SSN	Submarine (nuclear)
SWAPO	South West Africa People's Organization (Namibia)
UNAN	National Autonomous University of Nicaragua *(Universidad Nacional Autónoma (de) Nicaragua)*
UND	National Democratic Union (El Salvador) *(Unión Nacional Democrática)*
UNITA	National Union for the Complete Independence of Angola *(União Nacional para a Independéncia Total de Angola)*
UNO	United Nicaraguan Opposition *(Unidad Nicaragüense Opositora)*

URC	Revolutionary Communist Union (Cuba) *(Unión Revolucionaria Comunista)*
URP	People's Revolutionary Union (Honduras) *(Unión Revolucionaria del Pueblo)*
UWI	University of the West Indies
WPA	Working People's Alliance (Guyana)
WPJ	Workers' Party of Jamaica

Index

About the Author

Timothy Francis Ashby holds a Ph.D. in international relations from the University of Southern California. He is currently a policy analyst for Latin American affairs with the Heritage Foundation in Washington, D.C. He is a fellow of the foundation's Arthur Spitzer Institute for Hemispheric Development and also serves as chairman of the foundation's Working Group on Counterterrorism. Prior to joining the foundation, Dr. Ashby worked under contract with the U.S. State Department conducting counterterrorism and crisis-management exercises at U.S. embassies in Latin America and the Caribbean.

Dr. Ashby has published extensively in magazines and newspapers such as *BusinessWeek* and the *Chicago Tribune;* has appeared on CBS, NBC, ABC, and CNN; and has spoken at such forums as the National Press Club, the White House Working Group on Central America, and the Hoover Institution at Stanford University, where he was a visiting research scholar during 1983.

Between 1967 and 1980, Dr. Ashby lived and worked on the Caribbean island of Grenada.